I0810005

IMAGES
of America

CHERRYVILLE

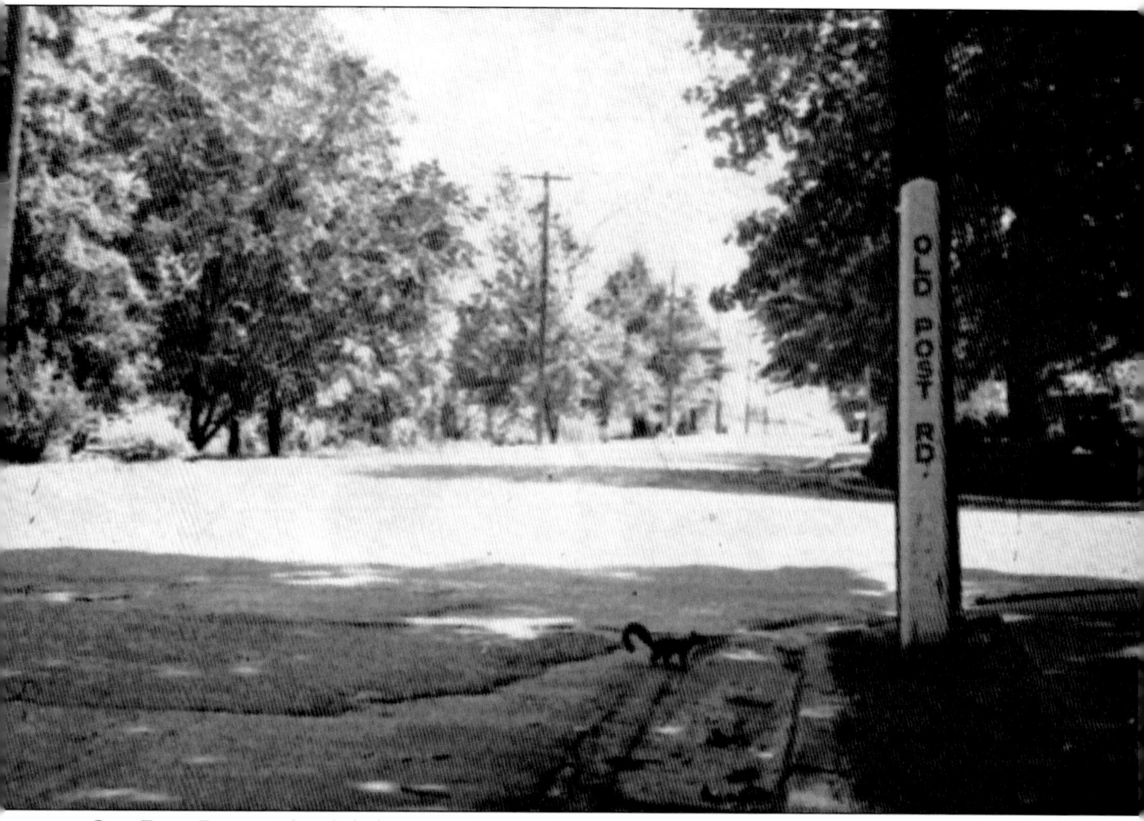

Old Post Road. This faded postcard, once distributed by Houser Drug Store, shows a peaceful scene on Old Post Road. Along this route in the 18th and 19th centuries passed the stagecoach and mail from the Deep South northward through Virginia and other points north. This route later passed by the Henry Summit Trading Post and General Store in the hamlet of Cherryville. (Courtesy of the Cherryville Historical Museum.)

On the Cover: It was a festive mood on Cherryville's Main Street at the square on "Big Celebration Day" held on a hot August day in 1916. These huge homecoming celebrations, combined with watermelon feasts, were held every year until the late 1950s, except for one year in the 1940s when there was a polio epidemic. There were hot-air balloon ascensions, brass bands, vaudeville shows, baseball games, a merry-go-round, "moving picture" shows, an address by the governor, old soldiers' dinners, and horseback tournaments. One balloonist was killed in the 1920s when he fell and landed on power lines in town. (Courtesy of the Cherryville Historical Museum.)

IMAGES
of America

CHERRYVILLE

Rita Wehunt-Black

ARCADIA
PUBLISHING

ISBN 978-0-7385-6855-3

Published by Arcadia Publishing
Charleston SC, Chicago IL, Portsmouth NH, San Francisco CA

Printed in the United States of America

Library of Congress Catalog Card Number: 2008935728

For all general information contact Arcadia Publishing at:
Telephone 843-853-2070
Fax 843-853-0044
E-mail sales@arcadiapublishing.com
For customer service and orders:
Toll-Free 1-888-313-2665

Visit us on the Internet at www.arcadiapublishing.com

This book is dedicated to my husband, John H. Black Jr., and to the Cherryville High School class of 1959, which is celebrating its 50th anniversary this year.

Contents

ACKNOWLEDGMENTS

This book is by no means intended to be a complete history of Cherryville but is a pictorial using vintage photographs from the Cherryville Historical Museum. Unless otherwise noted, all images appear courtesy of the Cherryville Historical Museum. In choosing photographs, I chose those with the sharpest image and best clarity, sometimes even over content. I also tried to include, if possible, images that have never been in print. In my research, I prefer to work alone with original archival photographs and original documents, such as census records, death certificates, and deeds. I also work with gravestone inscriptions and archival newspapers. I then weave these facts into the oral history. Sometimes local lore, handed down by word-of-mouth, may contradict the facts, but lore almost always has a nugget of truth within it.

The Sallie Stroup (born 1889) scrapbooks were invaluable in dating and identifying photographs. Little did she know that the newspaper clippings she compiled for many years would someday be of such great use to her beloved town. Many future pictorial volumes featuring Cherryville are possible; think of this as volume one. Hopefully someone will pick up the torch, continue the work, and compile a second and even third volume of Images of America: *Cherryville* using photographs from other sources and private family collections.

Encouragement from family and friends kept me going during the long hours needed to complete this project. I owe much to many people. Without the endless support and enthusiasm of the volunteer staff at the Cherryville Historical Museum, this volume would not have been possible. I especially want to thank Pat C. Sherrill, Lorie Pruett, Karleen Price, Bobbie Rudisill, Katherine Goins, Darrell Carpenter, Mary Peeler Wehunt, Ben Heavner, Nora Heavner, Thelma Sellers, Carl Dellinger, Hoover Quinn, and many, many others who have volunteered their time through the years to preserve the history of Cherryville. I also want to thank Diana Beam, executive assistant at the Cherryville Chamber of Commerce, and the staff at the *Cherryville Eagle*. And last, I want to thank the staff at Arcadia Publishing in Charleston, South Carolina, for their professionalism and help in getting this volume into print, especially acquisitions editor Lindsay Harris and publisher Maggie Bullwinkel.

Introduction

The area that is today Cherryville, North Carolina, in northwestern Gaston County was founded by Scots-Irish, English, and German settlers in the mid-1700s, with land grants signed by the king of England dating back as early as 1752. These immigrants brought with them their customs, languages, and religious beliefs, and organized Presbyterian, Lutheran, and German Reformed churches in the wilderness. These early settlers put down roots near the waterways of Indian Creek and Beaver Dam Creek. In the early years, iron working, gold mining, and state-licensed distilleries were successful pursuits, but farming was the major occupation of the area's early population.

Until 1768, the area was located in Old Mecklenburg County, but in that year, Tryon County was formed out of the land west of the Catawba River. This became effective on April 10, 1769, and the county was named for William Tryon, governor of North Carolina from 1765 to 1771. In 1779, Tryon was divided into Lincoln County and Rutherford County, and Tryon County ceased to exist. In 1846, Gaston County was formed from the lower part of Lincoln County.

The earliest permanent settlers to the area were the Mauney, Black, Reynolds, and Moore families. On November 23, 1762, Valentine Mauney purchased from Moses Moore 370 acres of land on the north side of Indian Creek (originally called Reynolds Creek), being a south branch of the south fork of the Catawba River. On the same day, Thomas Black bought 280 acres from Moses Moore. This land was on the south side of Indian Creek and joined Valentine Mauney's land.

Local lore says that four men by the name of Black all arrived in North Carolina around 1750. They were Thomas, John, William, and David Black, all descended from Scots-Irish immigrants from Ireland who settled first in Pennsylvania. A deed dated 1757 states that David Black, a resident of Rowan County, bought land in the region of what is now Rutherford County. Family tradition says that the David Black of Rutherford County was the father of Thomas, William, and John. Of the four, Thomas Black, born around 1741, is considered the founder of the Black family in the Cherryville area. Thomas Black settled in the valley near Indian Creek in the neighborhood of the shoal bridge in a house near Valentine Mauney's home.

Thomas Black had lived on this land for only a few years when, on September 12, 1765, he bought 320 acres lying on both sides of the Little Broad River in present-day Cleveland County. He left his Indian Creek property and moved with his family to the area that is today Cleveland County. He died there in March 1779, and his death is recorded in a land deed in Lincoln County dated October 11, 1800, between Morris Cox and Ephraim Black, who was the son of the deceased Thomas Black. Within the deed, it states that Thomas Black died on or about March 15, 1779. At his death, he had two tracks of land on Indian Creek and a larger track of 563 acres in Rutherford County on both sides of the Broad River.

After Thomas Black's death in 1779, Elizabeth Black left the Little Broad River property and returned to Indian Creek with her son, Ephraim. By 1800, Elizabeth Black, widow of Thomas Black, was married to Morris Cox. The deed on October 11, 1800, in Lincoln County was releasing her of all her dower rights.

Ephraim Abraham Black, son of Thomas and Elizabeth Black, was born on February 11, 1767. Around 1779, when he was about 12 years old, he came with his mother from the Little Broad River property to the Indian Creek property. Also living along Indian Creek now were Burrell Homesley,

Joseph Homesley, and Benjamin Homesley, all of English descent. Stephen Homesley also lived in the area at the time. In 1790, Ephraim Black (1767–1843) married Tabitha "Doshie" Homlesley (1778–1854), the daughter of Benjamin Homesley (1750–1813). Ephraim and Elizabeth Black had two sons, Thomas Black (1792–1880) and Stephen Black (1800–1856). Thomas and Stephen built homesteads along the "Old Post Road," as it was referred to in a land grant in 1796.

The county seat of Old Tryon County was located 3 miles outside of present-day Cherryville, and the courthouse for the county was in the home of pioneer Christian Mauney from 1774 to 1783. Mauney and his neighbors played an important part in the American Revolution. Residents of the area organized into committees of safety and later militia to prepare against the British following the Battle of Lexington in Massachusetts.

On August 14, 1775, forty-nine brave local residents, among the earliest colonists to do so, gathered at Christian Mauney's home and issued a declaration of grievances against the British, known as the *Tryon Resolves*:

> The unprecedented, barbarous and bloody actions committed by the British Troops on our American Brethren near Boston on the 19th of April and 20th of May last, together with the Hostile Operations and Traitorous Designs now carrying on by the Tools of Ministerial Vengeance and Despotism for the subjugating all British America, suggest to us the painful necessity of having recourse to Arms for the preservation of those Rights and Liberties which the principles of our Constitution and Laws of God, Nature and Nations have made it our duty to defend.
>
> We, therefore, the Subscribers, Freeholders and Inhabitants of Tryon County, do hereby faithfully unite ourselves under the most sacred ties of Religion, Honor and Love to our Country, firmly to resist force by force in defense of our National Freedom and Constitutional Rights against all invasions, and at the same time do solemnly engage to take up Arms and Risque our lives and fortunes in maintaining the freedom of our Country, whenever the Wisdom and Council of the Continental Congress or our Provincial Convention shall declare it necessary, and this Engagement we will continue in and hold sacred til a Reconciliation shall take place between Great Britain and America on Constitutional principles which we most ardently desire. And we do firmly agree to hold all such persons Inimical to the liberties of America, who shall refuse to subscribe to this Association.

The signers were John Walker, Charles McLean, Andrew Neel, Thomas Beatty, James Corburn, Frederick Hambright, Andrew Hampton, Benjamin Hardin, George Paris, William Graham, Robert Alexander, David Jenkins, Thomas Espey, James McAfee, William Thompson, Samuel Carpenter, Richard Woffer, Jacob Forney, David Whitesides, John Beaman, John Morris, Joseph Harden, John Robinson, Valentine Mauney, George Black, James Logan, James Baird, Christian Carpenter, Abel Beatty, Joab Turner, Jonathan Price, Jam. Miller, John Dellinger, James McIntire, Jacob Mauney, Jr., John Wells, Jacob Costner, Robert Hulclip, James Buchanan, Moses Moore, Joseph Kuykendall, Adam Simms, Samuel Smith, Joseph Neel, Samuel Loftin, and Peregrine Mackness.

Living in the area on Indian Creek at the time of the American Revolution was the infamous Tory Col. John Moore, who was later defeated at the Battle of Ramsour's Mill. His father, Moses Moore, was also accused of being a Tory and had to leave the area after the war. He was able to see that his two sons-in-law, who were good patriots, received his large land holdings. The Moore-Roberts Stagecoach Relay Station, thought to have been built around 1817 by Moses Roberts, grandson of Moses Moore, still stands today on this property. As for Col. John Moore, on April 11, 1783, London's *Political Magazine* published the statement of a North Carolina Loyalist who claimed that Col. John Moore had been taken prisoner by Col. Wade Hampton near Wateree River and hanged. Family tradition, passed from John Moore's sister to her grandson John H. Roberts, states that John Moore went to his father's birthplace at Carlisle, England, and was lost track of there. Moses Moore left North Carolina after the war and fled to West Florida (at that time possessed by the Spanish), which is today Washington County, Alabama.

After the Black, Moore, and Mauney families settled permanently, several other pioneer families came into the area; and the settlement that had begun along Indian Creek began to spread south and westward, and into the area first called White Pine, later to become the town of Cherryville. Among those settlers who came before 1800 were Stephen Homesley, who settled in what is today southwest Cherryville around 1790, and pioneer John Teeter Beam. Other early families were Reynolds, Carpenter, Dellinger, Heavner, Anthony, Brown, Neal, Kiser, Huss, Houser, Quinn, Summit, Craft, and many others.

At a crossroads on the old Stagecoach Road that ran from Salisbury to Charleston, South Carolina, the village of Cherryville emerged. Prior to around 1852, Benaja Black's home and store was used as a meeting place for the community. Benaja Black (1827–1917) was a son of Stephen and Elizabeth Black and father of Ben Black. It was in Benaja Black's home that the first post office was established in 1854. It was called White Pine Post Office because of a lone pine tree that grew out front. Soon the little hamlet began to grow.

The story is told that the village was renamed Cherryville when Elizabeth Black, the wife of Stephen Black (1800–1856), planted red heart cherry trees along the old lane in each corner of a split-rail fence of rails cut from oak and chestnut trees and laid out in a zigzag fashion on both sides of the lane. In the springtime, those who passed along the Old Stagecoach Road were attracted by the beautiful blossoms and gradually began calling the road "Cherry Lane." Later the little hamlet was renamed Cherryville.

Elizabeth Black (called Aunt Lizzie by most) told her grandchildren the following story. There were many cherry trees when the Wilmington, Charlotte, and Rutherford Railroad reached the small village of White Pine in 1862, and a civil engineer who had supervised the construction of the railroad bed and first depot suggested the name of White Pine be changed to Cherryville. The new name was given to the post office on November 2, 1865, three years after the railroad reached town. Some credit Ephraim Black with naming the town, although he had been dead for 22 years when the post office was given the name in 1865.

In W. T. Robinson's research in the 1960s, he reported the following information about the route of the original Old Post Road in talks with descendants of Stephen and Thomas Black. The Old Post Road entered the small village from Spartanburg, South Carolina, going east to approximately 100 yards from the present intersection of South Elm Street and Old Post Road. An extension going directly eastward to present-day Mountain Street was made years after 1850. After entering the village, the road crossed the strip of land that would become Elm Street. From here, it continued to the area of the present-day Presbyterian church. The old road picked up in the area of the "Old Depot," located near the point where the railroad crosses North Pink Street. The road crossed the railroad there and ran slightly northeast. From there, it went to the north, intersecting the Old Burke (Morganton) Road. It ran by the Blakely Place (Moses Moore's property), on which the Stagecoach Relay Station was located at Indian Creek, and then continued on to Lincolnton.

Henry Summit came to the area in 1852 and is credited with starting the first real business in what is today the town of Cherryville. Near where the Old Post Road crossed the Morganton (Burke) Road, Henry Summit built his distillery and mercantile business. Summit's store later became the new meeting place for the community. His store was so successful that he erected a second store, called "the long store" because of its shape and size, north of town.

Many other businesses would follow Summit's by men named Mauney, Rudisill, Hendricks, Kendricks, Beam, Elliot, Stroup, Aderholdt, Dellinger, Houser, Hobbs, McGinnis, Harrelson, Howell, Carpenter, Leonhardt, and many others. Cherryville also had one of the largest foundries in the state, run by C. C. Dellinger for many years.

In 1846, the first textile mill had been organized in Gaston County on the banks of the Catawba River, and Gaston County would eventually be known as the "Yarn Capital of the World." The introduction of steam power allowed the mills to locate other places besides along the rapidly flowing rivers and creeks. As a result, "mill towns" began to grow, and Cherryville was one of the fastest growing mill towns in Gaston County.

On February 18, 1891, the first cotton mill, Cherryville Manufacturing Company, was organized. The Cherryville Manufacturing Company later became known as the "Old Mill," and the neighborhood around it was called "Old Mill Hill." Next Gaston Manufacturing Company, later renamed the Dora Mill, was formed in 1896, and the company built its first plant in 1897. The Vivian Manufacturing Company, which later became the NuWay Mills, was organized on March 6, 1917, with the Rhyne-Houser Manufacturing Company being organized in 1919. The Carlton Yarn Mills was established in 1922.

What would grow into one of the nation's largest freight carriers started operating in Cherryville in 1932 as Beam Trucking Company. C. Grier Beam, his brother, Dewey F. Beam, and what would become Carolina Freight Carriers Corporation did as much to change the economy and the face of Cherryville as did the cotton mills earlier in Cherryville's history.

Today there are many new and exciting things going on in the Cherryville area. There is an effort to clean the waterways that our ancestors were dependent upon and used daily, and to restore and preserve these areas for the enjoyment of future generations. Each spring when the cherry trees bloom in Cherryville, a Cherry Blossom Festival is held in the town, and "Cherry Lane" is remembered and celebrated. This book is part of the effort to preserve the history of this wonderful area.

One

Charming Little Hamlet

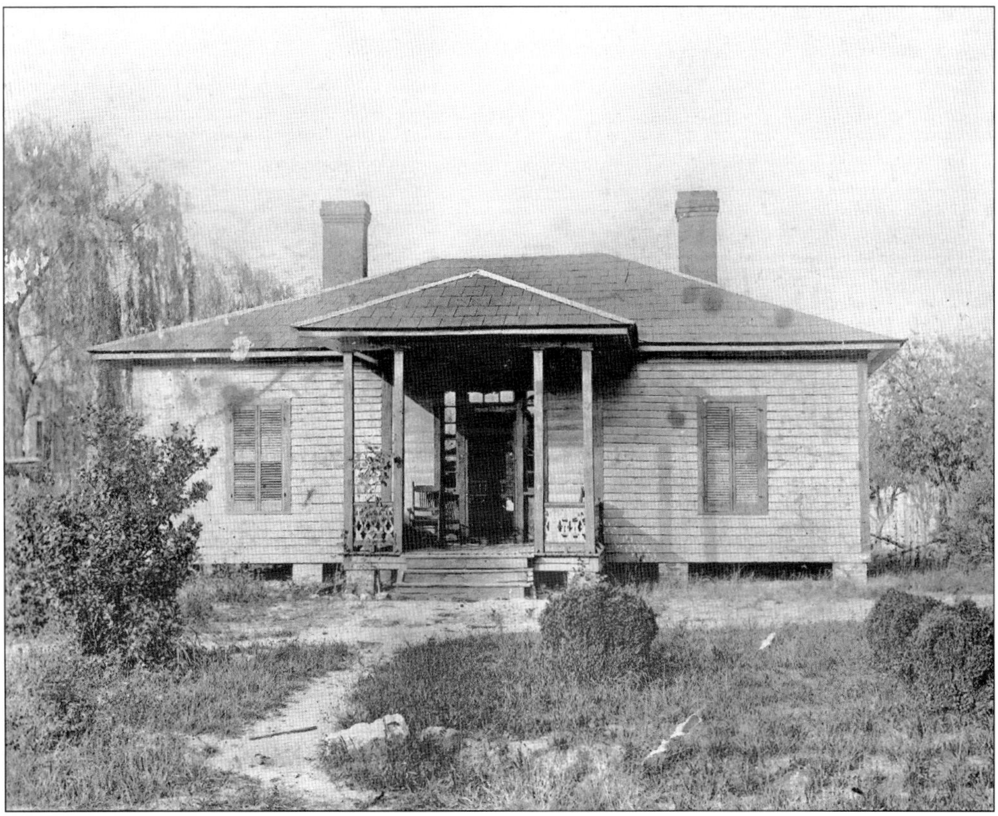

Henry Summit House. Built around 1854 by Henry Summit (1828–1894) on Mountain Street, then later moved to South Mill Street, this is said to be the first house built within the city limits of Cherryville. Summit occupied the house until the late 1880s. In 1889, M. L. Rudisill moved to Cherryville and occupied it until 1914. Then David P. Dellinger moved in and occupied it until the late 1920s after it was moved to South Mill Street.

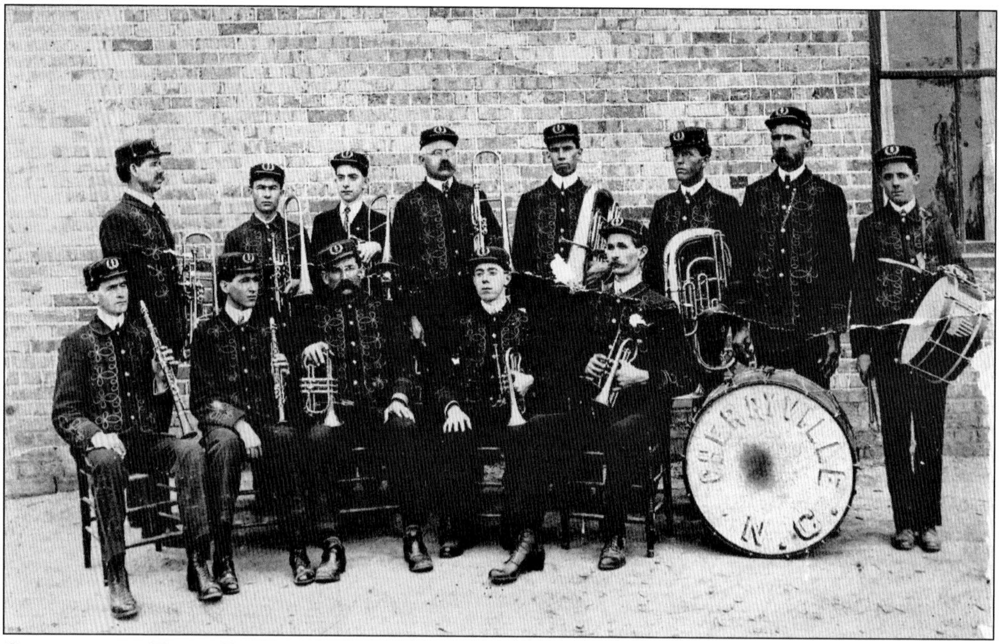

Cherryville Town Band, 1904. This highly rated band was organized around 1901. Widely known, it played for political meetings, school commencements, and many functions locally and as far east as Wilmington. From left to right are (seated) David Rudisill, Marcus L. Mauney, Lee McGinnis, John Moss, and Vitchel Q. Stroup; (standing) director Bishop Roberts, Ed Frye, Buford Moss, L. H. J. Houser, R. Frank Putnam, Stephen Stroup, J. B. Houser Sr., and Evon L. Houser.

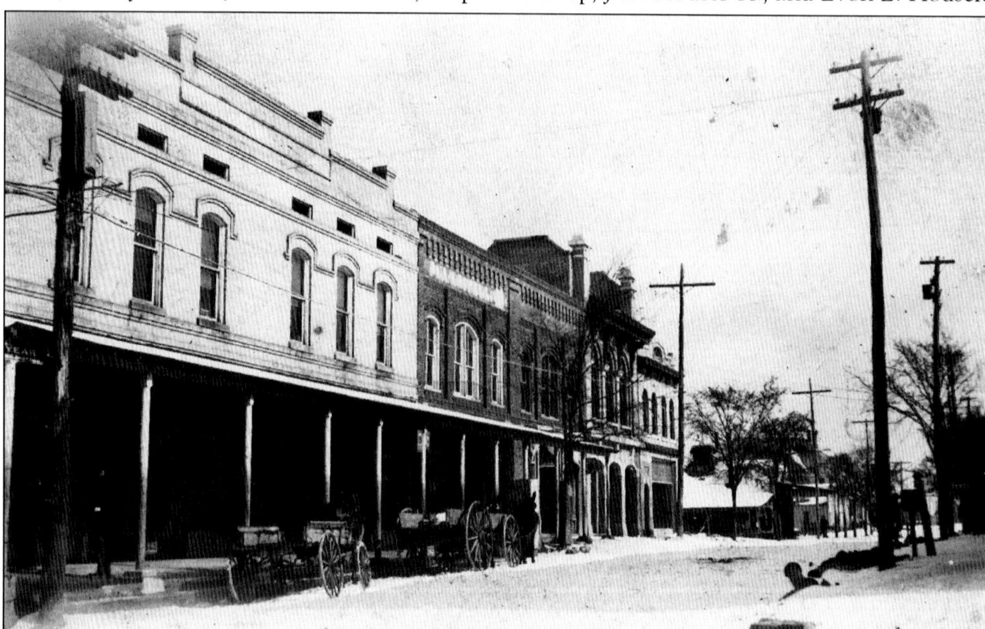

Cherryville Main Street, 1912. This early postcard view shows downtown Cherryville not long after the turn of the 20th century. The new Cherryville City Hall on the left had just been completed in 1911, but hitching posts were still located on Main Street, and the local livery stables and the wagon works did a lively business.

SHERIFF SAM MAUNEY. At the dawn of the 20th century, many towns had sheriffs instead of police chiefs. Sam Mauney was the sheriff in Cherryville when this picture was taken around 1915. Take note of the gun strapped around his waist, the badge pinned in clear view, and the billy club in hand. The jail in 1915 was located in the basement of the Cherryville City Hall.

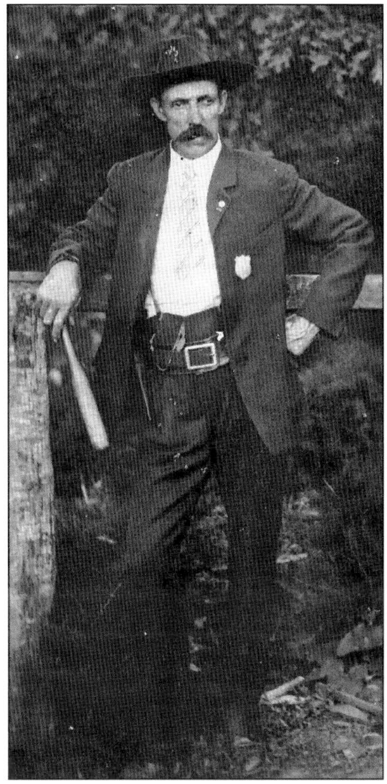

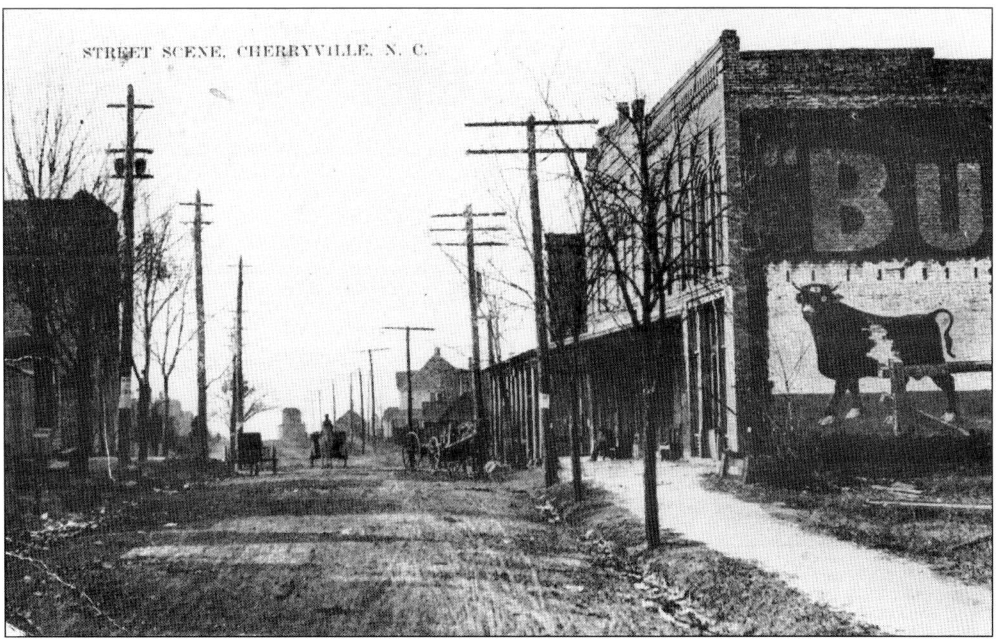

BULL DURHAM. The American Tobacco Company used the bull to advertise its Bull Durham Tobacco. Jules Kerner painted the advertisement in Cherryville around 1910. When the city hall was built next door in 1911, the existing wall of Brittain's Feed Store was used, covering the painting for 80 years. It was discovered in 1991 by Boy Scout Troop 323 while removing plaster at the old city hall, now the Cherryville Historical Museum.

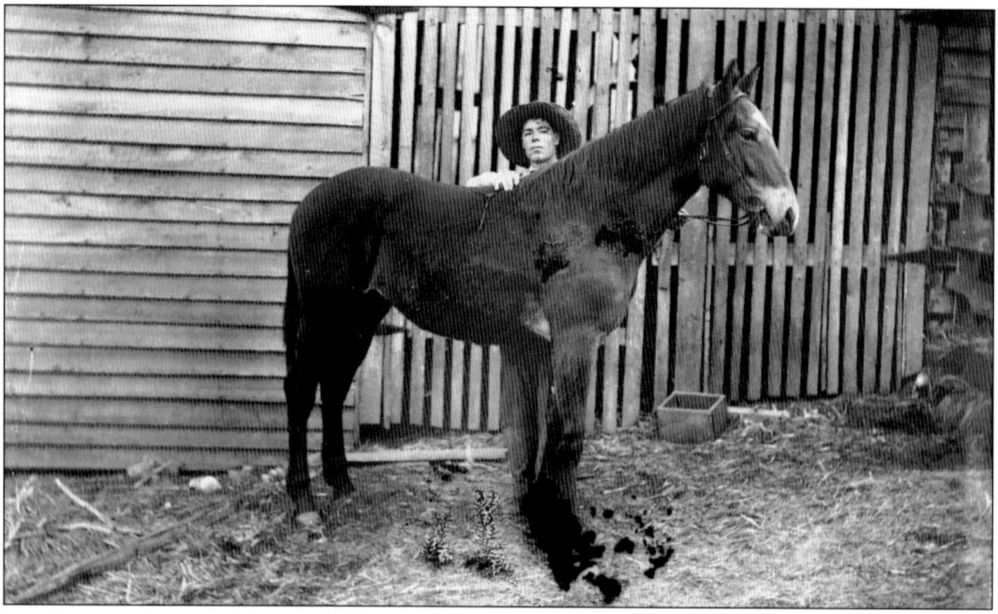

The Livery Stable. Cherryville has had many livery stables where one could board a horse, team of horses, or leave a surrey or buggy for the day. James M. Beam ran a livery stable in the Rudisill and Aderholt Building. Others who managed livery stables were James "Jim" Moss, Wiley McGinnis, Dr. A. W. Howell, L. Clay Harrelson, and John A. Stroup (in 1905 and 1906).

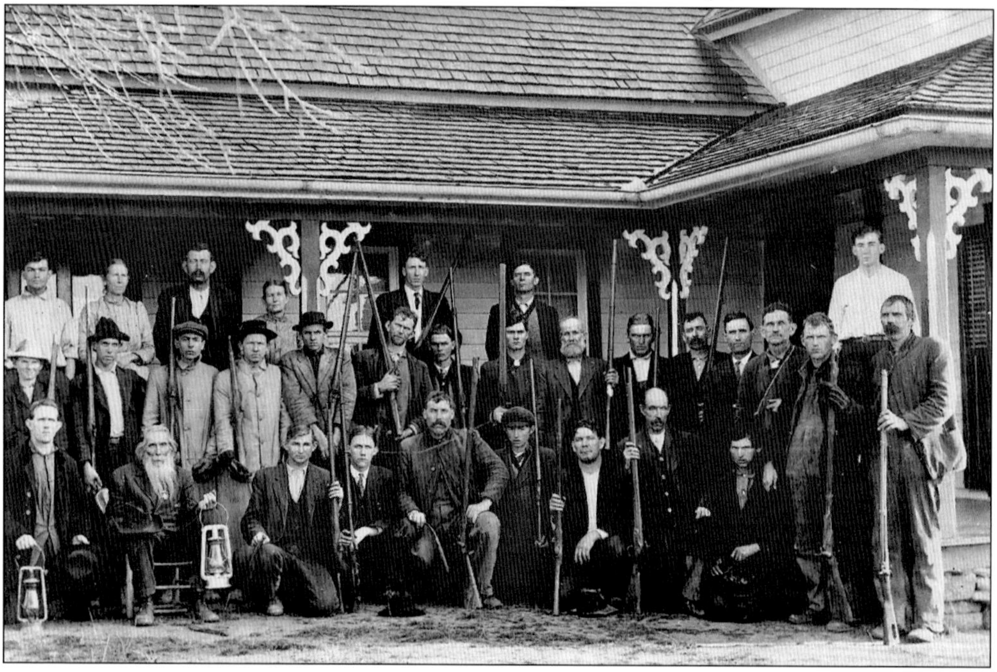

New Year Shooters, 1915. In and around the Cherryville area, black powder and the roar of muskets mark the end of one year and the beginning of another. Starting at midnight on New Year's Eve, these descendants of German and Scots-Irish settlers travel the highways and back roads, calling on families and businesses throughout the night and all through New Year's Day, wishing them well and shooting their guns.

FOREST MELVILLE HOUSER (1903–1998). Dr. Houser, a descendant of Monroe Houser of Cleveland County, North Carolina, was born and raised in Cherryville, the son of Dr. W. H. Houser. He is seen here at age eight in 1910. At that time, horses, chickens, geese, pigs, cows, and other livestock were common within the city limits of Cherryville.

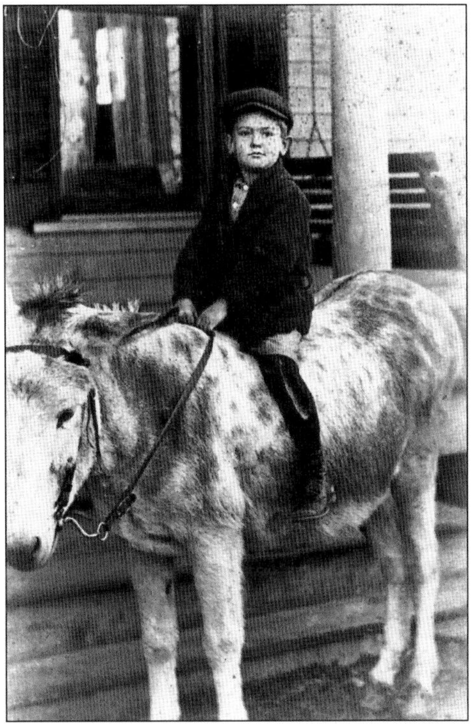

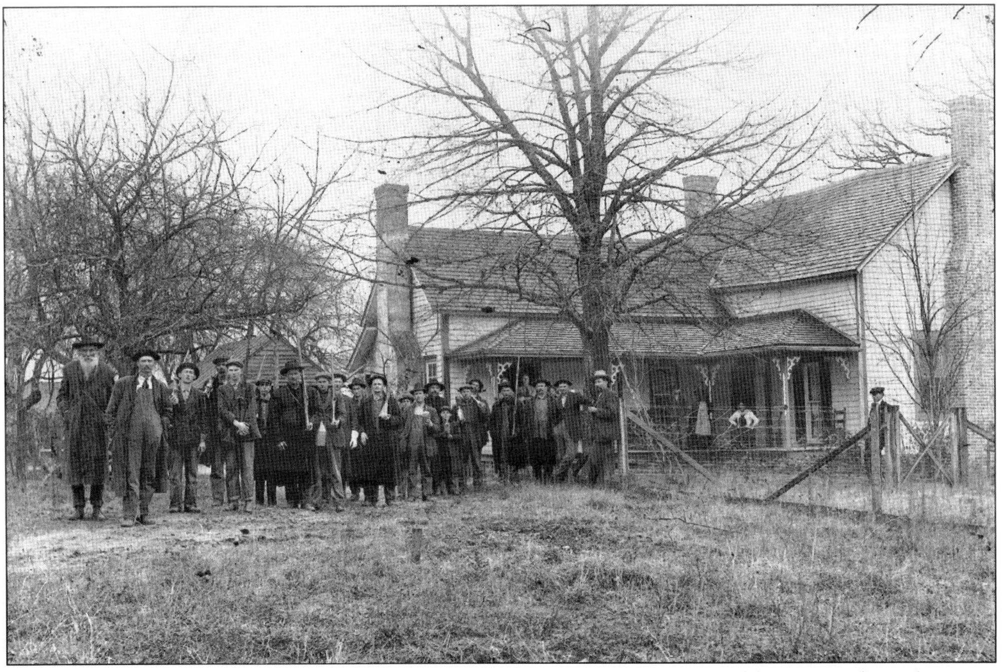

STEPHEN HOMESLEY HOUSE. The Cherryville New Year Shooters assemble on South Pink Street at the Stephen Homesley House around 1910. An English immigrant, Homesley (1778–1859) built his house, originally of log construction, around 1805 near a spring. He was married to Esther Roberts (1788–1874) and was the father of Amos B. Homesley (1818–1887) and Jemima "Mima" Homesley, who married Charles David Dellinger.

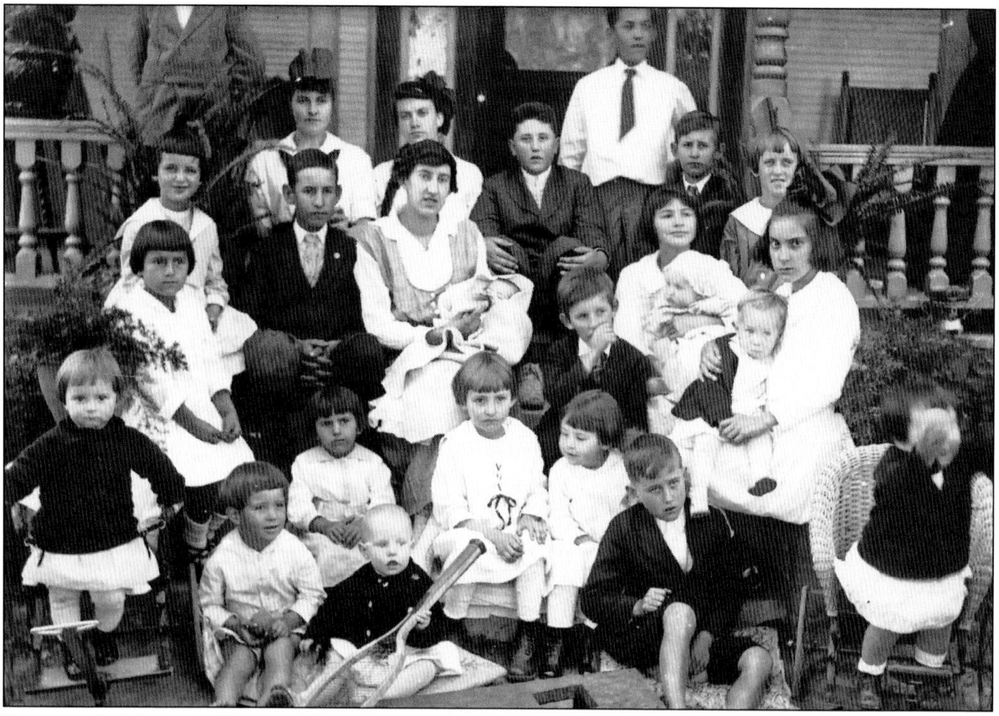

SAMUEL S. MAUNEY HOME. The Mauney family lived in this Queen Anne–style home on the corner of South Mountain and West Main Streets until around 1914. S. S. Mauney divided the home into three houses and moved them to clear the lot for a new bank building. One house remains and is located at 324 South Pink Street. Mauney was a state representative to the North Carolina Legislature from 1911 to 1915. The young people in the Mauney family (above) gather on the front steps for this delightful photograph.

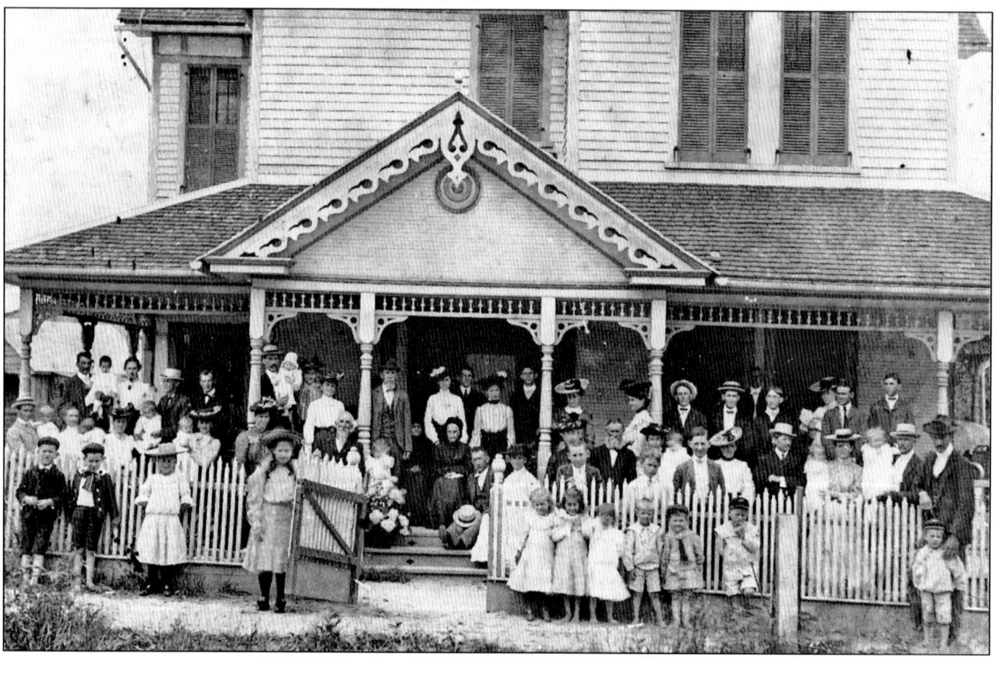

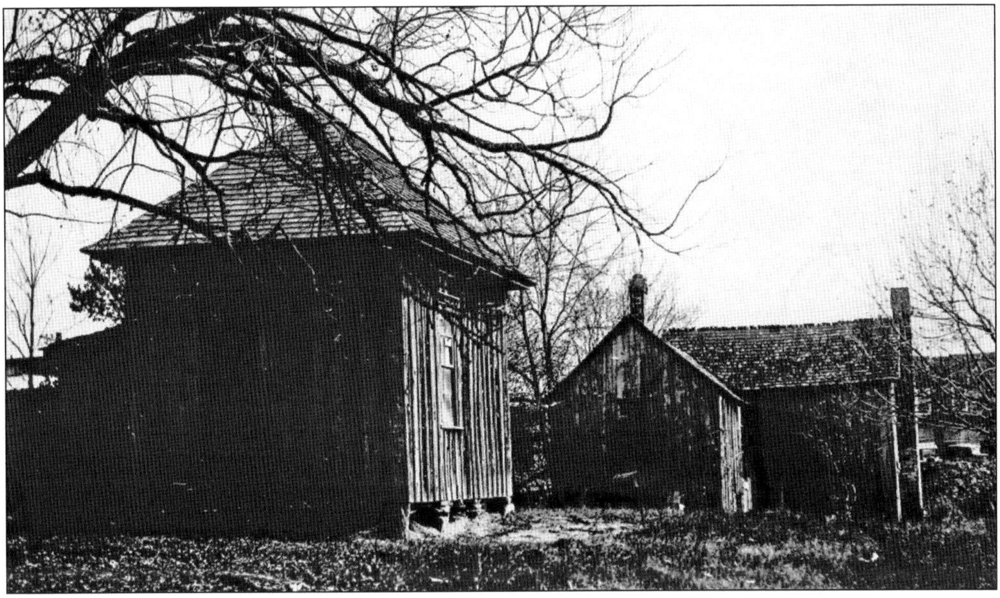

Maggie Litton's Hat Shop. A milliner known as "the Hat Lady," Maggie Quinn Litton was born in South Carolina in 1861, daughter of George and Genellia Putnam Quinn. She married Sanford Litton in 1900. They had no children, and he died around 1908. It is told that later in life Maggie ordered herself a mail-order husband. He came to Cherryville on the train, but things did not work out. Maggie died in 1924.

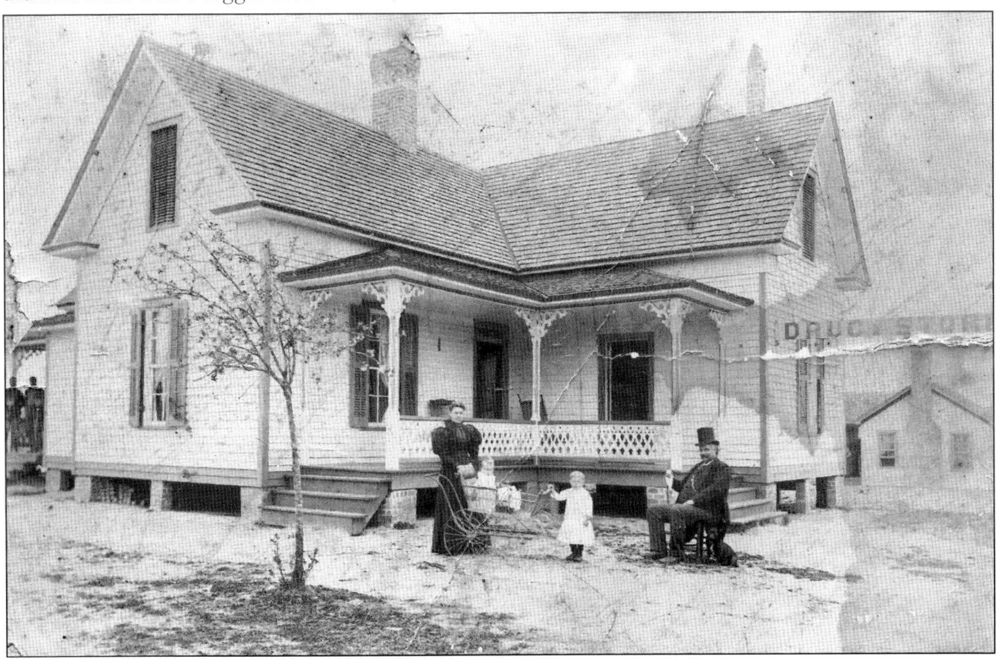

Dr. A. W. Howell. Seen here around 1896 with his wife and children, Alfred W. Howell came from Georgia in the late 1880s and built this house in Cherryville. He practiced medicine in Cherryville and at one time also ran a general store, drugstore, and livery stable while still practicing medicine. The house was used as his home, medical office, and drugstore. He later built an office on Main Street around 1901.

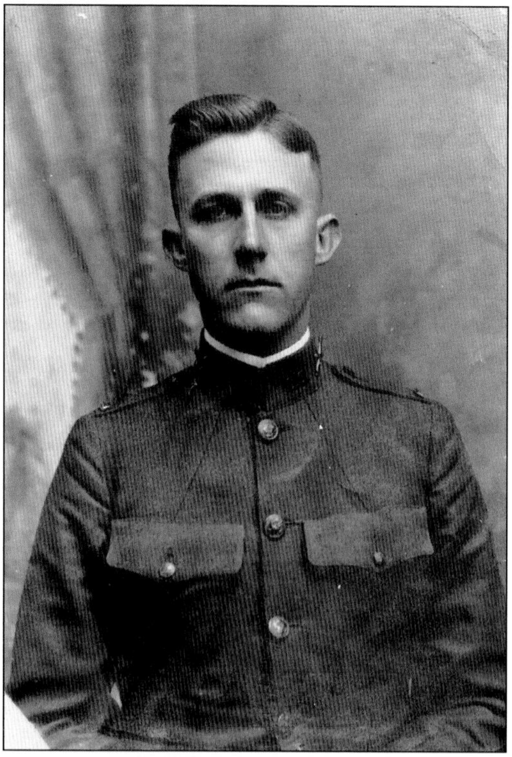

Henry Dellinger (1894–1964). The son of John Columbus Dellinger and Barbara Glen, Henry grew up in the Panhandle area. He left for World War I with the first men from Cherryville to go. He married Onie Eaker, daughter of Christie Eaker, and later had a long career as a rural mail carrier for the Cherryville Post Office.

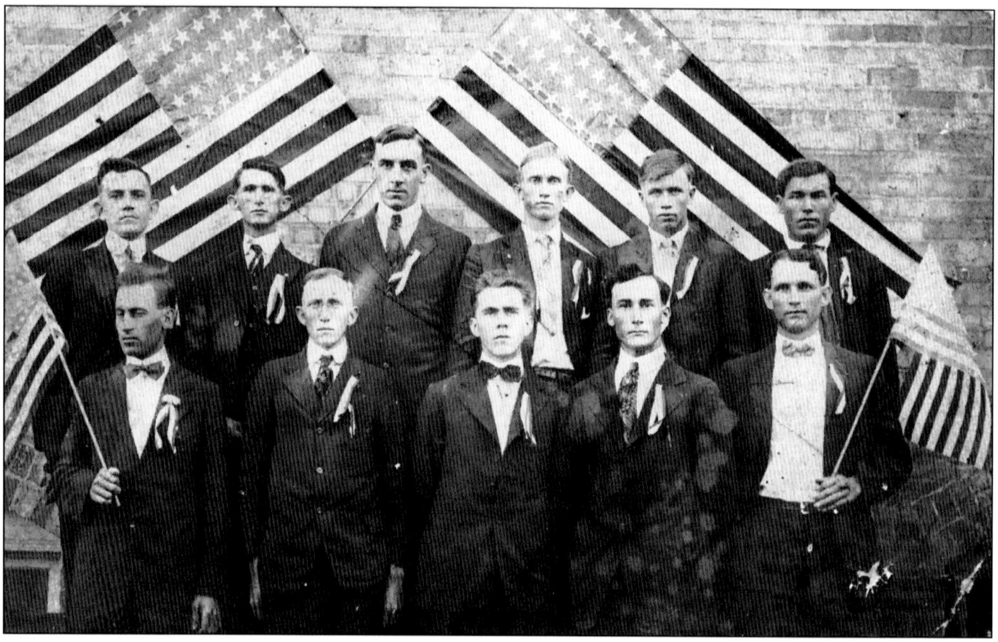

World War I Soldiers, 1917. Some of the first servicemen to leave Cherryville during World War I marked the occasion with this picture postcard on September 15, 1917. Many others would soon follow. Pictured are, from left to right, (first row) Sid Carpenter, Earl Costner, Jim Black, Webb Eaker, and Gus Mauney; (second row) John Whitworth, I. P. Long, Tom Self, Gyser Canipe, unidentified, and Arthur Dellinger.

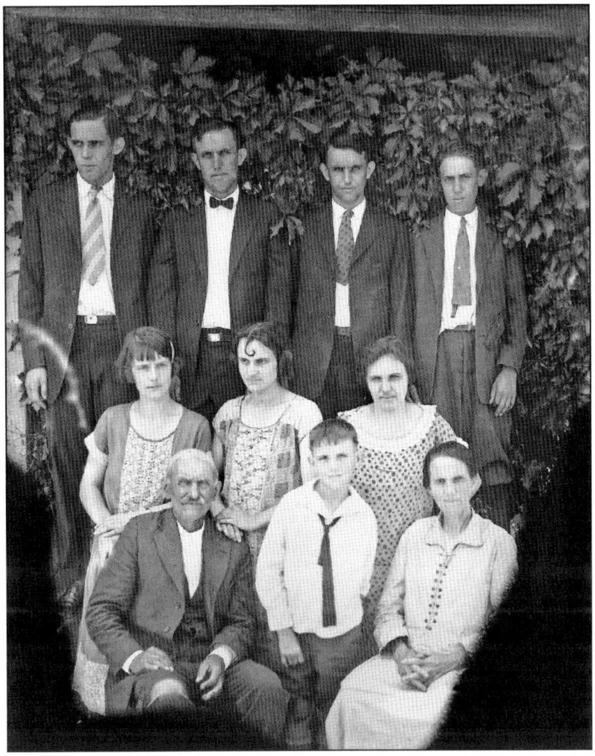

The McGinnis Family. Wiley N. McGinnis (1876–1962) was the son of Nathan McGinnis (1832–1908) and Susan Baker McGinnis. "Brought up" a few miles from Cherryville in the Beaver Dam section, he was one of the most widely known men in Cherryville. At one time, he was engaged in the livery stable business, worked at a brickyard, and was a teamster for the old mill. He later owned a general store and was in the general merchandising business at the mill store on West Academy Street near the Rhyne-Houser Mill No. 2. He also served as a town commissioner for many years. The mill workers (below) were photographed around 1908 at the Gaston Manufacturing Company (later Dora Mill), which was built in 1896.

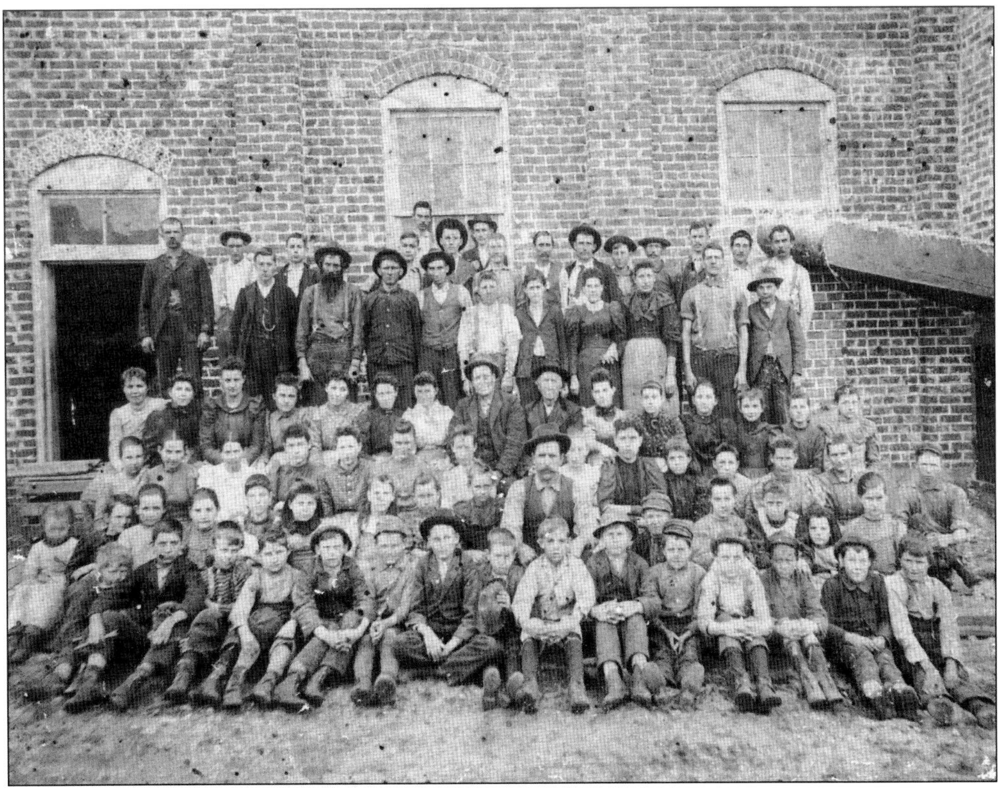

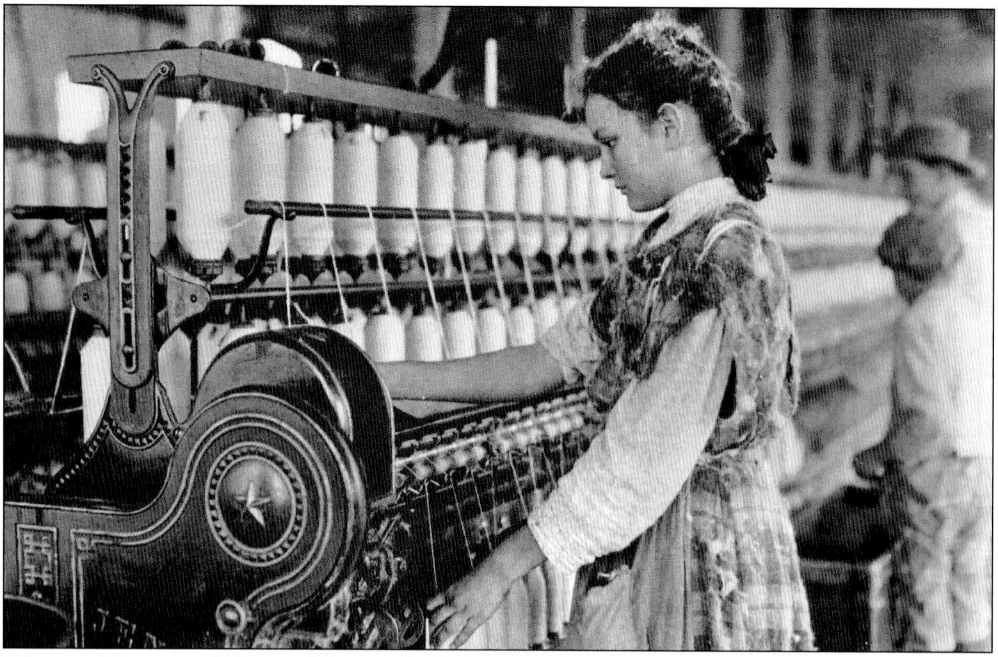

"Fair to Middling." Fair middling is the highest grade of nine grades of cotton, middling being No. 5 and the standard by which all grades are measured. This pretty young girl had been working two years as a spinner in the Vivian Cotton Mill when this photograph was taken in 1908 by Lewis Hine, a photographer for the National Child Labor Committee (NCLC). (Courtesy of the Library of Congress Photo Collection, NCLC, Lewis W. Hine No. 0271.)

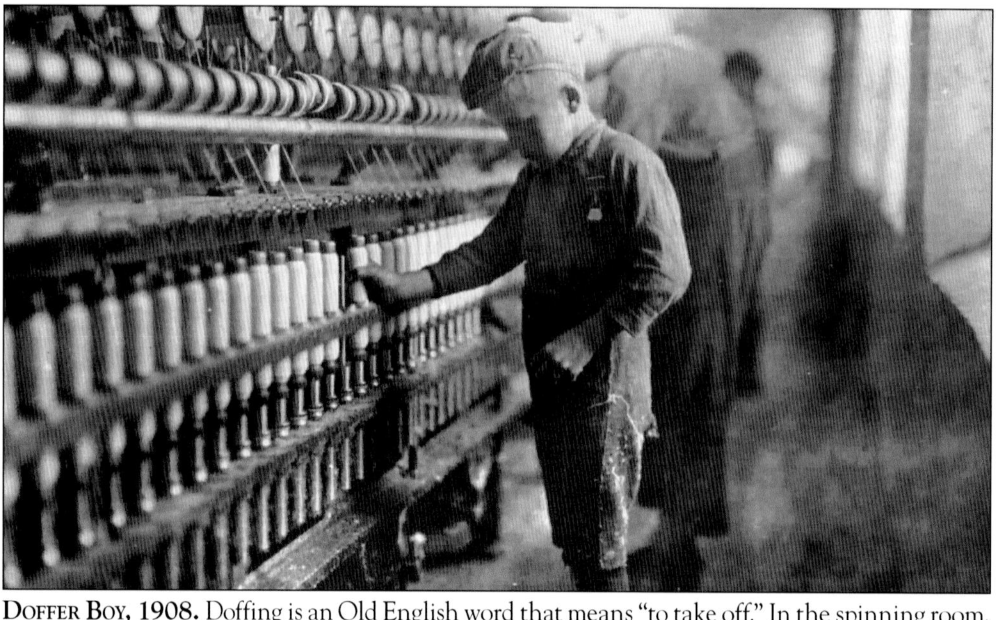

Doffer Boy, 1908. Doffing is an Old English word that means "to take off." In the spinning room, doffing was the task of removing filled bobbins and replacing them with empty ones. This child at the Melville Manufacturing Company in Cherryville said he had worked for two years. This photograph appeared on the cover of a report by the National Child Labor Committee around 1912. (Courtesy of the Library of Congress Photo Collection, NCLC, Lewis W. Hine.)

NOAH BENJAMIN KENDRICK. Kendrick Mercantile Company, a true department store located on the corner of Main and Mountain Streets, was organized and opened in 1903 by brothers J. W. Kendrick and Noah Benjamin Kendrick. The two-story brick building remains a landmark in downtown Cherryville.

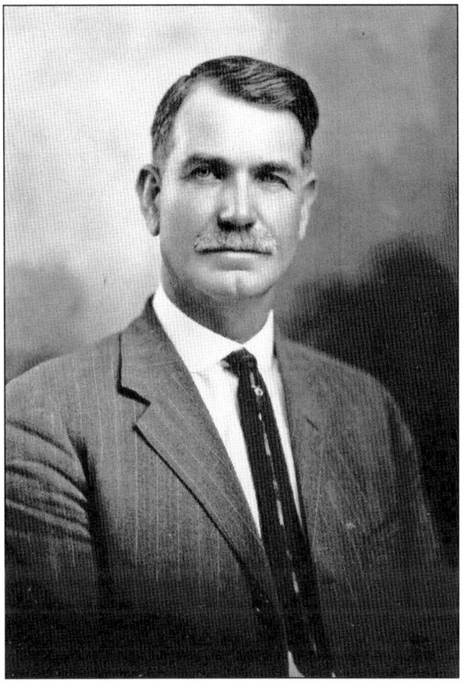

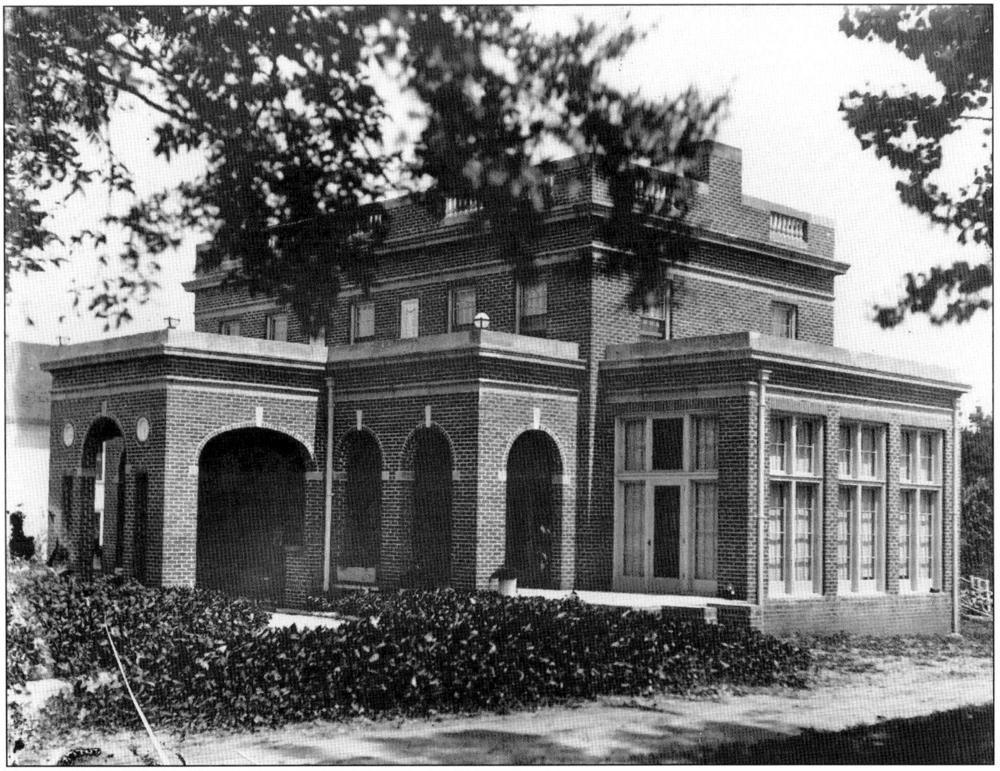

THE KENDRICK HOUSE, 1922. Noah Benjamin Kendrick of Cherryville built this house, designed by Hugh White, in 1922 as a showplace for the use of Kendrick Brick and Tile. Today it is a Gaston County Historic Property and is owned by Helen Homesley Lamoureux and family.

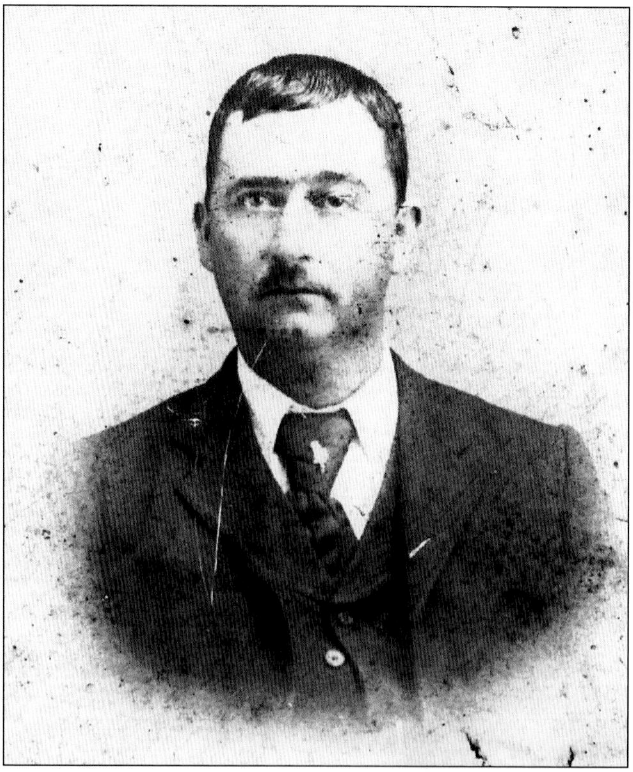

John Pinkney "Pink" Dellinger (1862–1921). Grandson of Moses Dellinger, Pink operated a whiskey store in Shelby before building a large home in 1908 on West Main Street in Cherryville, which is today owned by Charles and Pat Sherrill. Dellinger owned the Pink Manufacturing Company and Verner Oil Mill in Lattimore. While he and wife, Margaret Paulina Carpenter, lived on a farm on Buffalo Creek, near the South Carolina line, he operated the Ellis Ferry that crossed the Broad River. He was also postmaster in 1894 of Dellinger Post Office. (Courtesy of Charles and Pat Sherrill.)

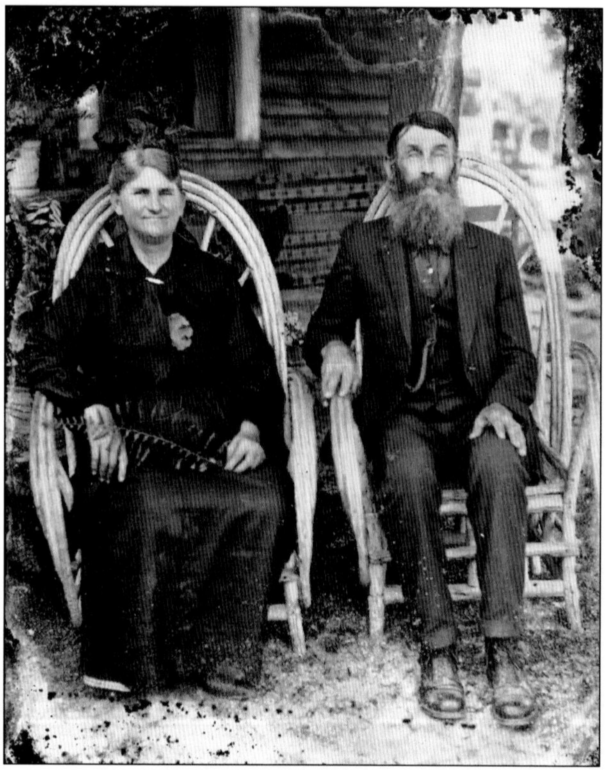

Lawson and Sally Glover Black. A grandson of Stephen Black (1800–1886), Lawson Black (1866–1955) was the son of Benaja Black and Annie Beam and a brother to Ben Black. Lawson, a farmer, married Sallie E. Glover (1870–1930), who was the daughter of Adam Glover. They are buried at Cherryville City Memorial Cemetery.

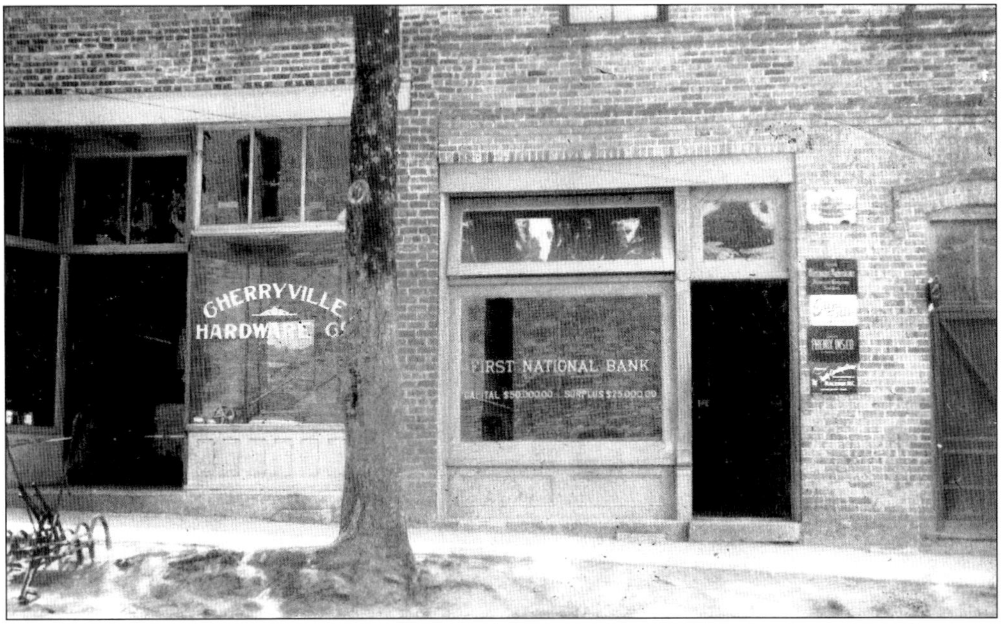

Cherryville, 1911. When this picture was taken around 1911, M. L. Mauney was cashier and M. C. Mauney assistant cashier of First National Bank. E. C. Brown was a railroad agent, Logan Craft and P. C. Beam dealt in fertilizer, and M. L. Rudisill was the secretary and treasurer of Melville Manufacturing Company. Dr. W. H. Houser and Dr. L. L. Self were prominent physicians, and Dr. R. J. Morrison was, at that time, a dentist and dealer in musical instruments.

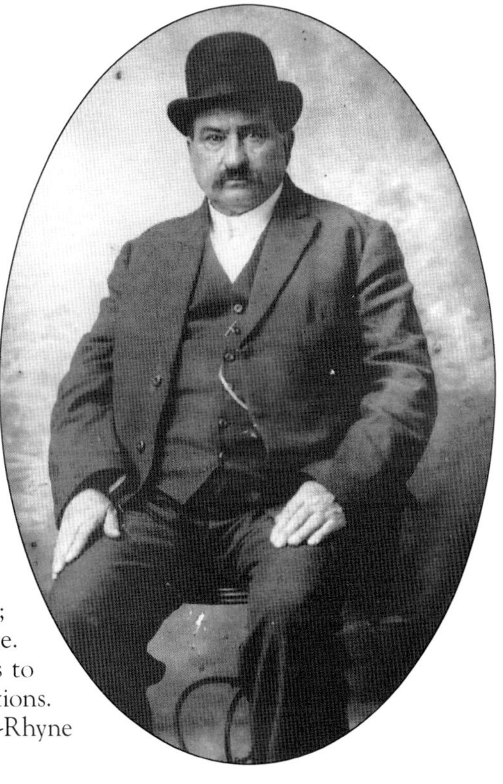

Industrialist Daniel Efrid Rhyne (1852–1931). Born near Mount Holly in Gaston County, D. E. Rhyne was a banker; textile manufacturer; owner of gold mines, tin mines, and a wagon factory in Hickory, North Carolina; and is said to have owned the first car in the state. He is remembered for his philanthropic gifts to religious, educational, and charitable organizations. Lenoir College in Hickory was renamed Lenoir-Rhyne College in his honor.

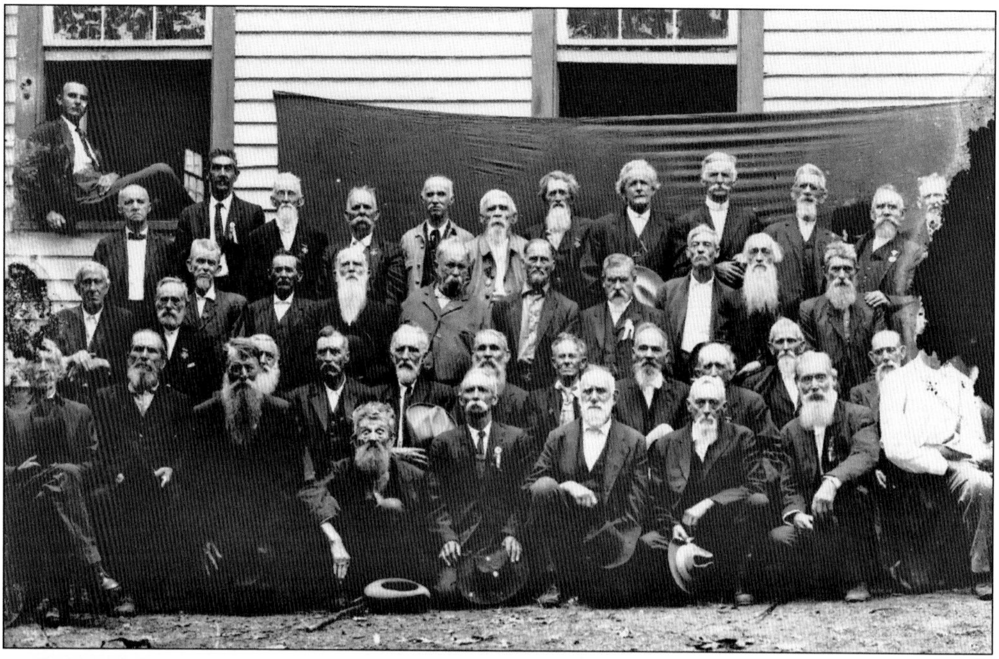

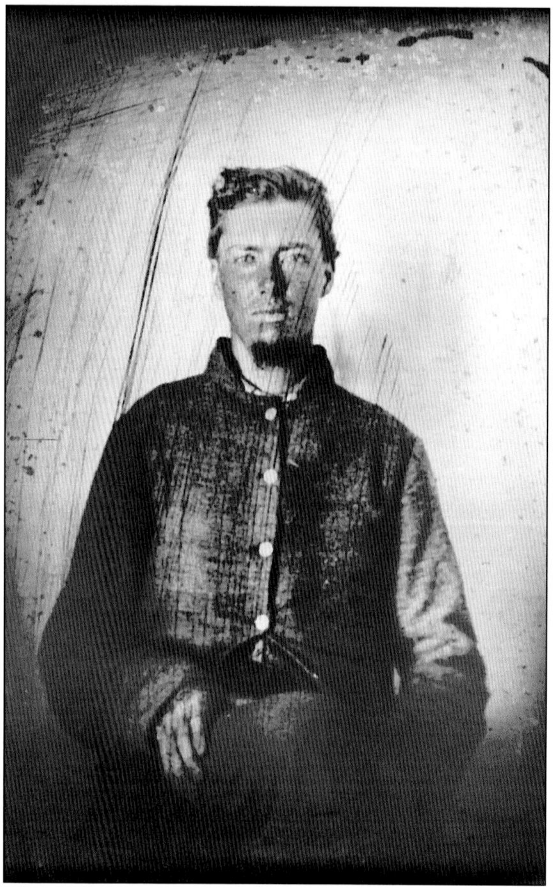

AMERICAN CIVIL WAR (1861–1865). "Lead Kindly Light, amid the encircling gloom, Lead thou me on; the night is dark, and I am far from home," from a hymn by John Newman. The Cherryville area sent its share of men and boys to fight in the Civil War. In the photograph above, Confederate veterans from the Gaston–Lincoln County area hold an Old Soldiers' Reunion around 1910 in Gaston County. Some are wearing Southern Crosses bestowed on them after the war by the United Daughters of the Confederacy. Among those pictured from the Cherryville area are John C. Carpenter (the grandfather of Cone Carpenter Sr.), Joe Black, George Self, Elam Houser, William Brown, Oliver Hallman, James Ledford, Joe Dellinger, Daniel Houser, Michael Carpenter, Capt. Isaac Self, and Peter Neill. Other Confederate soldiers from the Cherryville area were Robert G. Brown, James Crowder, John Dellinger, Nelson George, John Dellinger, Caleb Wehunt, W. O. Harrelson, Oliver Sisk, and Alfred, Thomas, and Daniel Black.

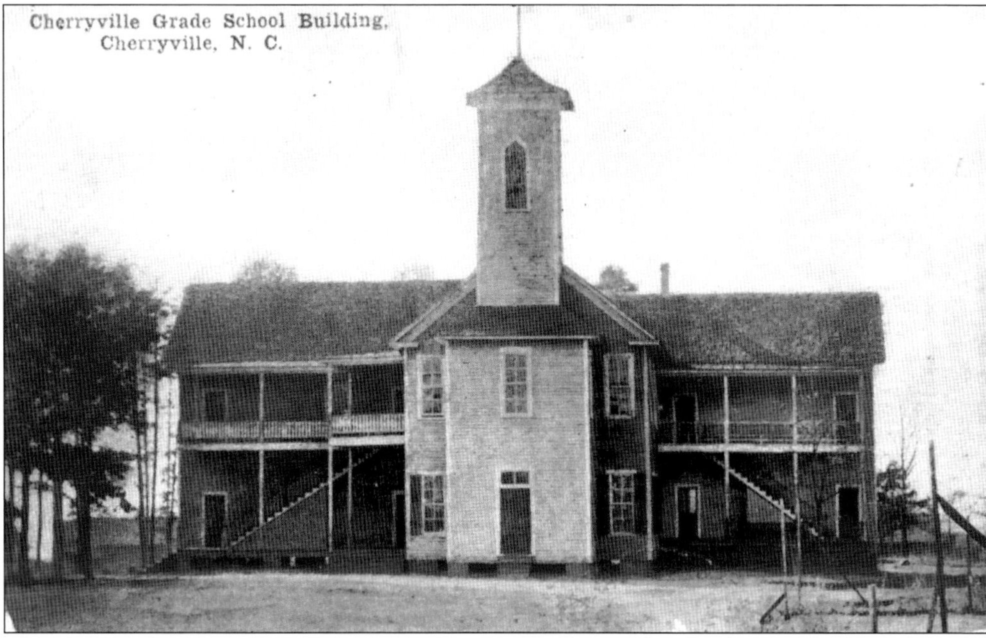

OLD CHERRYVILLE ACADEMY. Built in 1892, the two-story frame building was located at what was then the end of West Academy Street. The first graduating class received its diplomas in 1911. This image shows the school around 1911. Some of the early academy teachers were Zona Stroup Falls, Prof. S. P. Wilson, B. H. J. Houser, Capt. T. R. Bell, James Bell, Laura J. Wilson, Joe R. Nixon, and ? Zimmerman. The academy was used until 1915, when Cherryville High School was built.

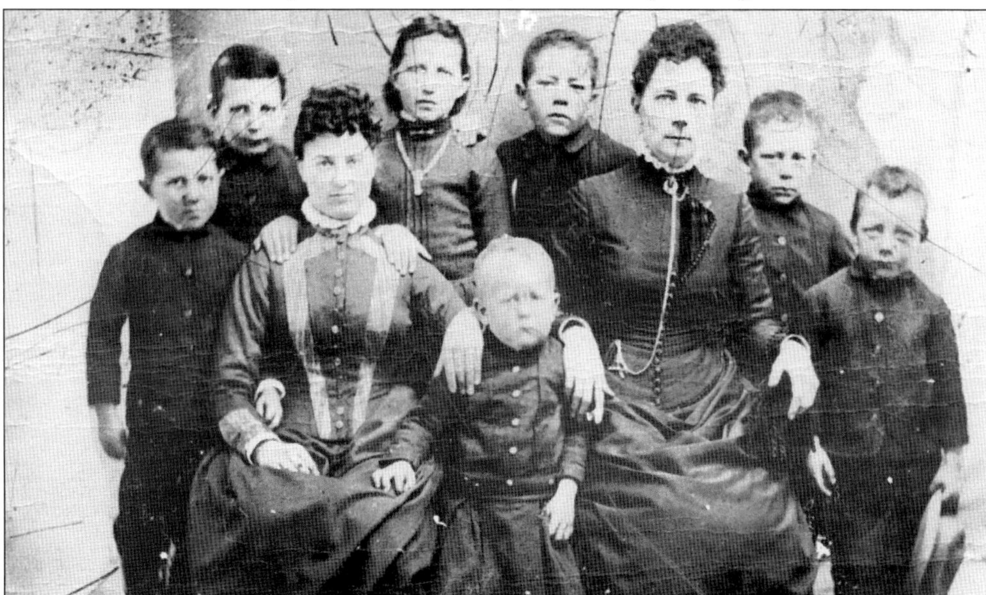

CHERRYVILLE PRIVATE SCHOOL. Before public schools and the Cherryville Academy, there was a private school for children around the beginning of the 20th century. It was operated by Lee Dellinger and Rufus Carroll for their children and engaged Lola Farnsworth (seated, right). The students are Dorus Dellinger, Grier Dellinger, Ava Dellinger (Rudisill), Will Carroll, Charlie Carroll, Audie Carroll, Clarence Carroll, and Sallie Thornburg.

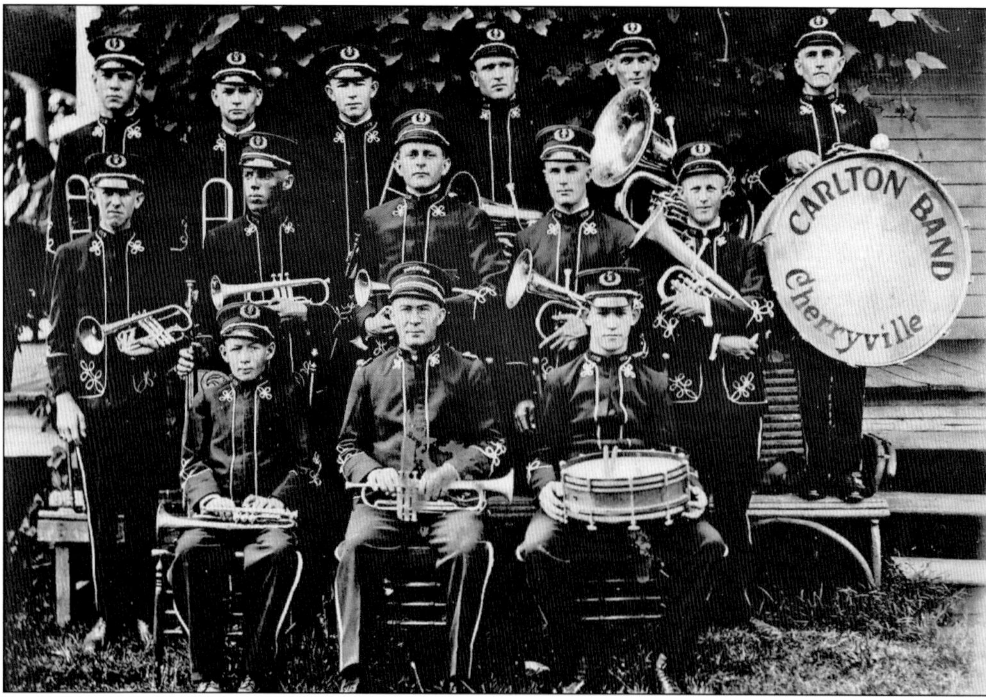

THE CARLTON YARD MILL BAND, 1925–1926. Band members are, from left to right, (first row) Streeter Frye, Ed Frye, and Monroe Randall; (second row) Lewis Sneed, Noah Mauney, Kelly Huss, Caldwell Farnsworth, and Guy Sneed; (third row) Howard Allran, Raymond Randall, Russell Frye, Floyd L. Mauney, Bill Harmon, and Rufus Mauney.

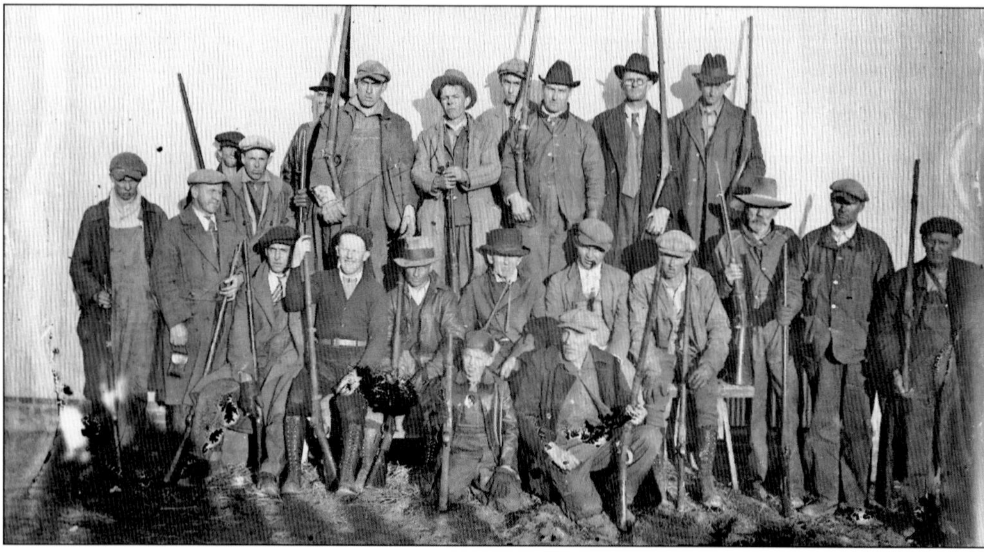

NEW YEAR'S DAY, 1921. Pictured in front of the Farmer's Union Fertilizer Building are the Cherryville New Year Shooters. From left to right are (first row) Floyd Mauney and Tom Mauney; (second row) Jake Mauney, Lewis Sneed, Ira Black, Ephraim Stroup, Houston Quinn, and Zeno Helton. Among the others are Sam Sellers, Vance Sellers, Noah Mauney, Sidney Beam, Von Heavner, Clarence Sneed, Berge Black, Wesley Helms, John Steve Stroup, Ben Black, James Mauney, and Tom Mauney.

Two

A Lasting Legacy

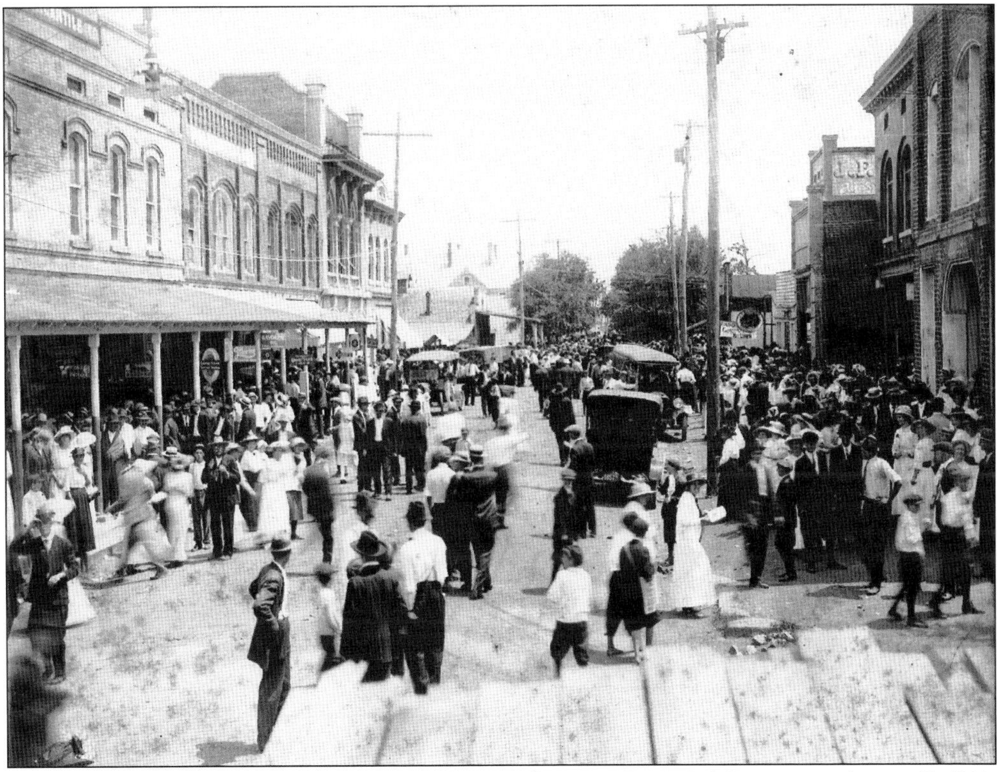

Big Day Celebration. The program for Cherryville's "Big Day" Celebration on August 5, 1911, made for a full day of fun. The local newspaper lists music by three brass bands at the square at 9:30 a.m., the first balloon ascension at the academy at 10:00 a.m., an address by Gov. W. W. Kitchin at the academy at 11:30 a.m., an Old Soldiers' Dinner at city hall at 1:00 p.m., brass bands again at 2:00 p.m., a horseback tournament at the academy at 2:30 p.m., the second balloon ascension at 4:00 p.m., and a baseball game at the academy at 4:30 p.m. There were also two moving picture shows, the vaudeville, one old-time minstrel show, a merry-go-round, and watermelon feasts. This photograph was taken in 1916.

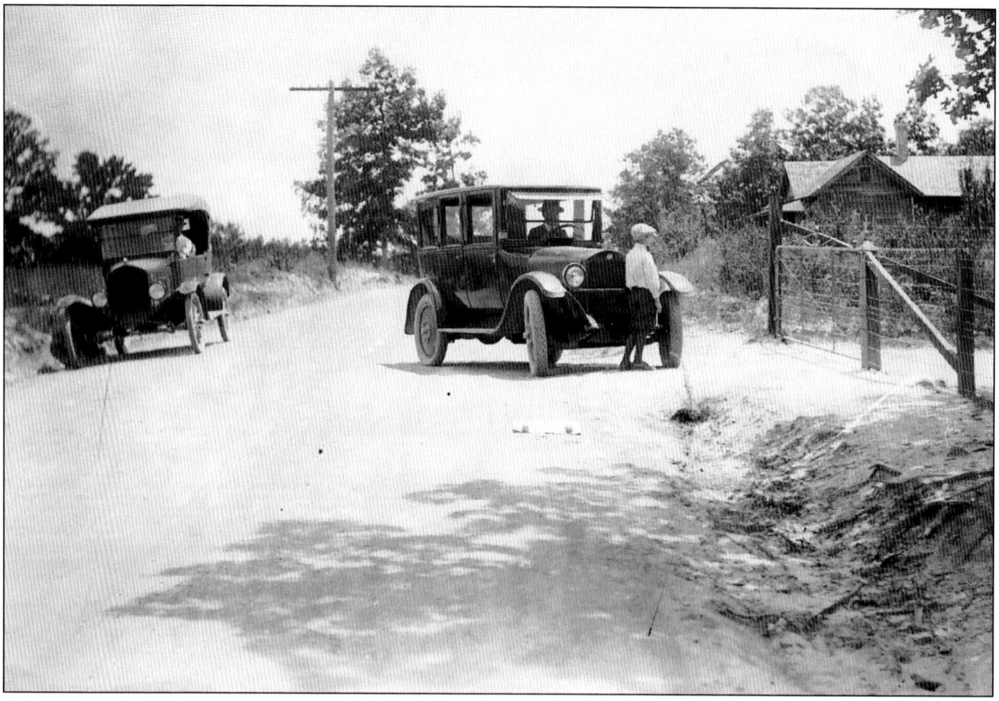

Cherryville–Bessemer City Highway. Railroads did a wonderful job of connecting cities in the early 1900s, but roads were another matter. Some areas during this time had "macadam" roads of close-packed gravel, but it was some time before these state-of-the-arts roads came to Cherryville. Dust or mud was expected!

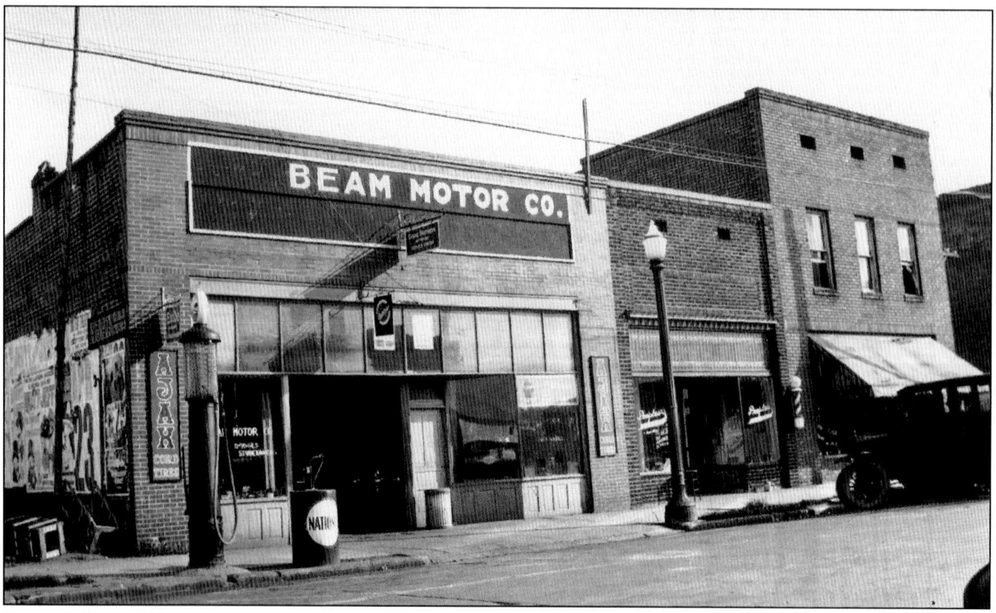

Beam Motor Company. After the automobile became commonplace in America, car dealerships, service stations selling fuel and tires, and garages sprang up in most small towns. In larger towns, "touring clothes" were sold. This city block, shown here in the 1920s, was located where Cherryville Savings and Loan is today.

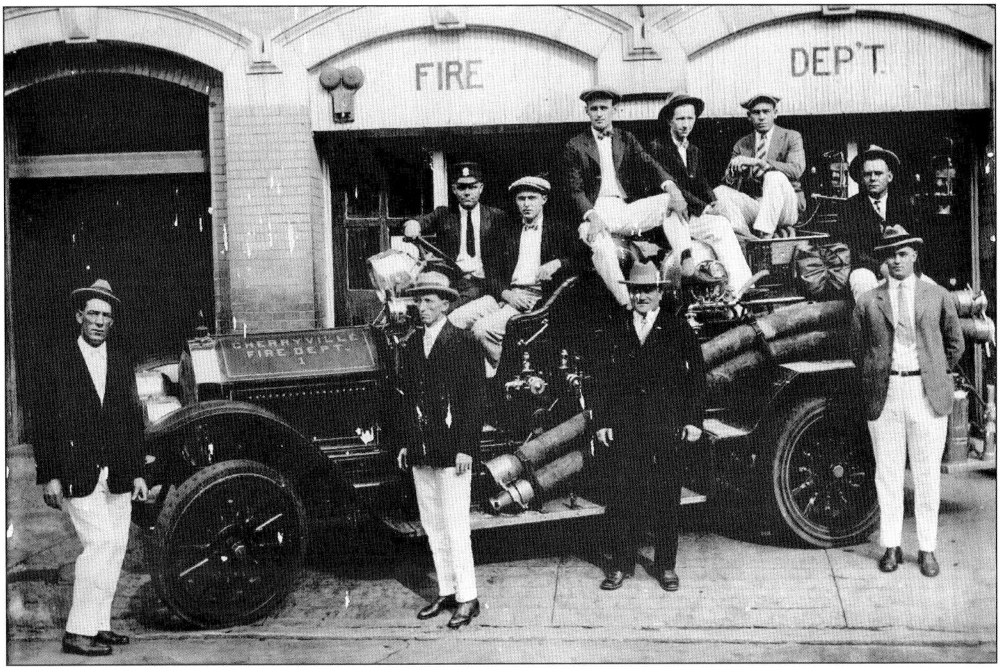

A 1921 Le France Fire Truck. Cherryville's first motorized fire truck was a Le France 1921 model. It can be seen today at the Cherryville Historical Museum. Volunteer firemen pictured are, from left to right, (standing) I. M. Burns, J. E. Costner (fire chief), Forrest U. Mauney, and driving instructor Albert Upton; (on the truck) Frank Garrison, Wiley "Sam" Whitesides (driver), Floyd Beam, Ed Hoyle, Vernon Beach, and Clyde Carpenter.

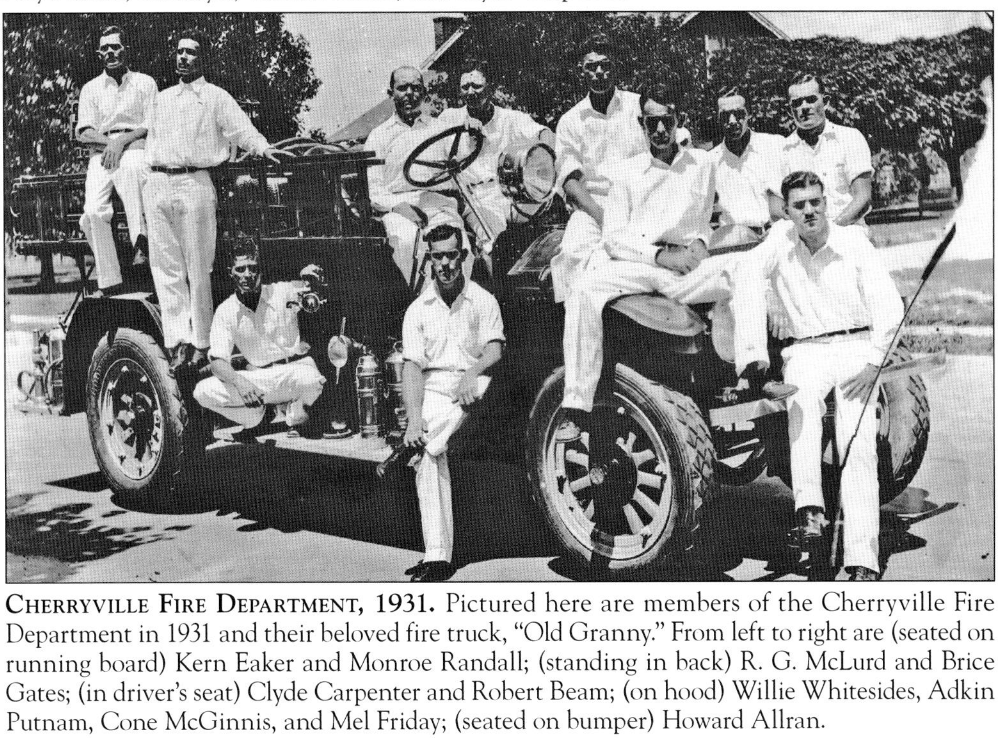

Cherryville Fire Department, 1931. Pictured here are members of the Cherryville Fire Department in 1931 and their beloved fire truck, "Old Granny." From left to right are (seated on running board) Kern Eaker and Monroe Randall; (standing in back) R. G. McLurd and Brice Gates; (in driver's seat) Clyde Carpenter and Robert Beam; (on hood) Willie Whitesides, Adkin Putnam, Cone McGinnis, and Mel Friday; (seated on bumper) Howard Allran.

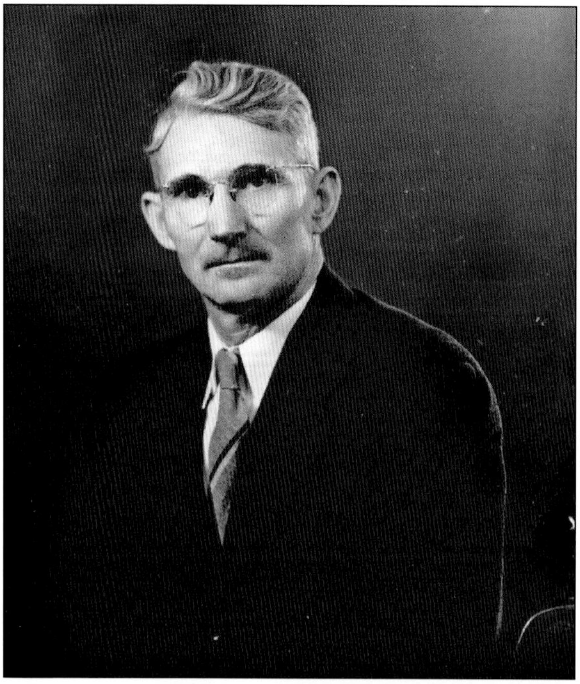

A. Click Beam (1895–1968). Arvle Click Beam was the son of George Lee and Junie McGinnis Beam. He served in World War I and later was a cashier at the Cherryville National Bank for many years. His daughter, Adrienne Beam Osborne, worked at the same bank for many years.

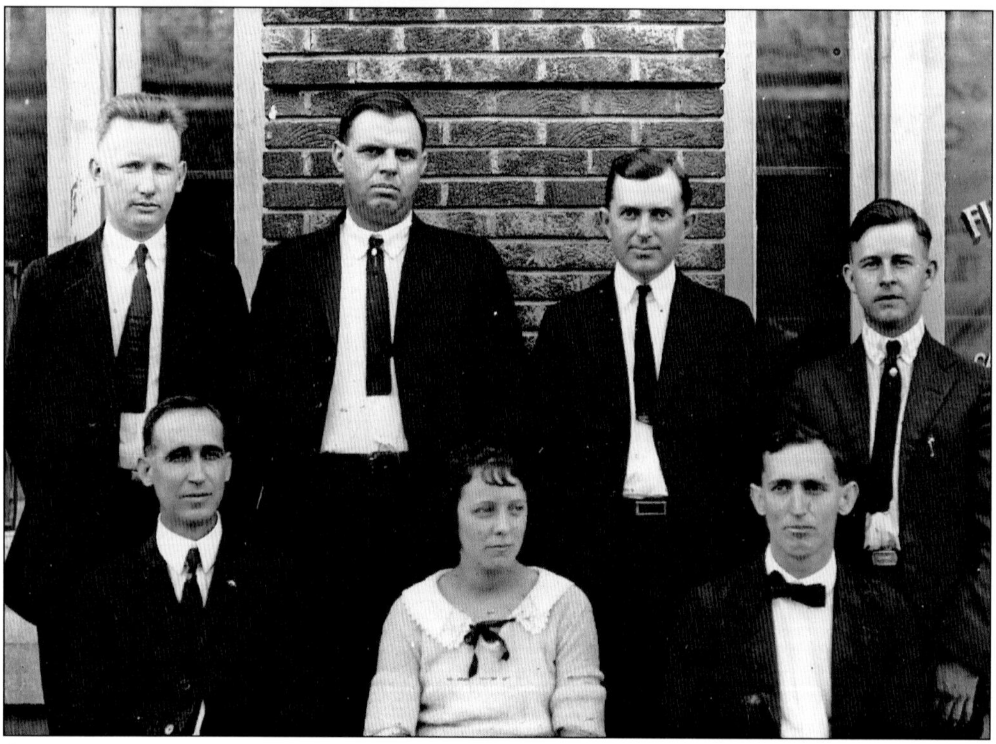

Cherryville National Bank, 1926. The staff of Cherryville National Bank can be seen here in 1926, ten years after the new building was constructed. They are, from left to right, (first row) Marcus L. Mauney, Carolyn Heafner, and M. C. Mauney; (second row) Andrew Mauney, Dorus C. Upton, E. V. Moss, and Dewey F. Beam.

EZRA VERNON MOSS. Cashier of Cherryville National Bank in 1934, Moss was executive vice president in 1961 at his death. In 1938, the directors were Hoke Huss, J. T. Allen, Dr. L. L. Self, C. A. Rudisill, and Dr. F. M. Houser. The bank was founded in 1904 by S. S. Mauney and M. L. Rudisill. It moved from its first location, where the Cherryville Savings and Loan now stands, to the corner of Mountain and Main Streets in 1916.

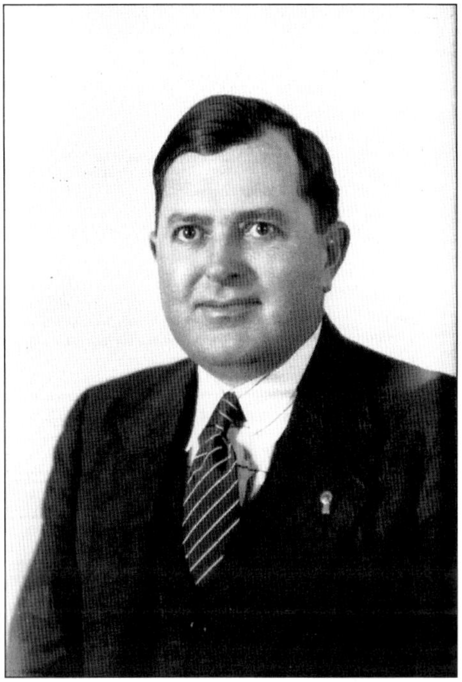

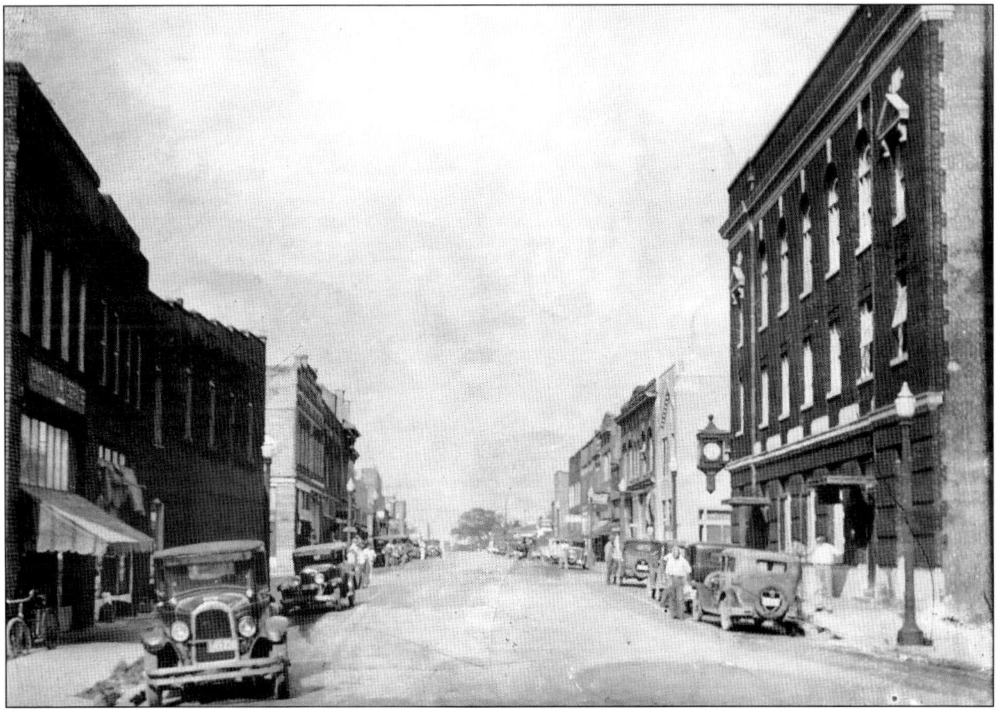

CHERRYVILLE NATIONAL BANK. Designed by architect Willard Rogers, the neoclassical Cherryville National Bank is at right in this photograph of Main Street, looking east. It was built in 1916 at a cost of $35,000 and had fixtures of bronze, marble, and mahogany. There was a public ladies' restroom and a public farmers' room. The first floor housed the bank, the second housed offices, and the third floor was used for lodge meetings.

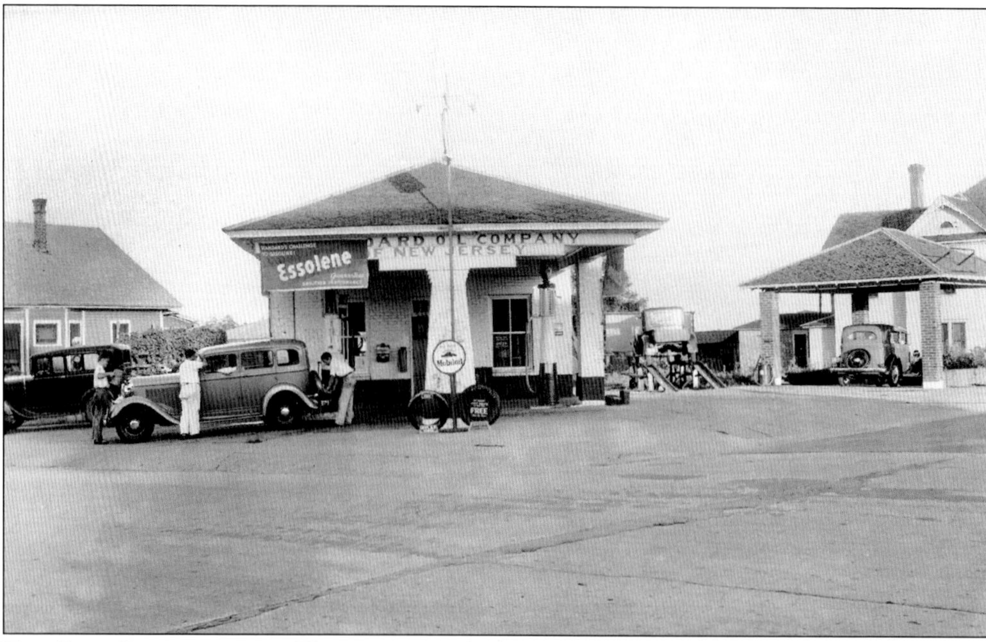

The Esso Station, 1933. This was one of Cherryville's busiest corners on Main Street in 1933, when the above photograph was taken. The Esso Station (shown above) was operated by Ralph Sharpe and was located on the corner of Main and Jacob Streets. Standard's new motor fuel, Essolene, and Essolube, its new motor oil, were introduced that year and greatly increased Sharpe's sales. In the 1930s, the 44 Auto Inn (pictured below) was located on Mountain Street near the railroad tracks. Its motto was, "Give Us a Try and Be Convinced," and the telephone number was 44. Regular gas cost 20¢ a gallon. Patrons could have their automobiles "washed and greased" for only $1. There were also many other stations in and around Cherryville during this time period.

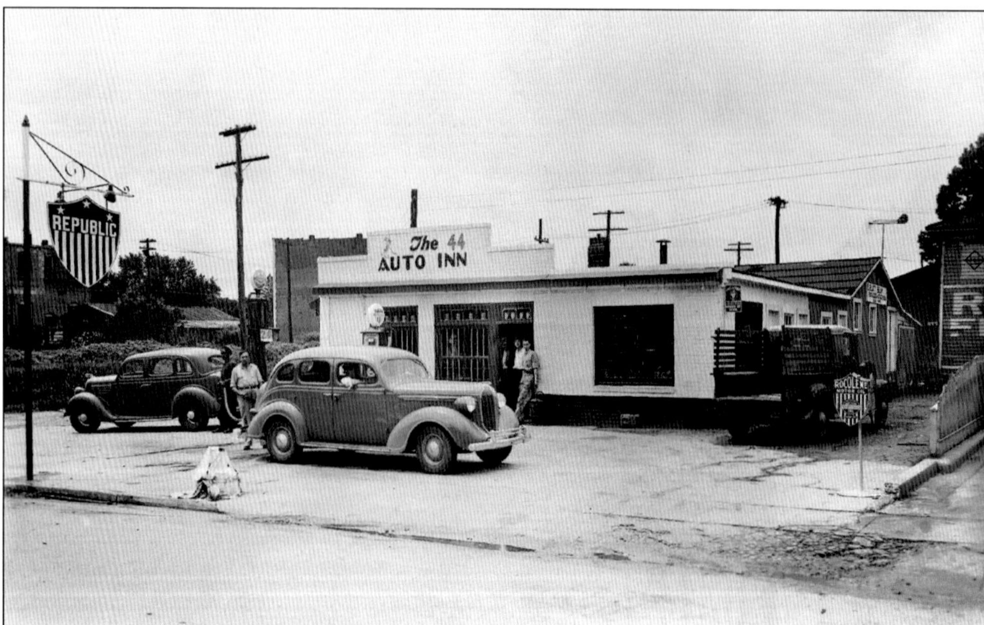

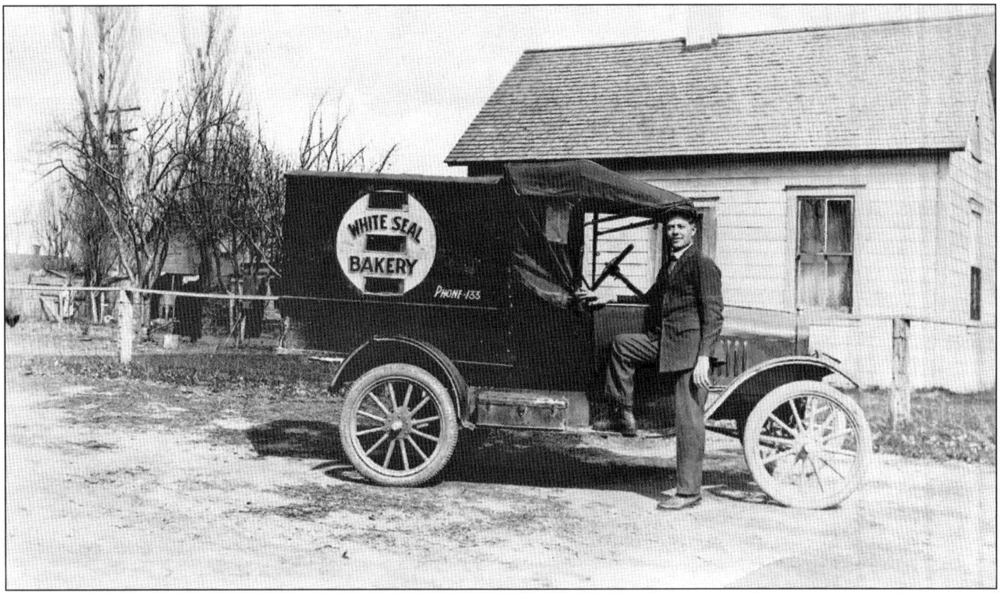

White Seal Bakery. White Seal Bakery was a wholesale and retail bakery in Cherryville during the 1920s. The bakery was owned by H. O. Halstead, seen above standing beside his White Seal Bakery delivery truck in the 1920s. Bread was delivered to local homes, hotels, boardinghouses, and businesses. The bakery's motto was "The Best We Have in Every Loaf." One of the boardinghouses the bakery delivered to was the Nu-Way Spinning Mill's boardinghouse. Many mills had boardinghouses for single workers and those who had not brought their families to the mill village yet. Some workers boarded with private families. The large dough bowl seen in the photograph below is on display at the Cherryville Historical Museum.

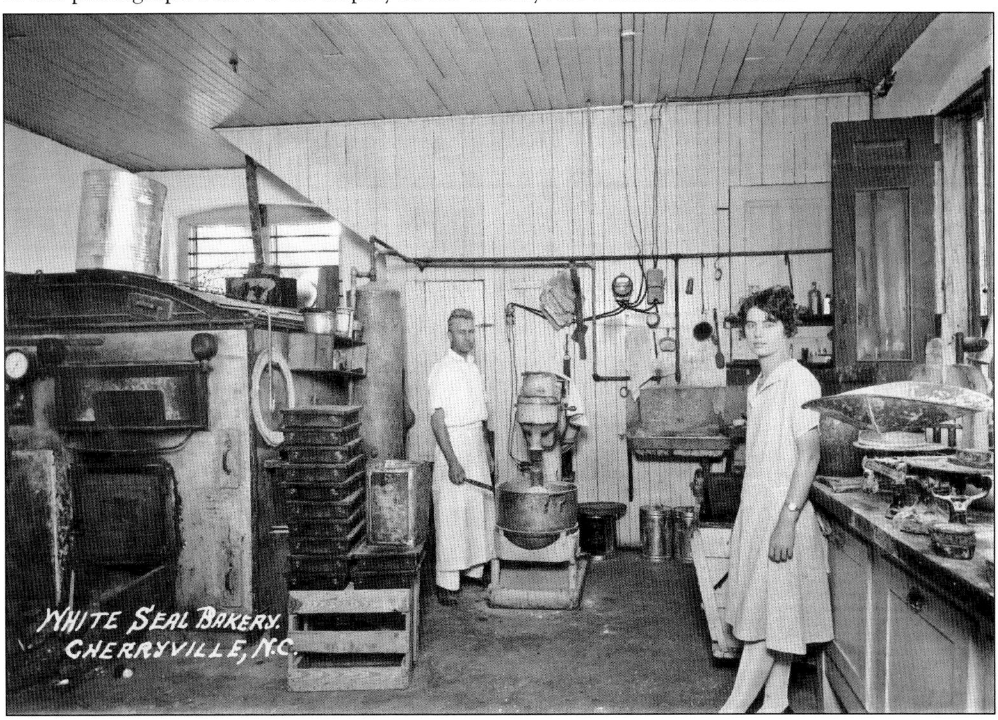

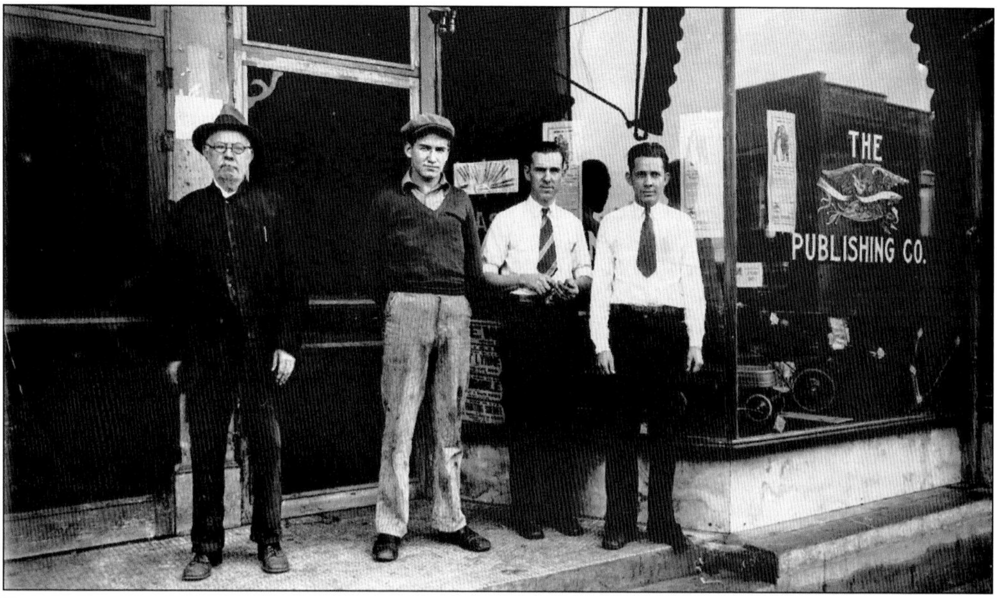

The Eagle Publishing Company. In February 1926, the *Cherryville Eagle* staff takes a break outside their office for the photographer. They are, from left to right, Levi (L. H. J.) Houser, editor of the *Eagle*; Harvey Lankford; J. P. Costner; and Fred K. Houser.

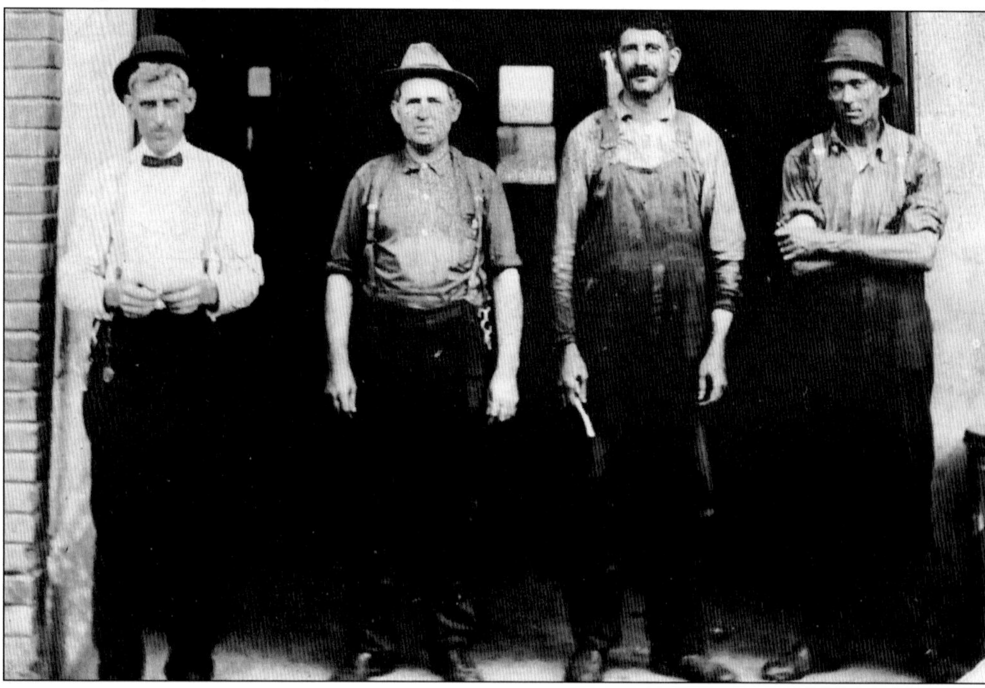

Cherryville Foursome. Stopping their work for a photograph, these four Cherryville citizens are (from left to right) Dr. Robert J. Morrison (1877–1960), dentist and optometrist, who came to Cherryville around 1904; William Thomas Gates, merchant; Tom Seagle, local blacksmith; and Henry Summit, son of Henry Summit (1828–1894), who built the first house in town. The older Henry Summit, buried at St. John's Lutheran Church, was dead by the time this photograph was taken.

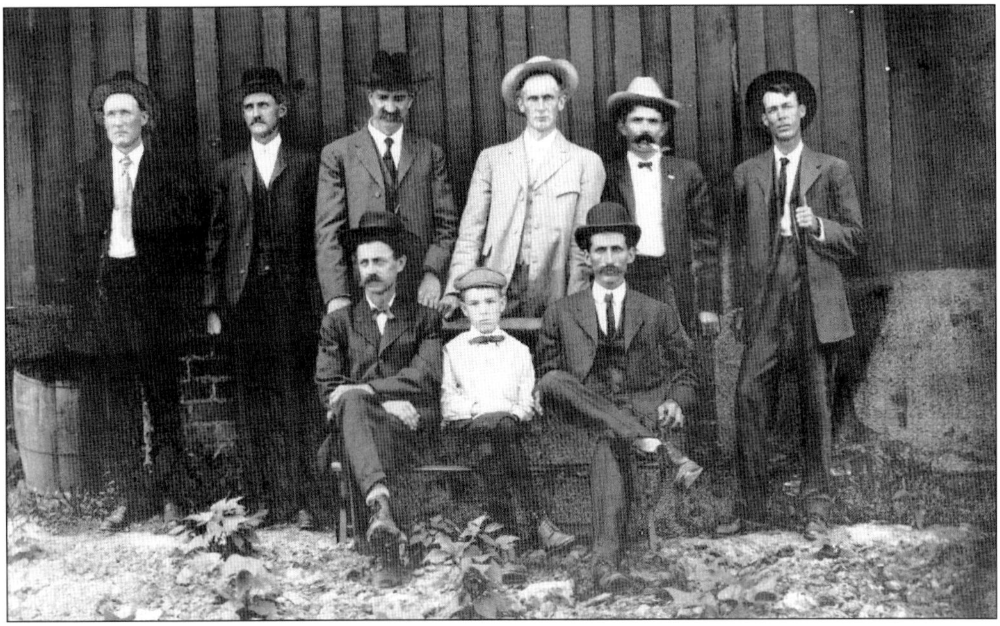

The Cherryville Train Depot. The first depot was a frame building located at Pink and First Streets. The Seaboard Airline Railway, first known as the Carolina Central Railroad, was extended from Lincolnton to Cherryville about the close of the Civil War. The second depot of brick construction was built in the early 1900s. W. D. Brown was the Cherryville depot agent for many years, starting around 1914.

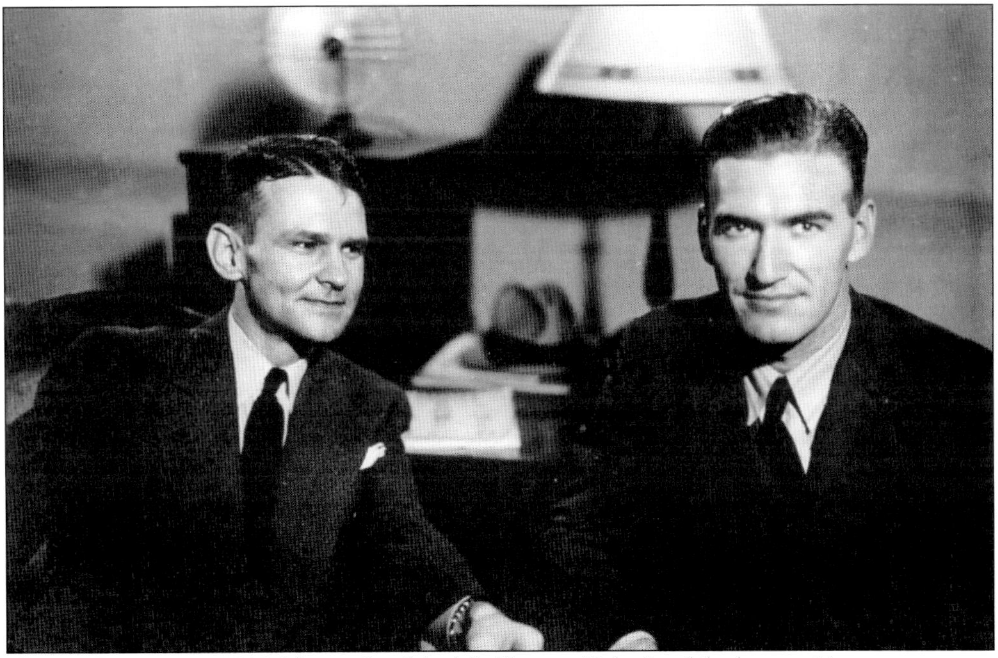

Harvey Lankford, 1933. Harvey Lankford (left), son of John Lankford, was a Linotype operator and machinist for the Eagle Publishing Company. He was thought to be the youngest machinist in the state. Also shown is J. P. Costner, who was head of the mechanical department at the publishing company.

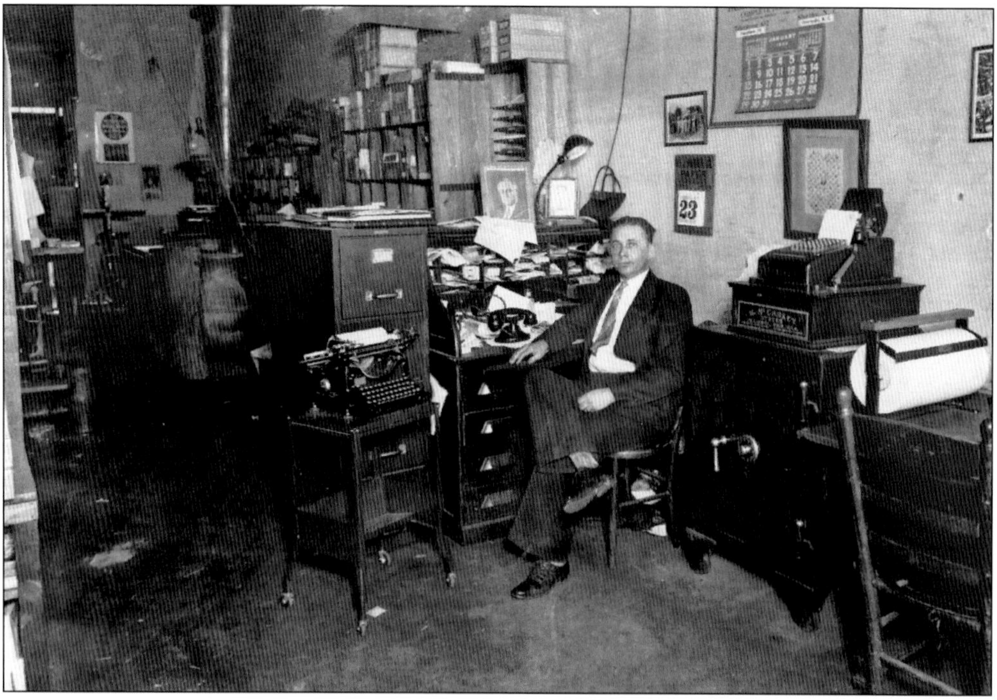

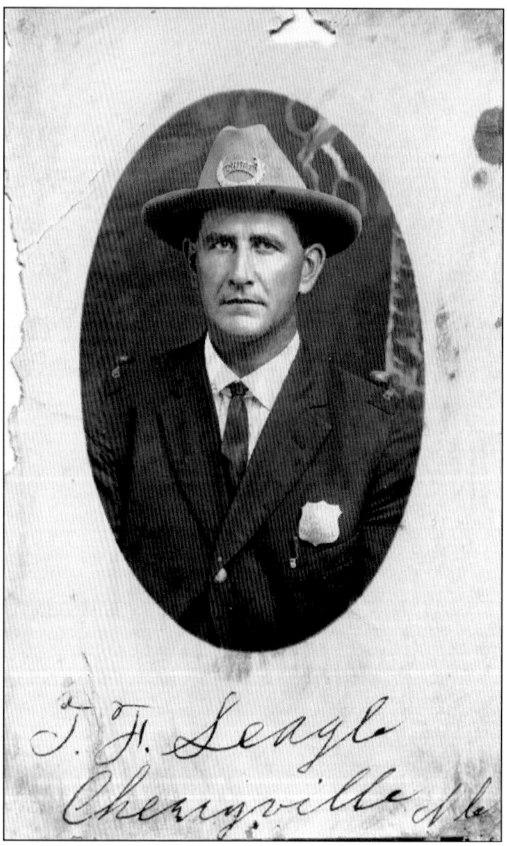

Fred Kohn Houser. Son of newspaper editor Levi Jacob Houser (1856–1933), Fred Houser was born on April 8, 1905, and married Creola Griggs from Chesterfield, South Carolina. He took over the job of editor of the *Cherryville Eagle* after his father's death. Fred and Creola had no children but worked side-by-side at the newspaper.

Cherryville Police Chief Tom Seagle (1879–1930). Thomas Frances Seagle was born in Lincoln County, the son of John Adolphus Seagle and Mary Catherine Mosteller. He first married Maude Stroupe, and after her death, he married Lona Heavner. He belonged to St. John's Lutheran Church in Cherryville and was a gifted blacksmith, mechanic, and carpenter.

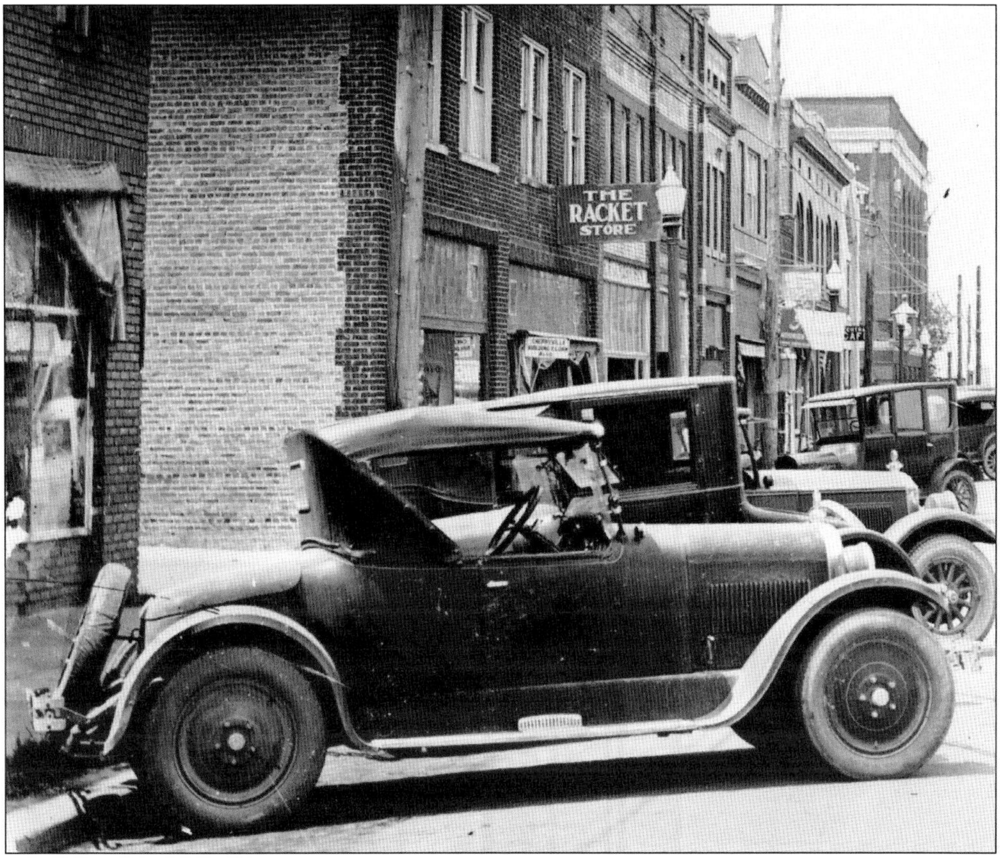

Main Street Cherryville, 1927. Even in the 1920s, backing into a parking place was the cool thing to do. Looking west on Main Street, Cherryville Building and Loan Association, a Ford dealership, Central Café, and the Racket Store were all located on the block where Houser Drug Store is today.

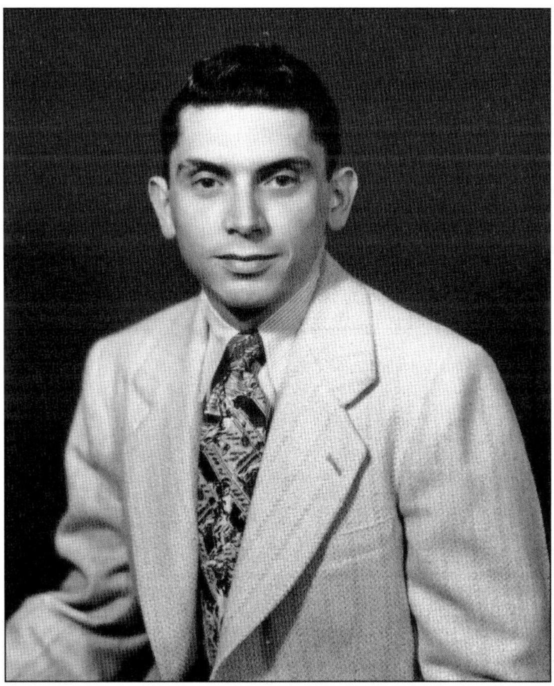

Irvin Goldiner. Max Goldiner (1896–1964), born in New York of Russian immigrants, came from Hickory, North Carolina, and opened the Racket Store on Main Street in Cherryville in the 1920s. Max Goldiner later added a more substantial line of dry goods, clothing, and shoes to his store in Cherryville and then changed the name to Goldiner's Department Store. His son, Irvin Goldiner (shown here), continued with the business for many years.

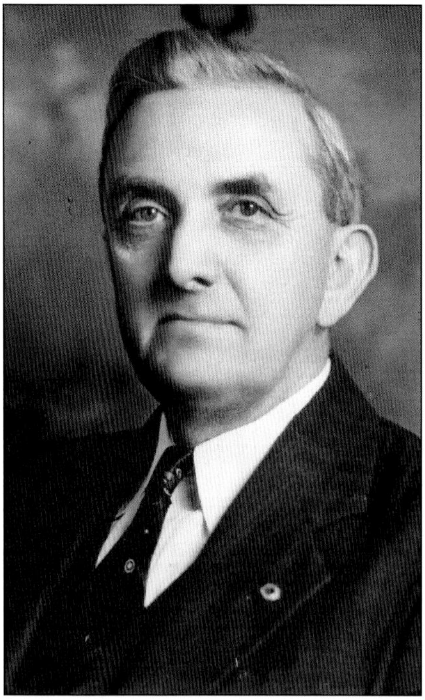

G. V. Lohr. G. V. Lohr served as recorder (judge) from 1948 to 1952 in Cherryville. He was a descendant of pioneer Valentine Lohr. Another well-known Lohr was Dr. Luther L. Lohr (1862–1939), a Lutheran minister and professor, who was trained at the Lutheran Theological Seminaries in Gettysburg and Philadelphia, Pennsylvania. Others known to have served as judge in Cherryville were Ray Ballard, Lester Houser, and Yates McGinnis.

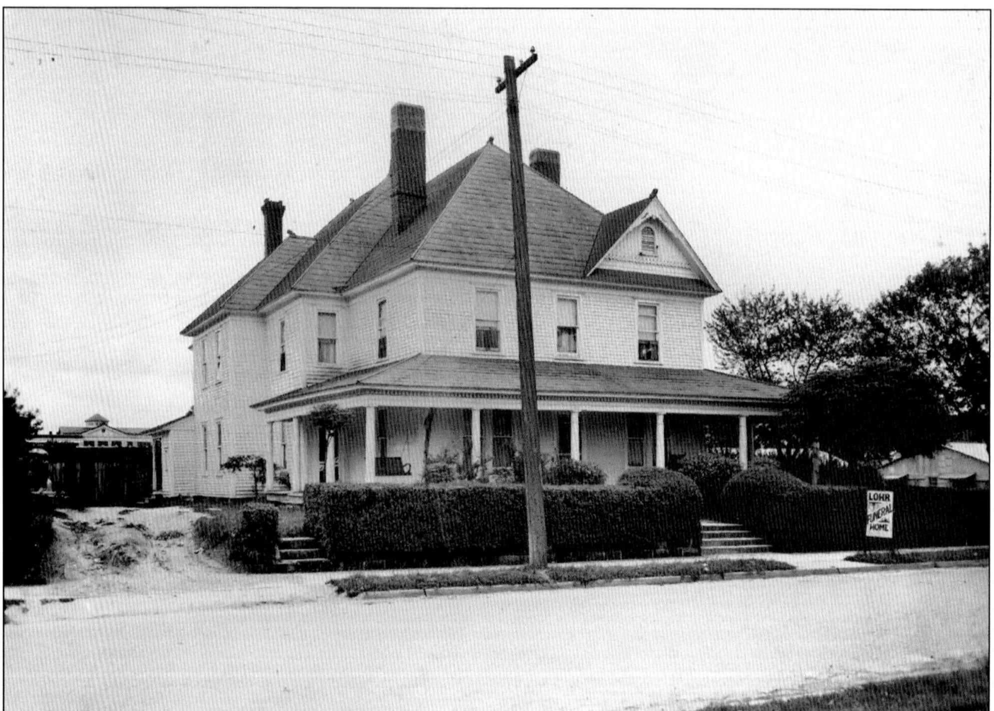

Lohr Funeral Home. Lohr Funeral Home and office of the Lohr Mutual Burial Association was located on North Mountain Street in the 1930s. G. V. Lohr was the proprietor and undertaker, and his wife, Bessie L. Lohr, was his assistant, with G. S. Lohr as ambulance driver. Note the view of First Baptist Church in the background.

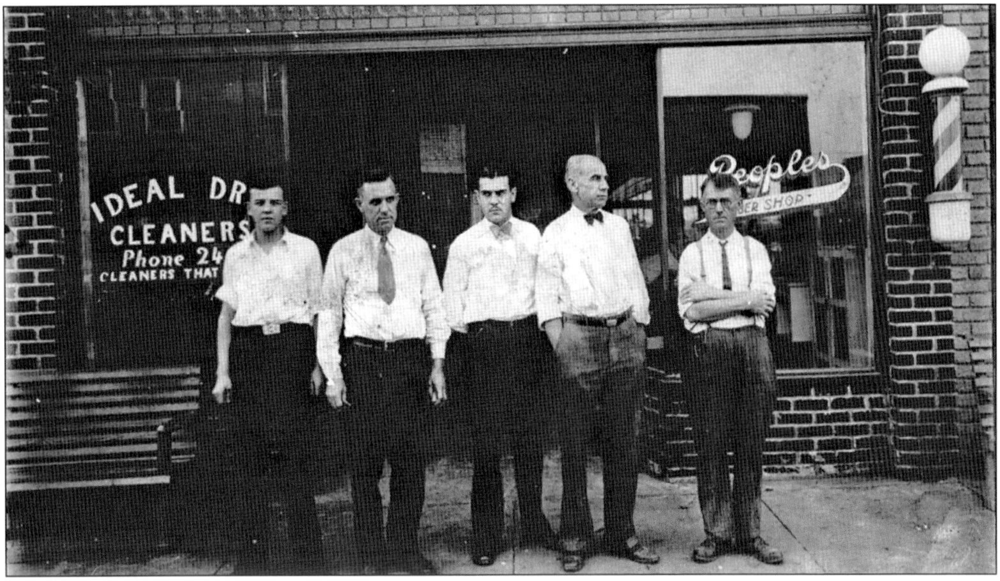

PEOPLE'S BARBER SHOP. Standing in front of his place of business, Ideal Dry Cleaners, is Jesse Jarrett (far left). The Peoples Barber Shop barbers in this photograph are, from left to right, Lawrence McGinnis, Howard Allran, Henry Allran, and John Hendricks. Henry Allran was born in Lincoln County in the settlement called Henry in 1881 to James Asbury Allran and his wife, Frances Shuford. Asbury was the postmaster of the new post office, and he named it Henry after his son. At the age of seven, Henry worked near his home in Jugtown in a pottery factory. He moved with his family to Cherryville in 1890. Allran worked for a while in the old Gaston Mill and a mill in Bessemer City. In 1907, local barber Frank Black died, and Allran was asked to run the local barbershop. Clayton Crocker and Floyd Waters joined him in the barber business. The Mauney Building, where the shop was located, was where the savings and loan is today. The City Beauty Parlor was owned by Grover Beam and was located upstairs in the Houser Building. The contraption seen in the background (below) was an electric permanent wave machine and can be seen at the Cherryville Historical Museum.

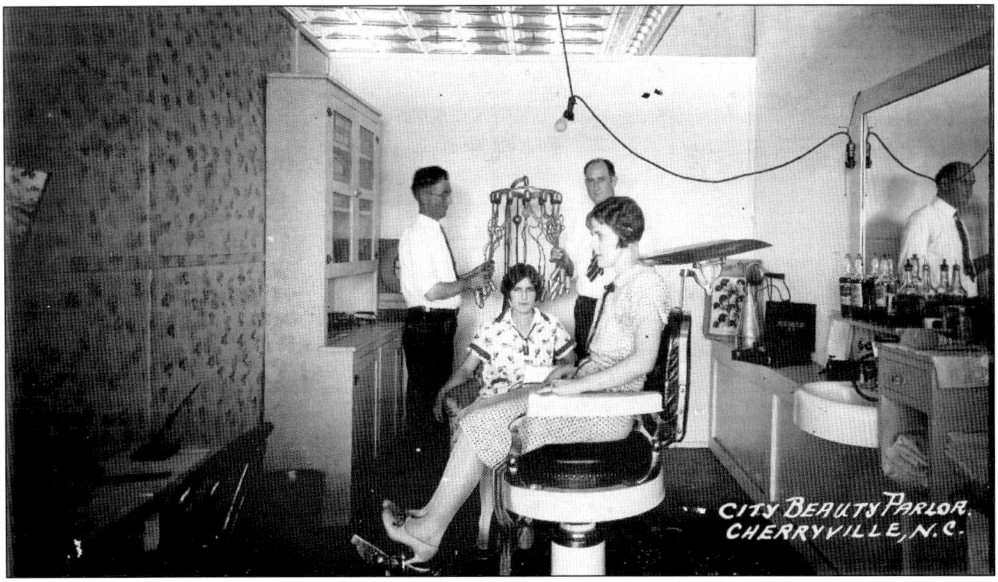

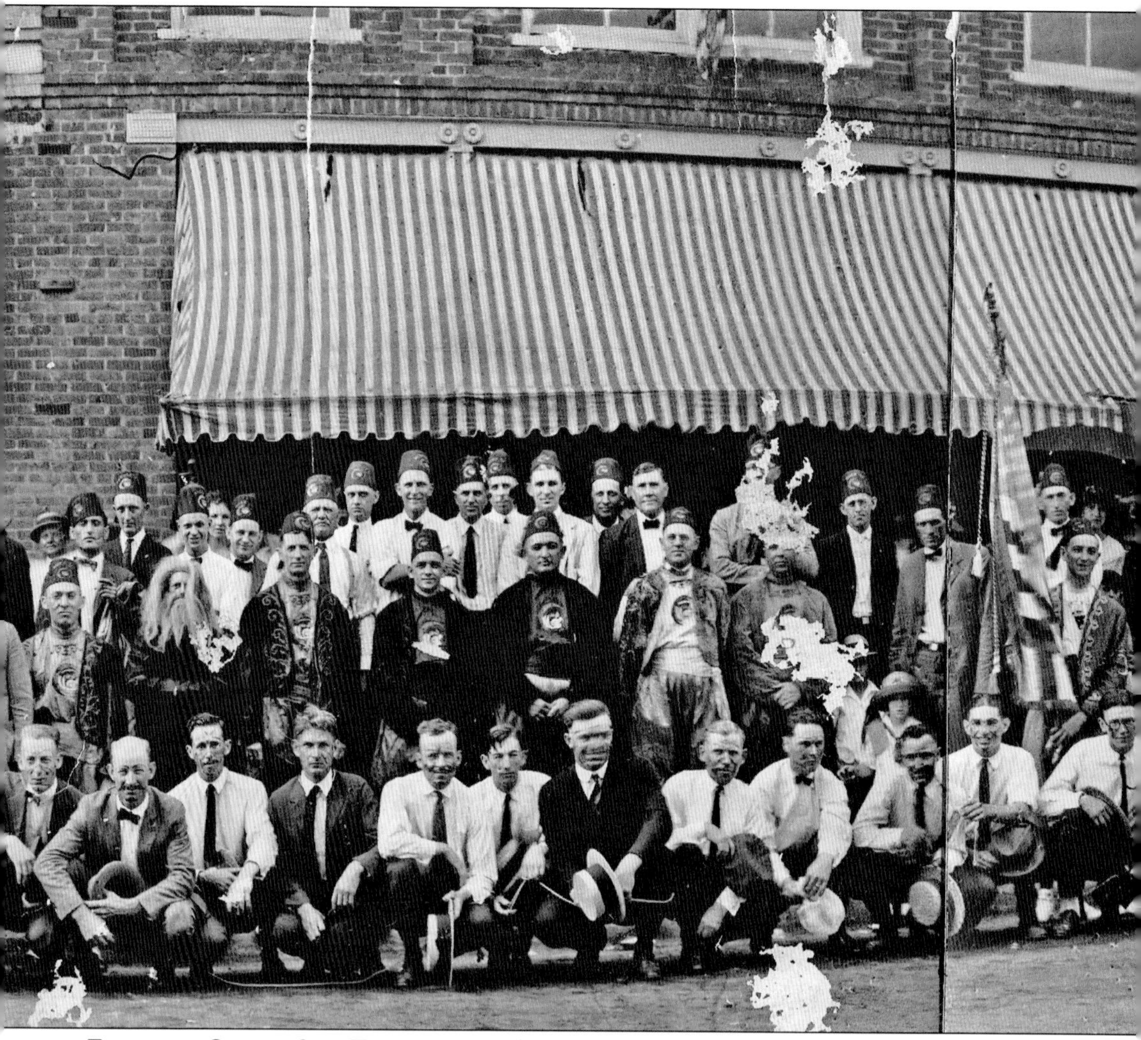

Fraternal Orders, Suez Temple, 1923. The first lodge of fraternal order to organize in Cherryville was the Masonic Order, with fewer than 20 members. A charter was granted to Cherryville Lodge No. 505 AF&AM in January 1900. The charter shows Dr. J. Lee Beam of Crouse as worshipful

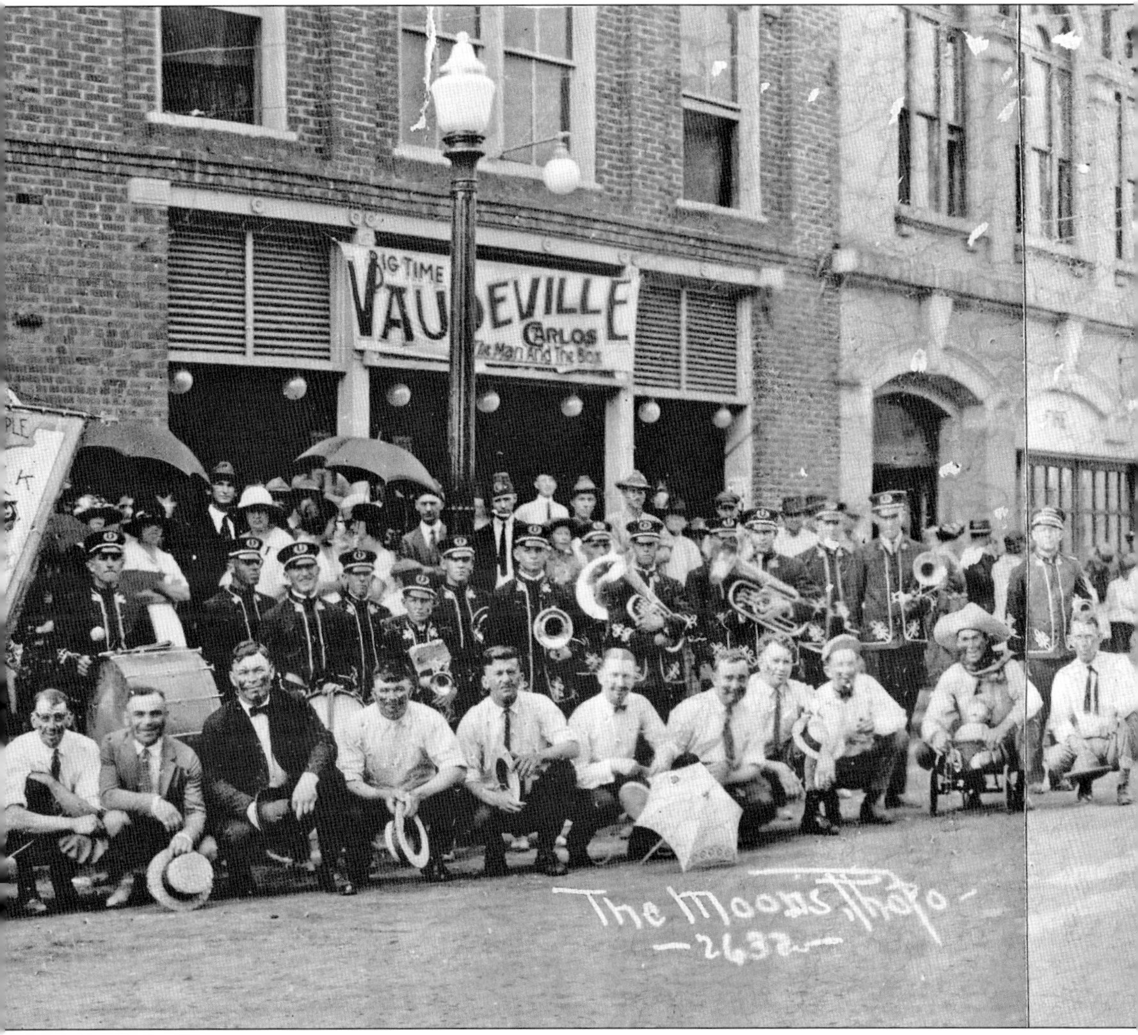

master, Charles P. Stroup as senior warden, and John Carpenter as junior warden. In this photograph, the Masons line Main Street during a convention held in Cherryville in 1923.

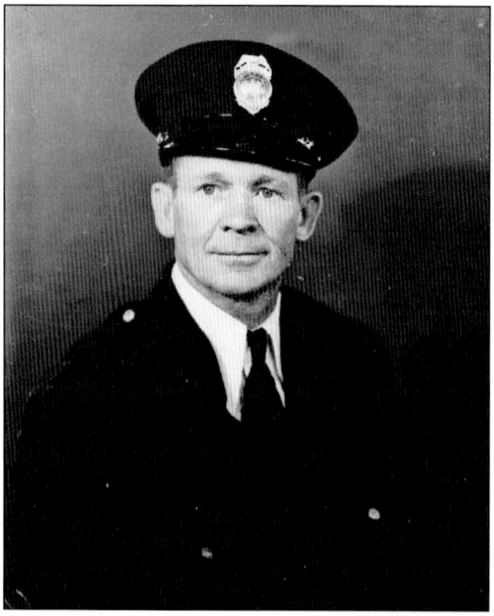

Reedy Sloane Ballard (1903–1977). Although born in Catawba County, son of Thomas B. and Barbara Smith Ballard, Reedy was one of the most colorful characters in Cherryville's past. He served in World War II, was at one time the Cherryville chief of police and a tent evangelist, and brought clothing back to Cherryville to sell that he had acquired in his travels. He traveled extensively in the United States, and many stories abound about his eccentricities.

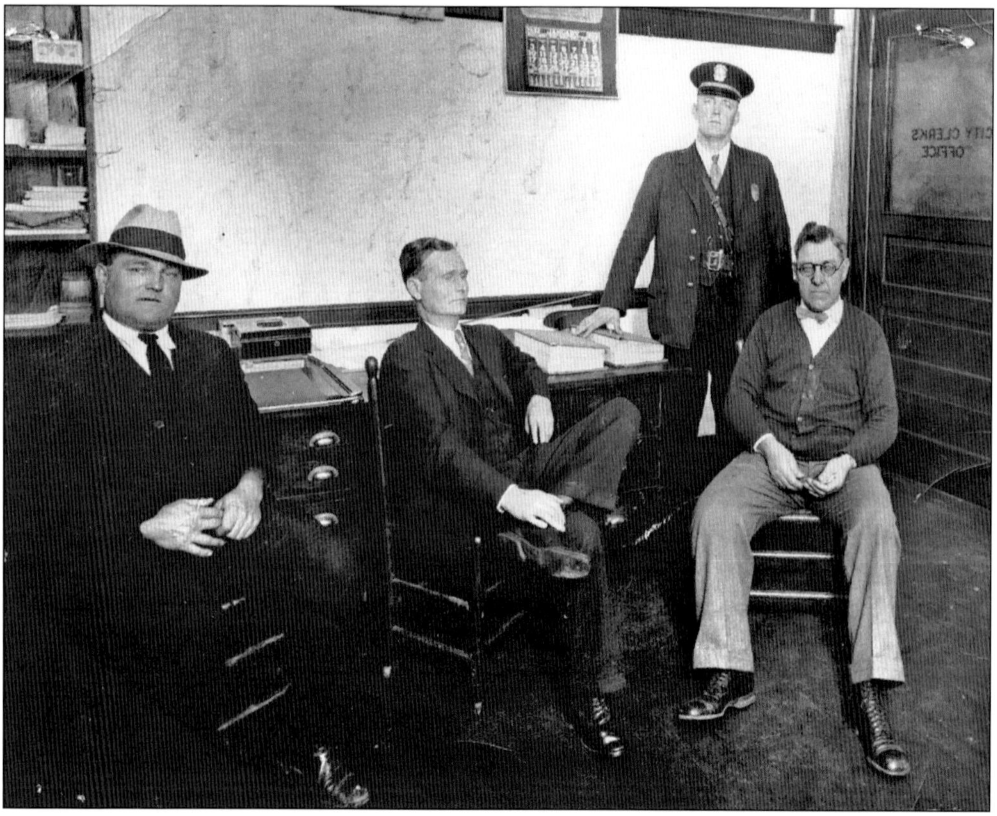

Cherryville City Hall, Built 1911. City hall employees are shown in the "Old City Hall" in January 1932. Paul Crocker was city clerk from 1947 until 1968. The first city hall was built in 1892 by M. L. Rudisill, mayor of Cherryville at the time. Today the 1892 city hall can be seen at the J. Ralph Beam Jr. Heritage Park, along with the city jail, John F. Black School, Benaja Black Bonded Warehouse, Smoke House, and the New Year Shooters statue.

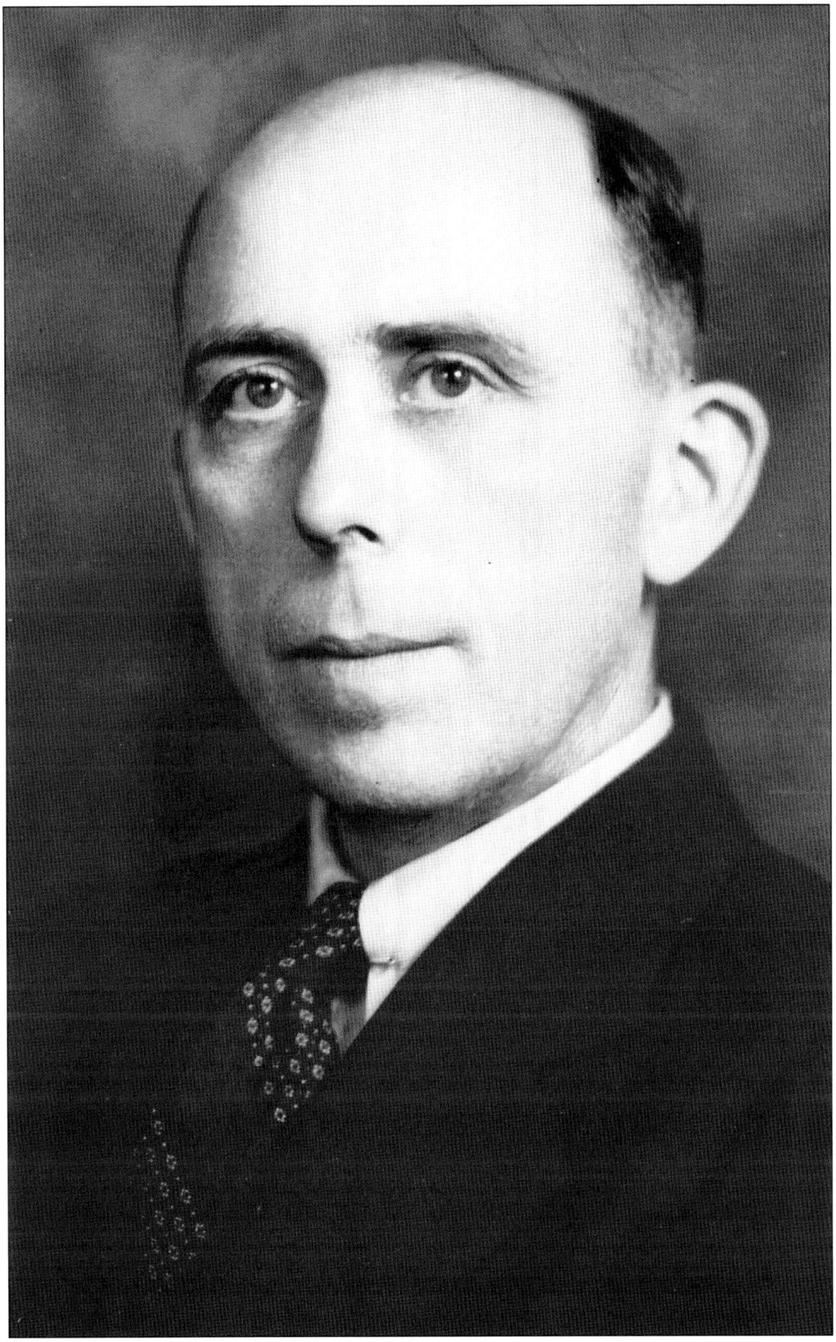

ALLEN DRUG COMPANY. H. H. Allen graduated from the School of Pharmacy in Atlanta in 1913 and worked there until 1916, when he came to Cherryville and bought a drugstore from John F. Weathers. In 1918, his brother J. T. Allen joined him in the business. H. H.'s son, Harry Allen Jr., joined the firm in 1943 and son William F. Allen in 1955. The local drugstore on Main Street also served as the Trailways Bus Station and sold school books, gardening seeds, almanacs, Philco radios, washers, and dryers. At one time, the soda fountain even offered curb service. H. H. Allen worked as a pharmacist until his death in 1967.

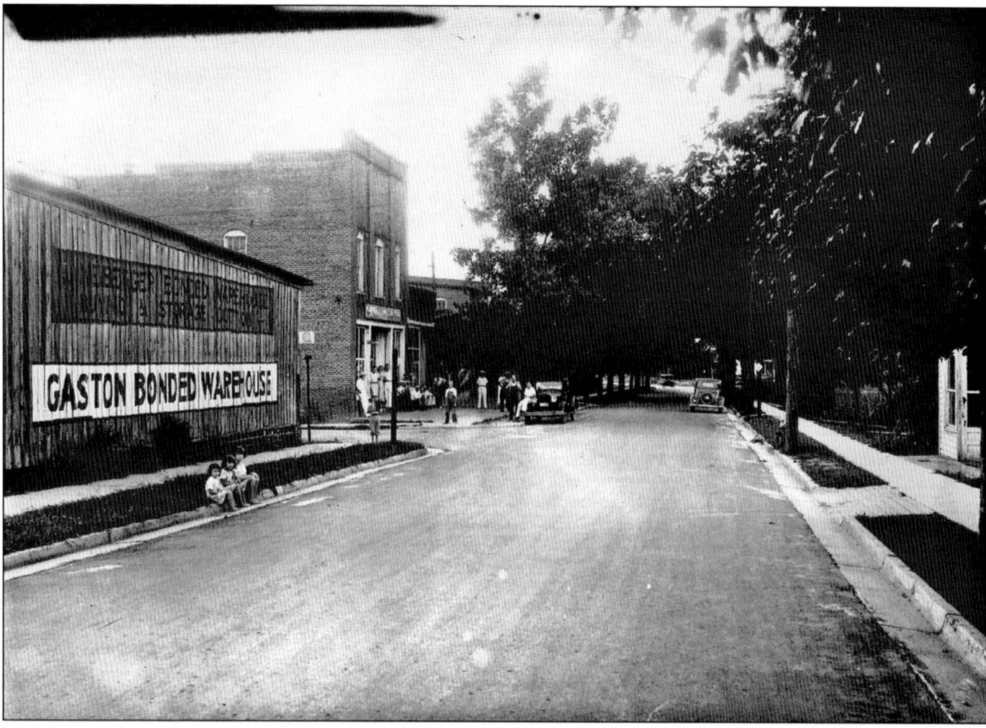

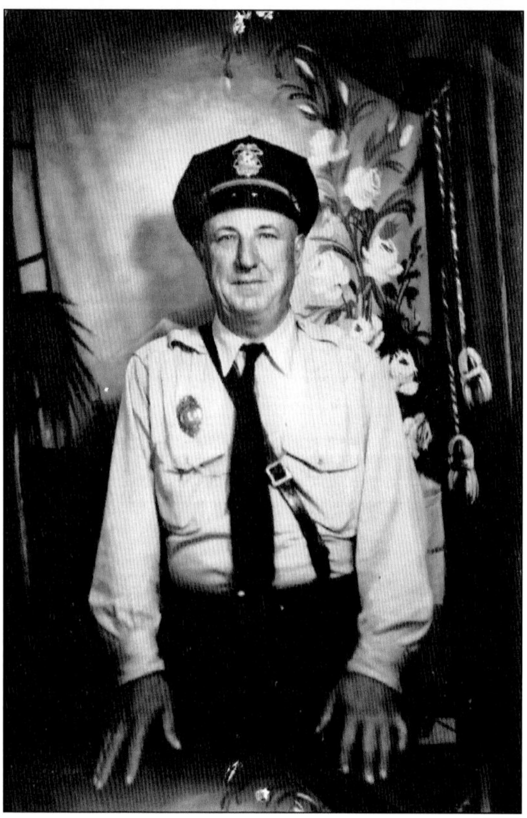

North Mountain Street. Shown here is an early view of North Mountain Street looking north. The street got its name because the Morganton (or Old Burke) Road led north to the Great Smoky Mountains, where treks were often made to buy apples, picnic, camp, and escape the summer's heat. Visible in the photograph is the Gaston Bonded Warehouse, Gaston Mill (later Dora Mill), and the Ben Boyles Store.

Police Chief E. P. Mitchell. Appointed chief of police on December 9, 1947, after serving as the assistant chief for four months, Mitchell replaced Karl M. Warlick. Before coming to Cherryville, Mitchell had been a policeman for 25 years in Franklin, Taylorsville, Granite Falls, Landis, Pinehurst, Aberdeen, and Roxboro, North Carolina; McCall and Bennettsville, South Carolina; and Henry County, Virginia. During World War I, he was with the military police and later the Secret Service department in Detroit, Michigan. Others on the Cherryville Police Force in 1947 were E. H. Yerton, Paul Honeycutt, and R. E. Guffey.

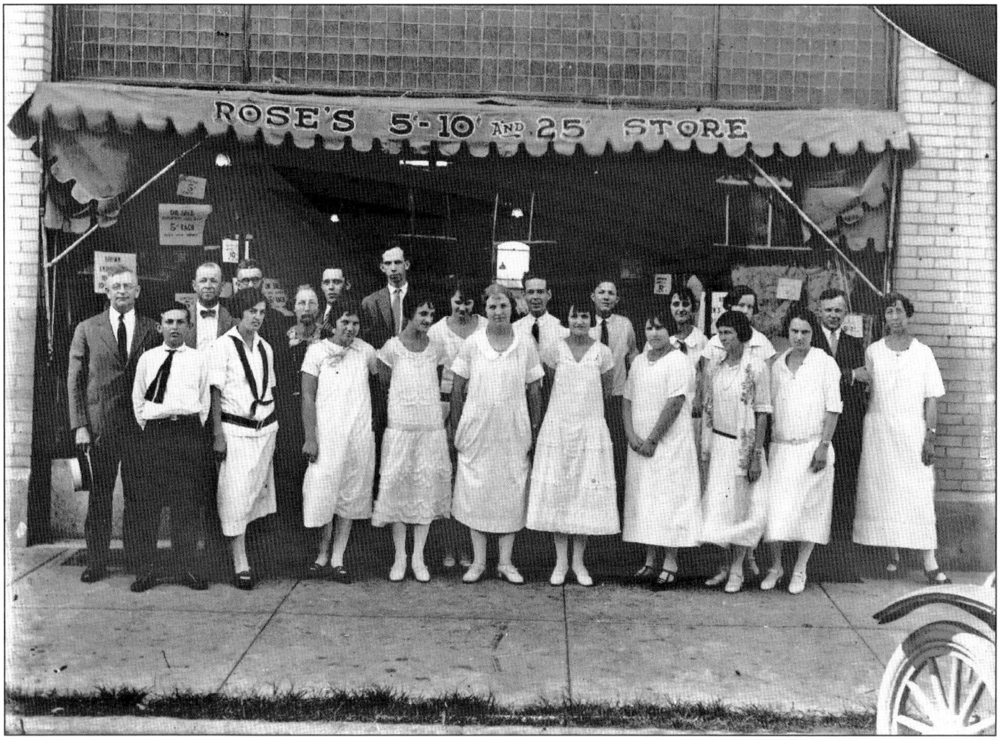

ROSES FIVE AND DIME. A large and competent-looking staff poses on opening day at the Rose's 5, 10, and 25¢ Store located on Main Street in the 1920s. Opening-day specials were advertised in the store windows. Some high school girls begged their parents for permission to work at the "Dime Store" but were not allowed to interrupt their studies.

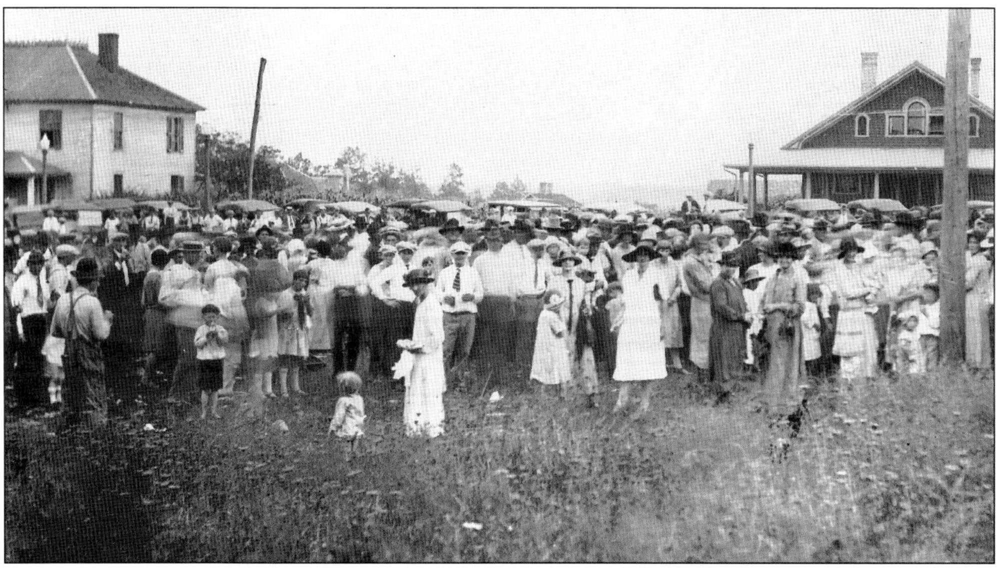

CHERRYVILLE HOMECOMING CELEBRATION. In the early days of the "Big Day" celebrations, people would come early from nearby towns and rural areas. They would park their buggies in town behind Dr. W. D. Houser's house. Here the children are enjoying soda pop, a treat on a hot August day in the early 1900s.

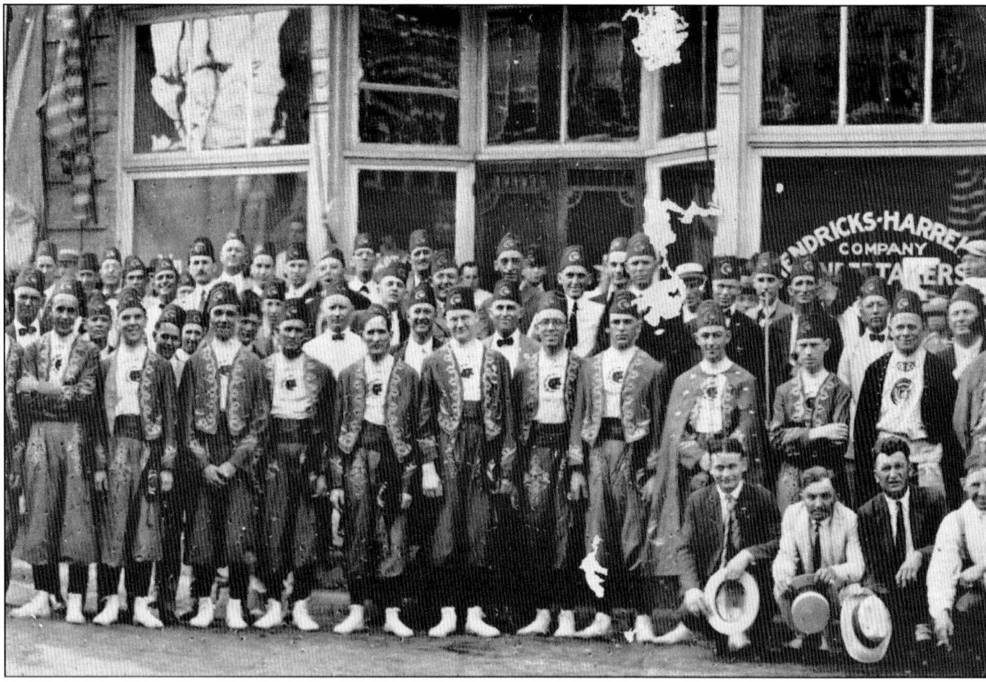

CARPENTER'S FUNERAL HOME. Mauney Mercantile sold the first caskets in Cherryville. The store also sold dry goods and furniture. The business was sold to Columbus Hendricks and Craig, Carl, and Adkins Harrelson. Cone Carpenter, a nephew of the Harrelsons, joined the firm after graduating from embalming school in 1921. In 1930, the business was divided into Harrelson's Dry Goods, which was run by Craig and Hillard Harrelson, and Cone Carpenter took over the undertaking and furniture business. His son Cone Jr. joined him in 1947, then his grandson Carroll joined the family business in 1961.

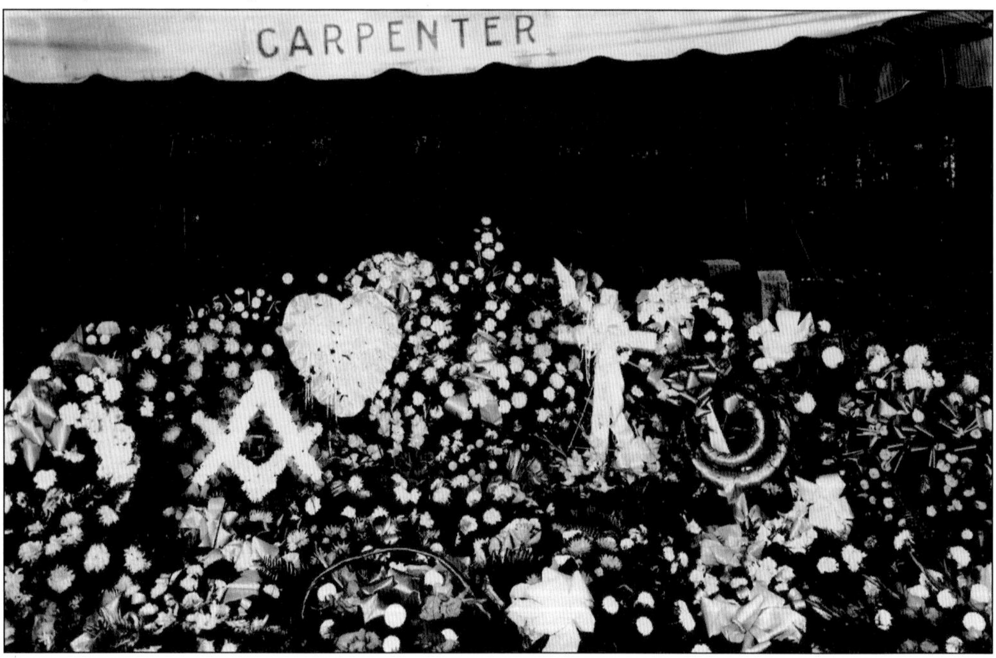

DR. EVAN SHERRILL WEHUNT (1890–1956). Son of Eligah Alexander Wehunt and Ida Lola Wood, Dr. Wehunt attended Piedmont Academy in Cleveland County and dental school in Atlanta. He married Bessie Dixon, and after her death in 1929, he married Vida Lee Heavner, his dental assistant. He was a dentist in Cherryville for many years and was a faithful member of the First Methodist Church of Cherryville. He is shown here with his first wife, Bessie Dixon Wehunt (1894–1929).

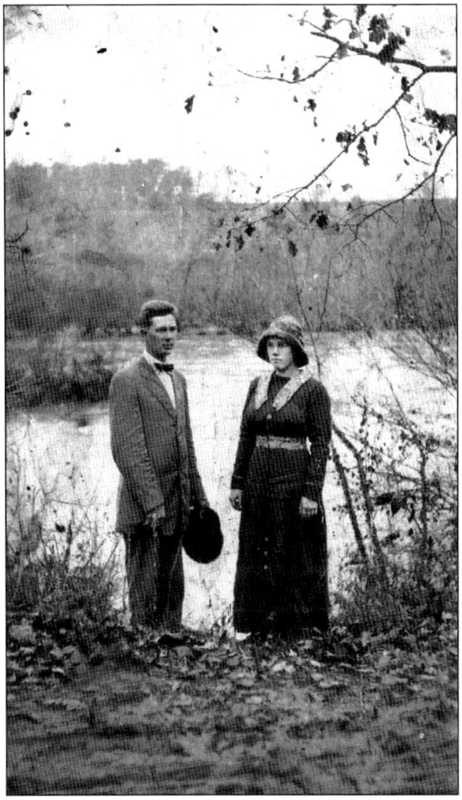

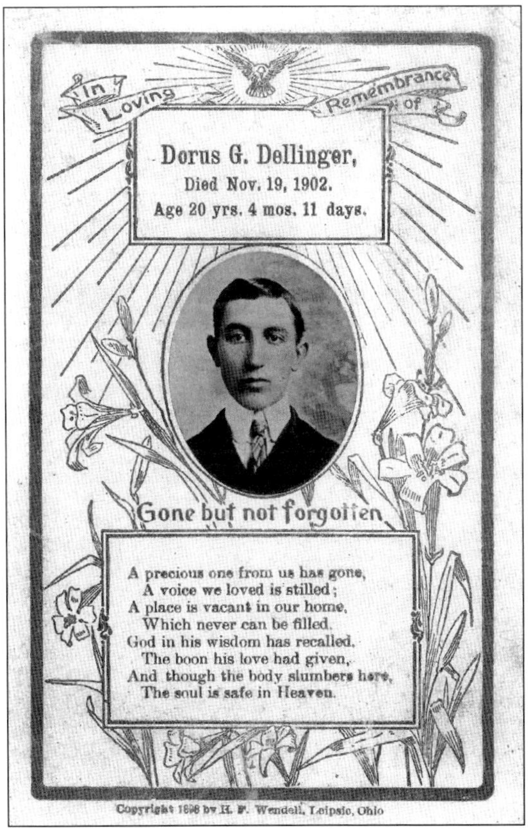

FAMILY MEMORIAL CARD. Memorial cards such as this one were common and were distributed by funeral homes around 1900 as a kind of memorial and as a remembrance for family and friends of the loved ones. This one is for Dorus G. Dellinger, who died on November 19, 1902, at the age of 20.

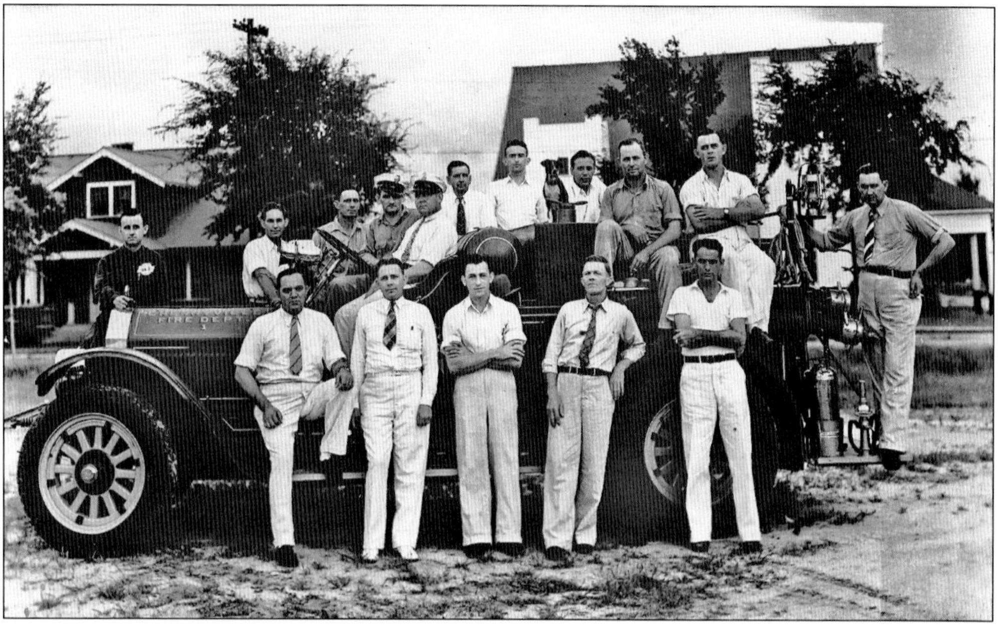

CHERRYVILLE FIRE DEPARTMENT, 1938. Pictured here in 1938 is the efficient Cherryville Volunteer Fire Department. From left to right are (first row) Giles W. Friday, chief; Fred K. Houser, secretary-treasurer; Hollis Eaker; Robert McLurd, assistant chief; and Adkin Putnam; (second row) Marcus Hoyle; Roosevelt Canipe; Fred Neill; Clyde Carpenter, driver; Lander Carpenter, night driver; Brice Gates; Roy Carpenter, second assistant chief; Hugh Harrelson; Maurice Beam; Melvin Friday; and Dee Elmore; (sitting on top of truck) mascot "Brownie McLurd," the fire dog.

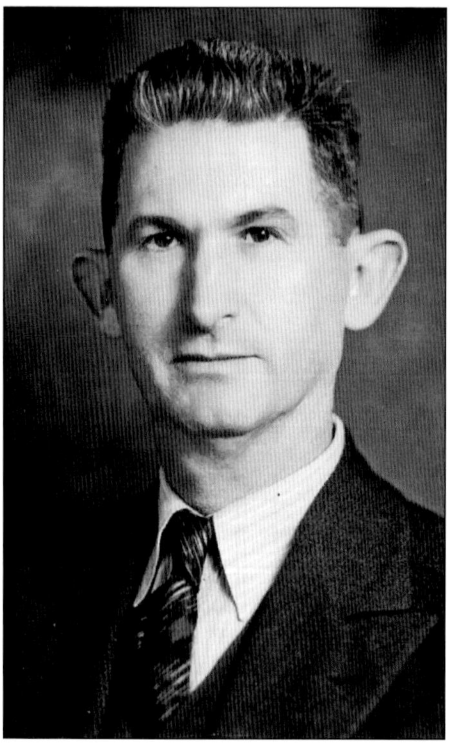

I. P. LONG (1890–1951). Preston Long was born in Gaston County and was the son of Johnson and Margaret Beatty Long. He established Long's Metal and Tin Shop around 1913. He served his country in World War I and his town as judge of Recorders Court. He was a member of the Cherryville Board of Commissioners, the American Legion, and the Board of Deacons of First Methodist Church. He was married to Ina Homesley.

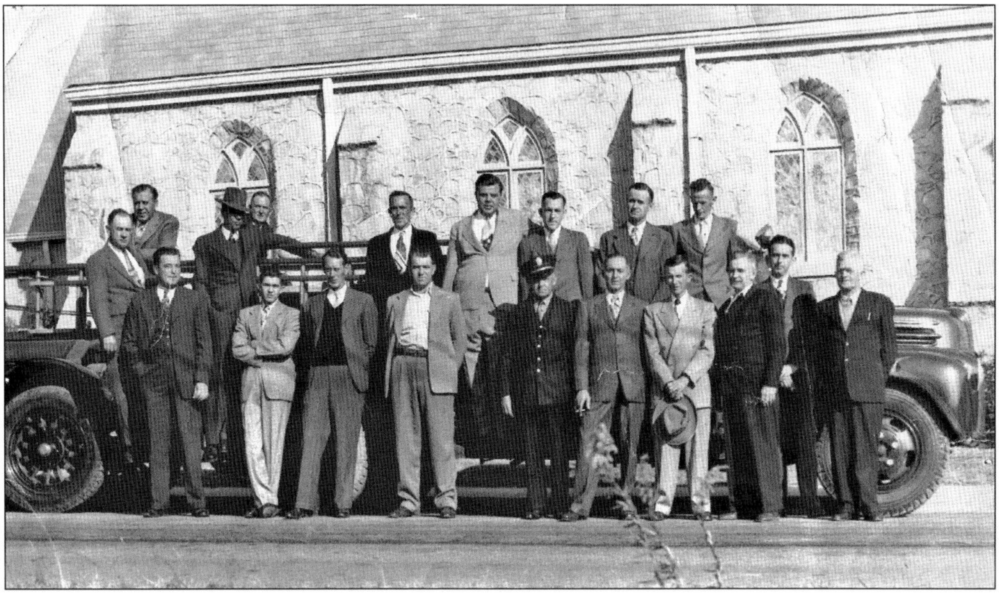

Cherryville Volunteer Fire Department. Beside the Cherryville Presbyterian Church in the late 1940s, in no certain order, are Hugh Harrelson, Thad Kilby Sr., Kent Jenkins, Hazel Williams, E. C. Sullivan, Brice Gates, Paul Hudson, Marvin Mitchem, E. F. Whitaker, Monk Sellers, Jack Clawson, Basil Dellinger, Clyde Carpenter, Mark Hoyle, Ray Carroll, Hollis Eaker, William Lloyd, Bub Beam, Robert McClurd, and Roy Carpenter.

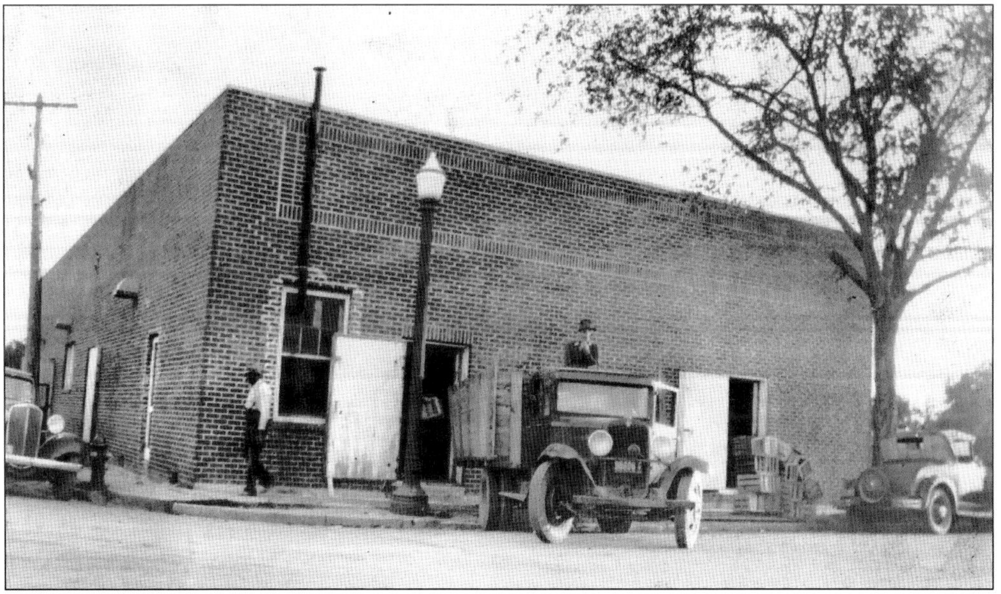

The Potato House. The Cherryville Potato Storage House was located on East Main and Pink Streets, and was owned by attorney M. A. Stroup and Stephen Stroup. It was erected in 1931 and was designed by the State Agricultural Department of Raleigh. Equipped with the most modern heat control and ventilating system for the storage of sweet potatoes, it had a capacity of 18,000 bushels. Local farmers brought their potatoes, and any surplus was sold for them. The potato house burned in November 1945. At that time, it had changed hands and plans had been made to install textile machinery in the building.

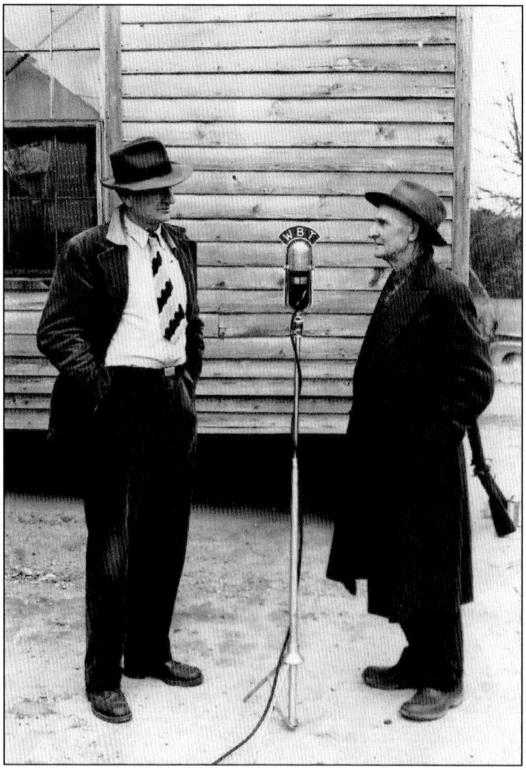

WBT Radio Broadcast. Veteran Cherryville New Year Shooters W. Blaine Beam (left) and Sidney Beam (1872–1960) are ready for a radio broadcast at the Panhandle home of Ruffin White on New Year's Day in the 1940s. Sidney Beam, "Speech Crier" for the New Year Shooters for more than 60 years, starting in 1889, learned the chant from his two brothers, Jacob and Lee Beam, while picking cotton one fall in the 1880s.

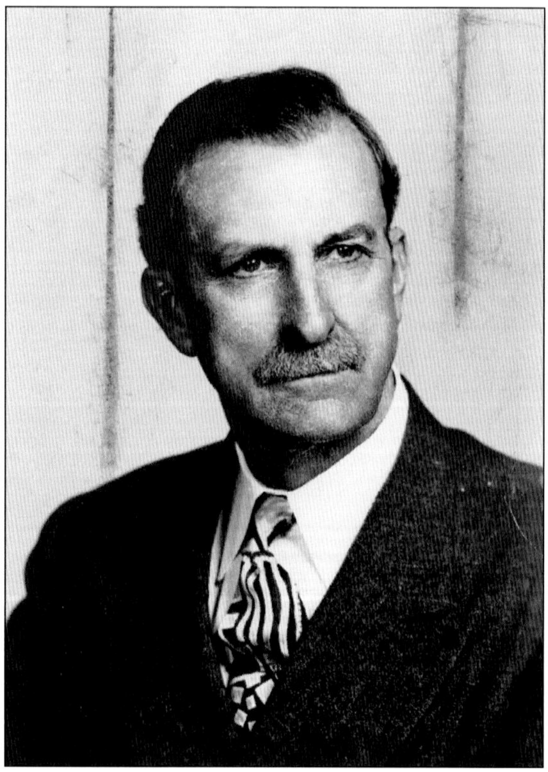

David P. Dellinger. David was a veteran member of the North Carolina General Assembly from Gaston County starting in 1912 and served 19 years. A lawyer, he served as mayor of Cherryville many times and was solicitor of the Recorders Court here for many terms. He loved history and wrote many articles about local history in the 1950s that were printed in the *Cherryville Eagle*.

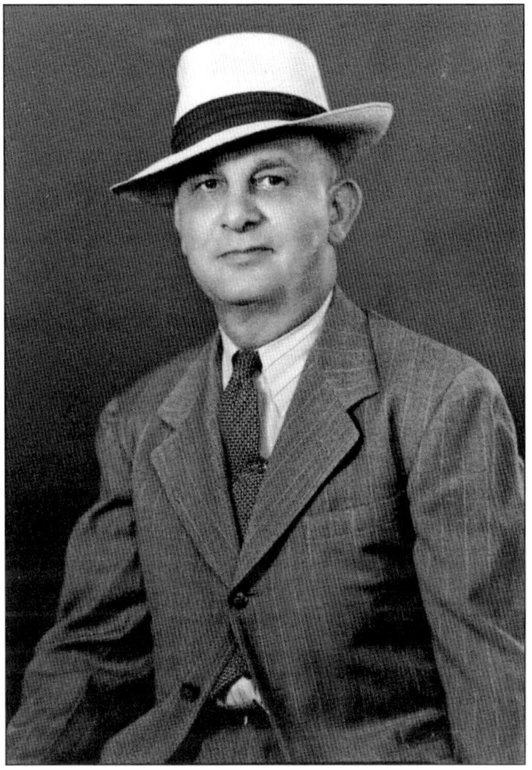

John Wesley Mosteller Sr. (1893–1952). John came to Cherryville from Lincoln County to work in the C. and S. Chevrolet Dealership and later at Homesley Chevrolet. He married Irene Bess, daughter of Dorus Clarence Bess and Ada Black. In 1933, he was appointed postmaster and held that position until he retired in 1950. He was stationed in France in World War I.

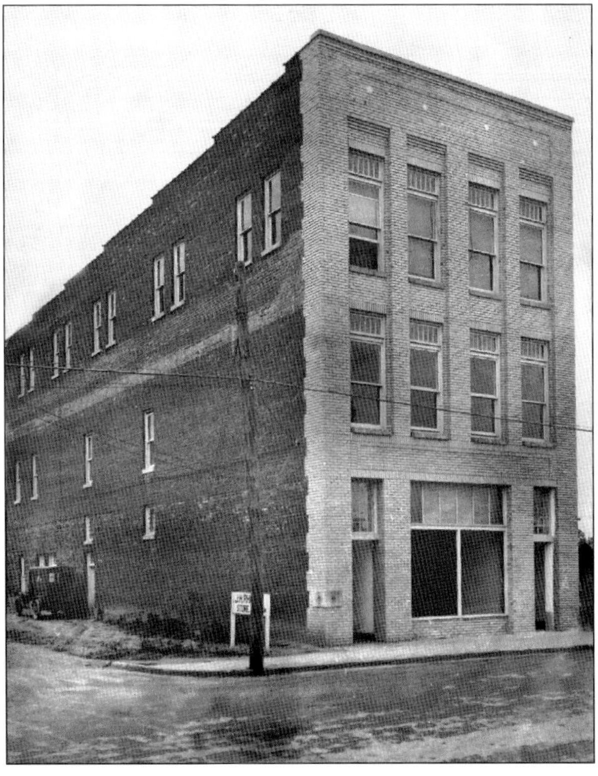

Post Office in Masonic Building. This white brick Masonic Temple was completed in 1924 after a time capsule made of copper was put in place. The federal government rented the bottom floor from the Masons to house Cherryville's post office, and the post office remained here until 1958. The lot for the Masonic Temple was donated by Minnie Ava Dellinger Rudisill (1878–1963), wife of David A. Rudisill, and David Grier Dellinger (1880–1958) in memory of Lee M. Dellinger, their father, who died on March 21, 1901.

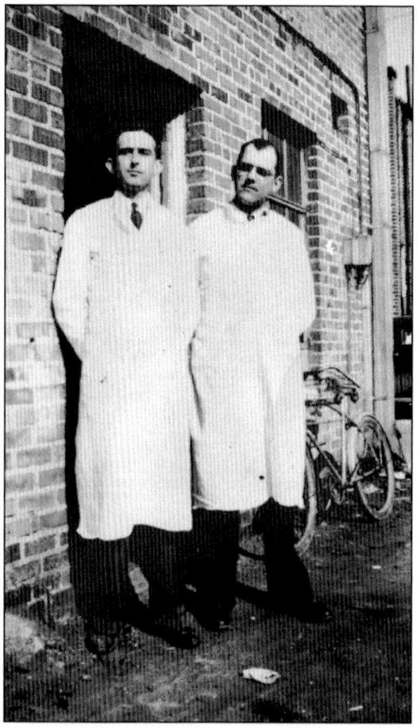

ROY AND TROY GROCERY. Brothers Roy and Troy Carpenter ran a local grocery store in Cherryville for many years. Other grocery stores in the Cherryville area were run by Mon Hallman, Hollis Eaker, Conley Kiser, and members of the Farnsworth, Weatherly, Ballard, Randall, and Stroup families, just to name a few.

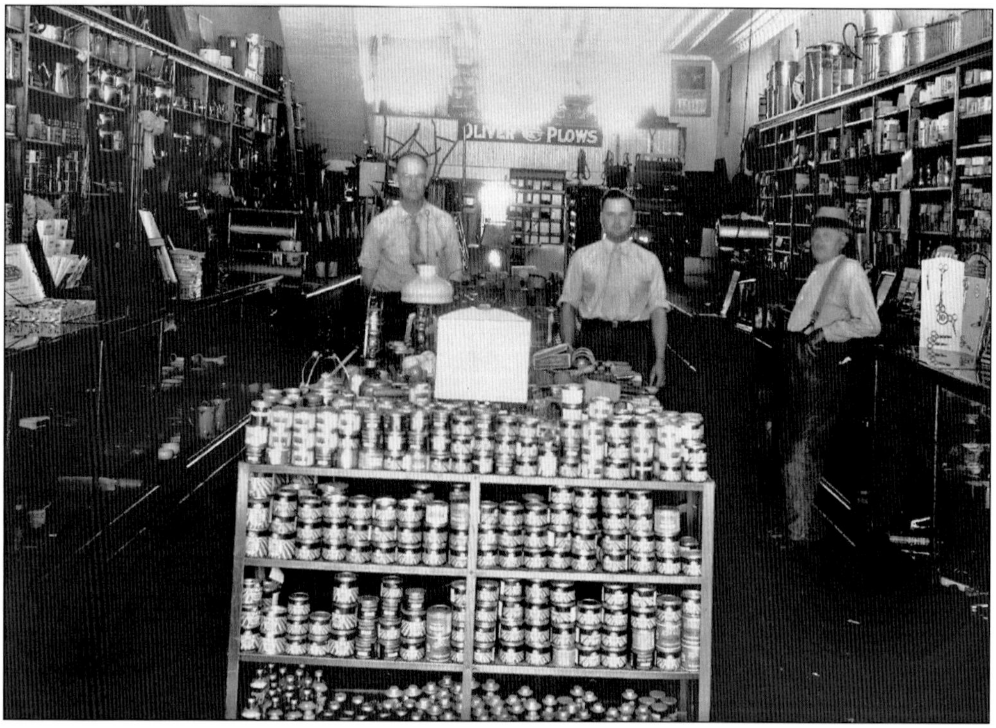

CHERRYVILLE-HALL HARDWARE COMPANY. The first hardware store in Cherryville was run by J. H. Trott and E. L. Webb. It was called the Cherryville Hardware Company. Later the business was taken over by E. B. Scruggs. Fred N. Hall bought out the business and ran it for many years under the name Cherryville-Hall Hardware Company. This picture, taken in August 1933, shows, from left to right, clerks L. A. Cabiness, E. B. Scruggs, and Rupert Camp.

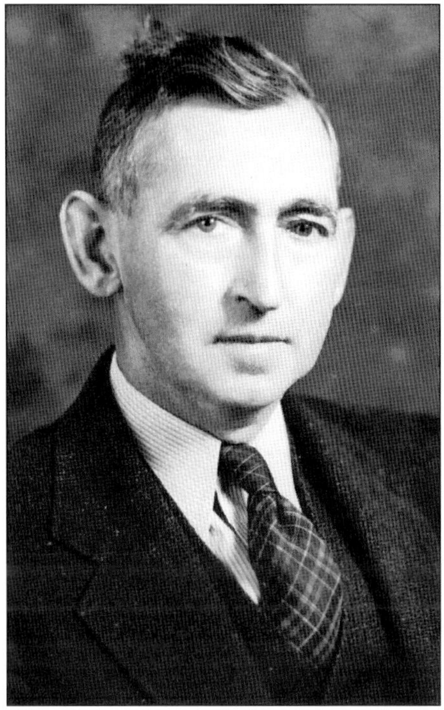

David Rudisill Mauney Sr. (1886–1972). Son of Samuel S. Mauney and Margaret Rudisill, David was widely known throughout the cotton trade and textile industry. He was organizer and owner of the Josephine Knitting Mills and the Vivian Mills. In 1936, he founded the Mauney Cotton Company, Inc. His son, D. R. Mauney Jr., continued in his footsteps.

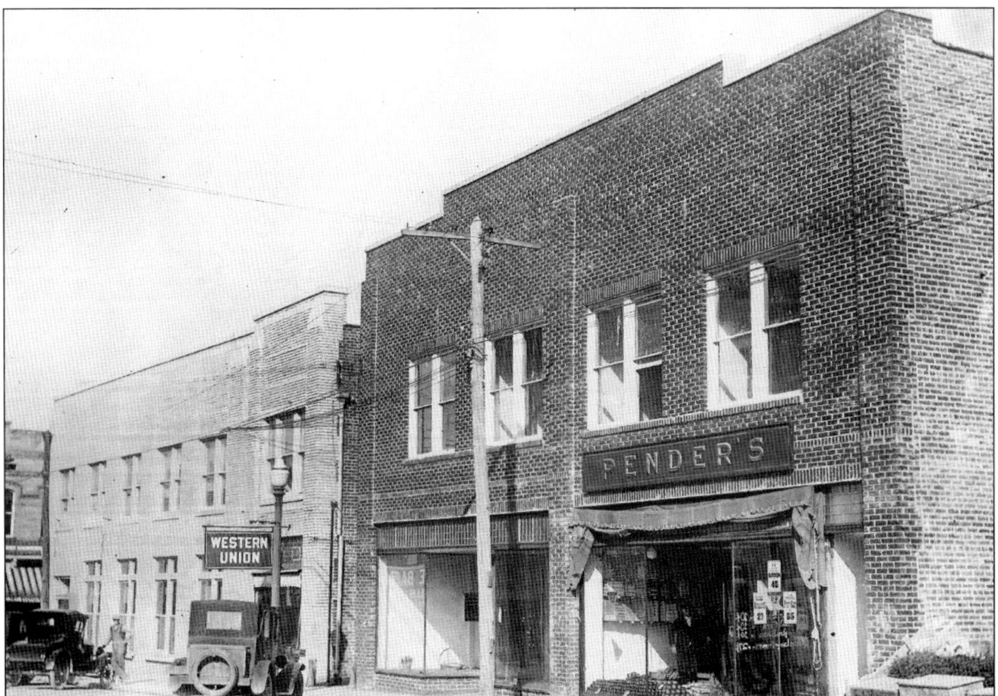

Mountain Street at the Square. The Houser Building, Western Union Office, and Pender's Variety and Grocery Store can be seen in this photograph, taken around 1927. By this time, uptown had modern lighting in its stores and streetlights along its paved streets, and people came from miles around to shop in Cherryville.

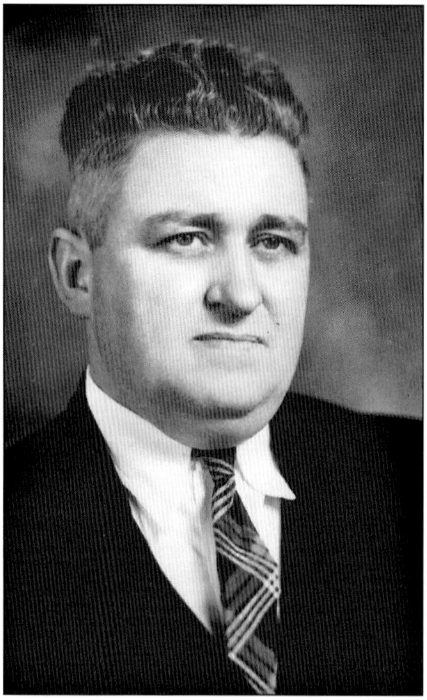

Troy C. Homesley Sr. (1899–1972). Born in Gaston County, Troy was the son of Commodore D. and Kathryn Bolick Homesley. He came to Cherryville in 1932 and bought out the Chevrolet Agency, owned by Stephen Stroup and John W. Mosteller Sr., located on East Main Street. He later moved it to Mountain Street and operated this business until his retirement in 1968.

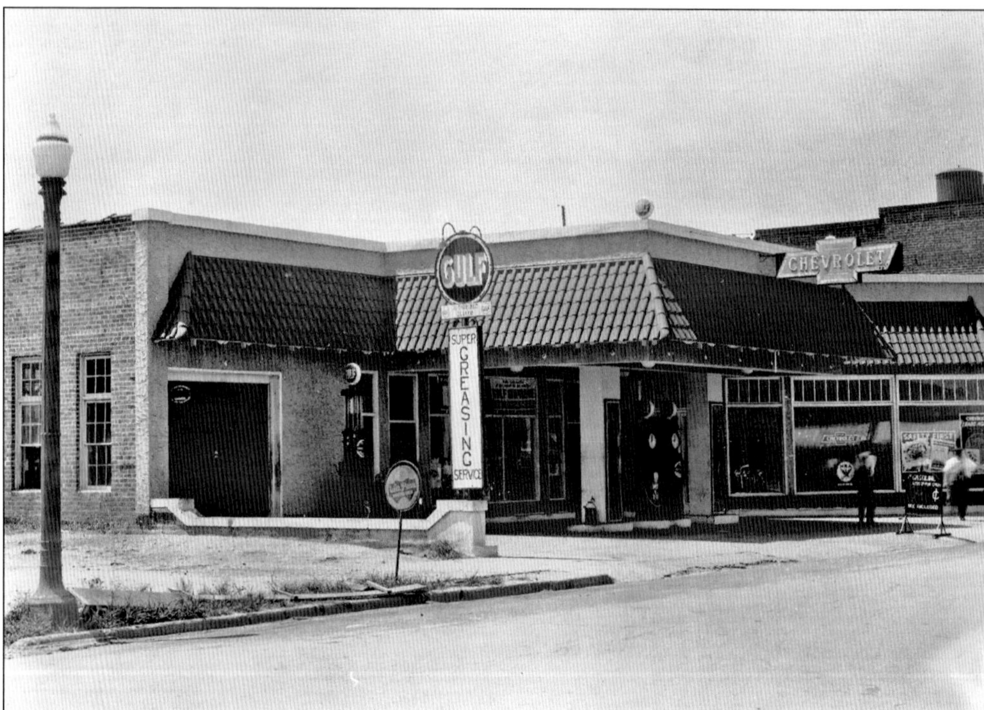

Homesley Chevrolet Company, 1933. In the 1930s, the Homesley Chevrolet Company garage and service station building on Main Street was open daily from 6:00 a.m. until 10:00 p.m. but was closed during church hours on Sundays. The business offered 24-hour wrecker service, and Troy Homesley was the manager.

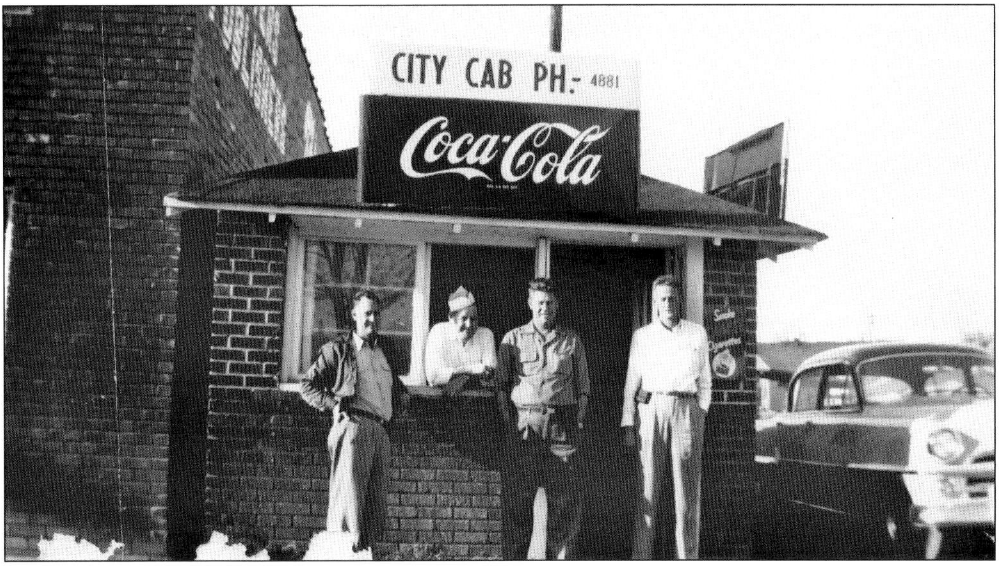

Cherryville City Cab Company. Taxis were more common in the 1940s, 1950s, and early 1960s. Today most small towns do not have taxis. City Cab was located in the 1950s on West Main Street near the Eagle Publishing Company. In February 1954, (from left to right) Ralph Towery, John Hovis, Ed Abernethy, and Ray Carroll pause in front of the City Cab building for a photographer.

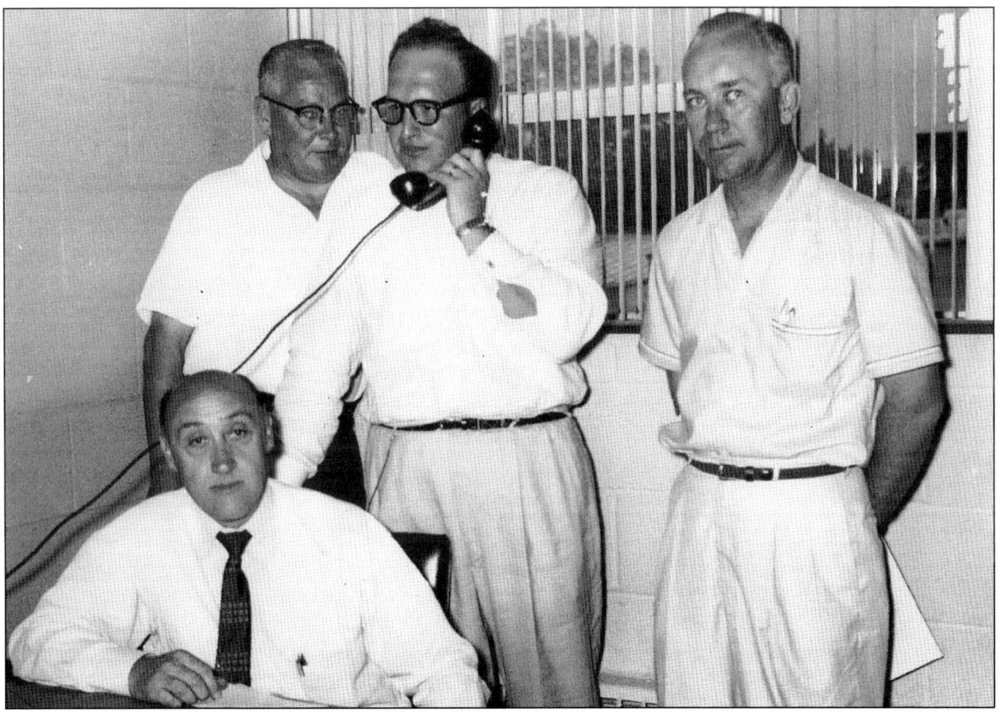

Local Businessmen. In this undated photograph, (from left to right) Cherryville businessmen Dr. W. H. ("Bill") Houser, a Cherryville pharmacist; Henry Michael, manager of Belk's Department Store; an unidentified person; and James L. Beam, a building contractor, conduct business in what appears to be the new city hall on a hot summer day, as all appear in shirtsleeves.

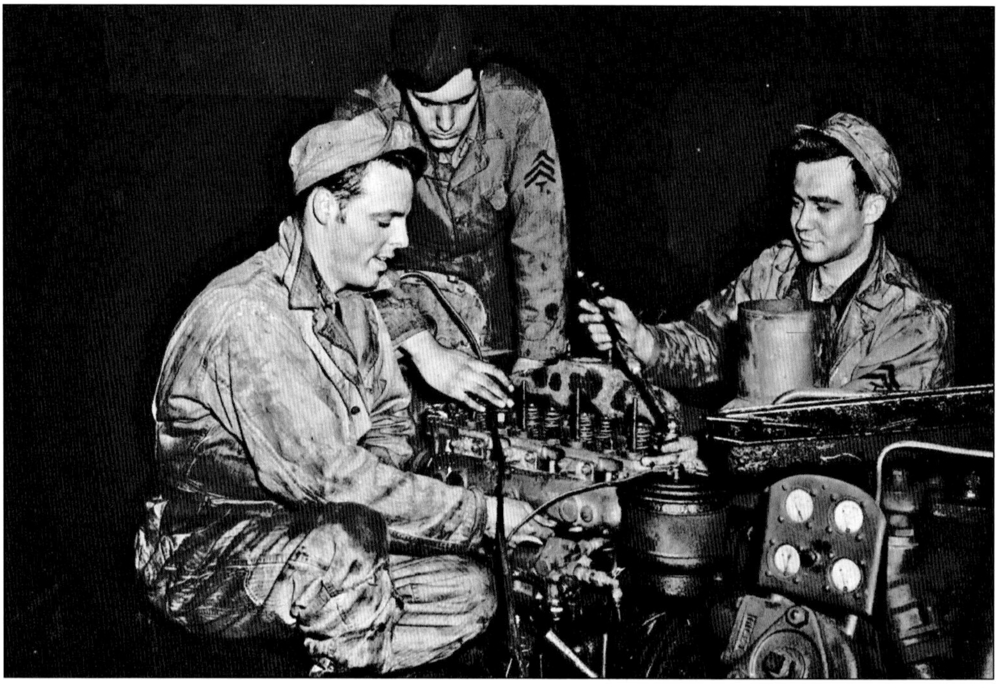

World War II, February 19, 1945. A group of servicemen operating in a major Belgium port kept the cranes, tractors, forklifts, air-compressors, and all other mobile dock equipment there in good working order during World War II. Three men of the 3521st Ordnance MAM Company overhaul an air-compressor. From left to right are Cpl. Howard Foxhoven of Iowa, Sgt. Blaine W. Eaker of Cherryville, and Cpl. Kenneth Ausborn of Mississippi. All three men listed their occupations before the war as farmer. (Courtesy of U.S. Army Signal Corps Photography.)

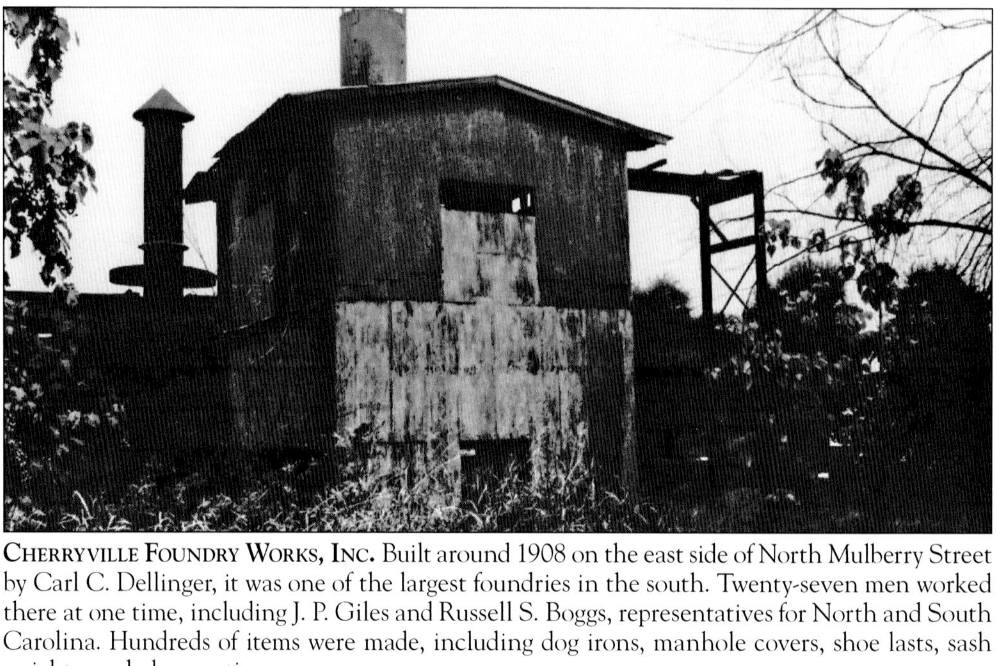

Cherryville Foundry Works, Inc. Built around 1908 on the east side of North Mulberry Street by Carl C. Dellinger, it was one of the largest foundries in the south. Twenty-seven men worked there at one time, including J. P. Giles and Russell S. Boggs, representatives for North and South Carolina. Hundreds of items were made, including dog irons, manhole covers, shoe lasts, sash weights, and plow castings.

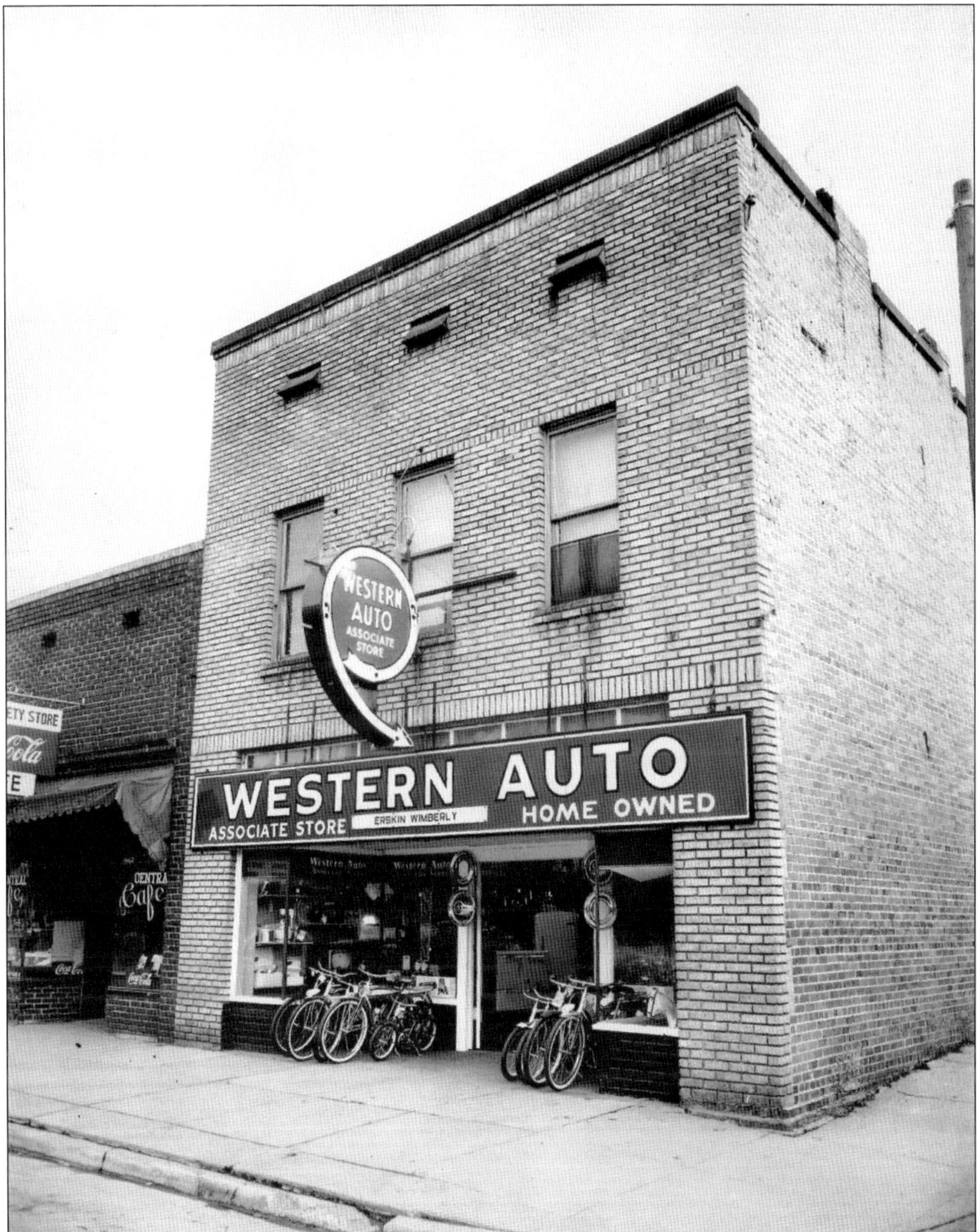

Western Auto Store. Managed by Erskine Wimberly in the 1950s, the store was a busy place, especially at Christmastime when bicycles were a popular item for sale. Next door to Central Café, it was located on the corner of Main and Oak Streets. Some families lived upstairs above the businesses on this block, and it holds many memories for those families. Today the building is owned by Red Dellinger.

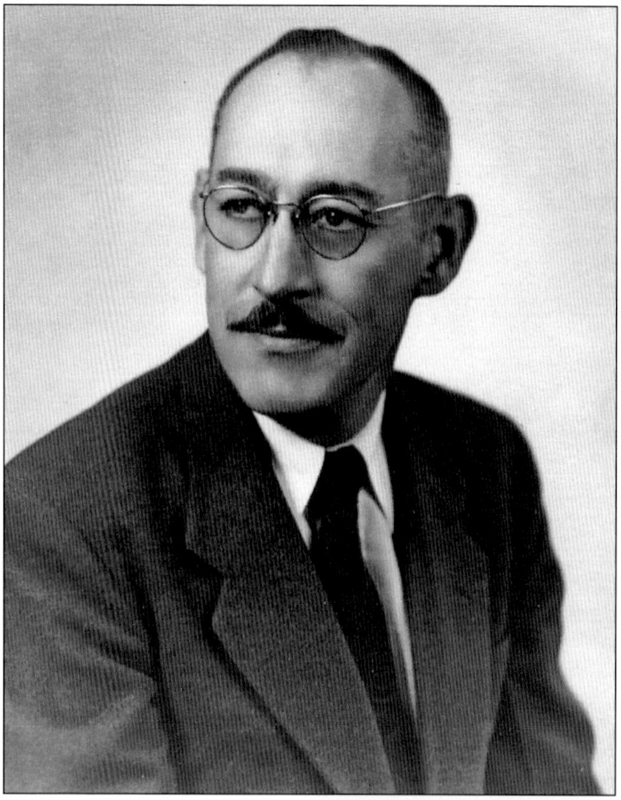

Dr. Loren Lee Chastain (1907–1965). Dr. Chastain, a Cherryville general practice physician, lived on Ballard Street and was a member of the First Baptist Church. A 32nd-degree Scottish Rite and a member of Cherryville Lodge No. 505, he served in the Korean conflict as a captain in the U.S. Army. He graduated from Carson-Newman College in Jefferson, Tennessee, Vanderbilt College, and Bowman Gray School of Medicine.

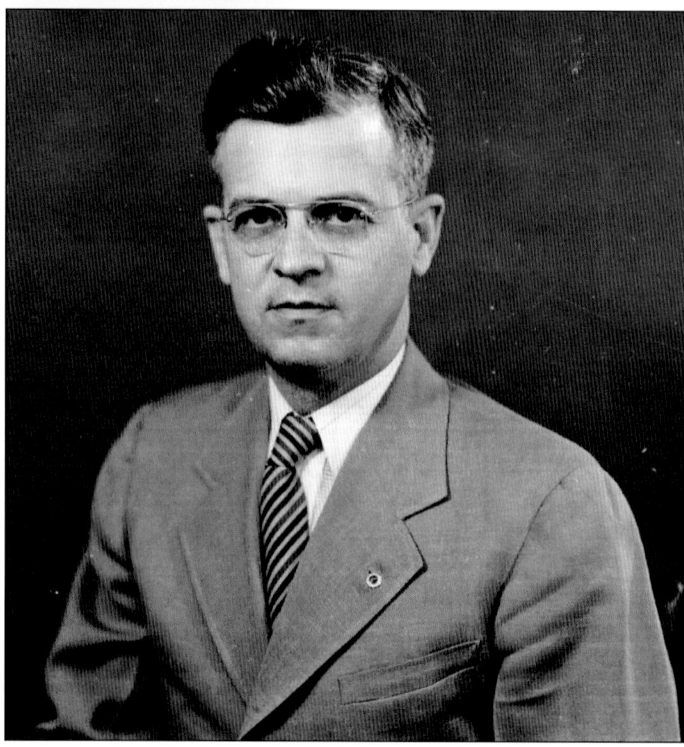

Kenneth Beam (1908–1980). Son of Austin A. Beam and Hester "Mima" Dellinger, Kenneth owned K. B. Beam, Inc., an insurance and real estate business. In the 1960s, his agents were Blaine Childers, Frank Hoyle, Milton Loy Jr., and Milton L. Hardin. He moved his family to Cherryville in the 1950s and purchased the Kendrick House on the corner of Mountain and Church Streets. He was married to Irene Peeler of Lincoln County.

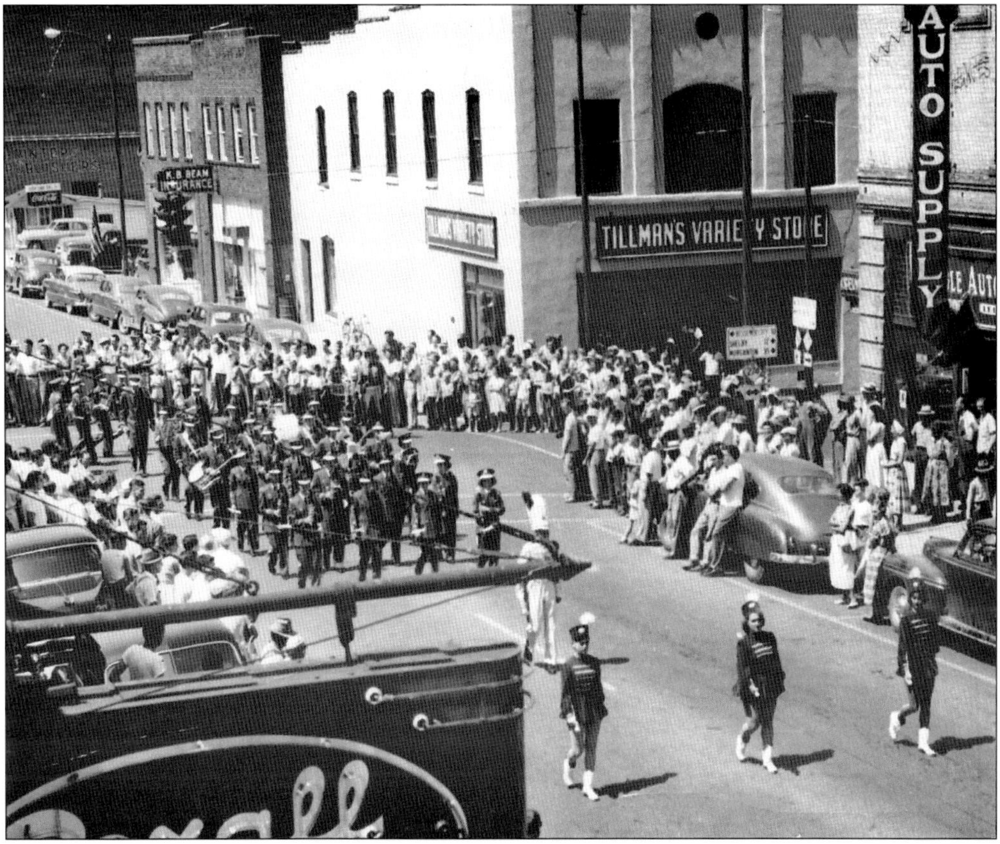

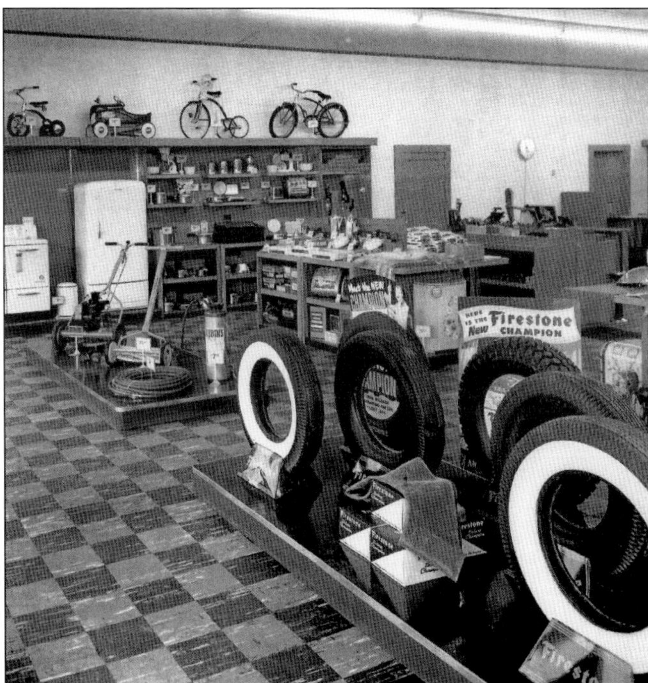

CHERRYVILLE PARADE, 1940s. Beauty queens, majorettes, marching bands, and clowns make up most small-town parades. Parades drew large crowds to Cherryville during the holiday season, and merchants hoped they would stay and shop in their establishments, such as Woodrow Beam's Shell and Firestone Store, which was on Main Street for many years. Woodrow W. Beam (1913–1977), son of Austin A. and Mima Dellinger Beam, drowned at Sunset Beach on September 3, 1977. Other stores were Tillman's Variety Store on the corner of Main and Mountain Streets at the square and Cauble's Auto Supply Store.

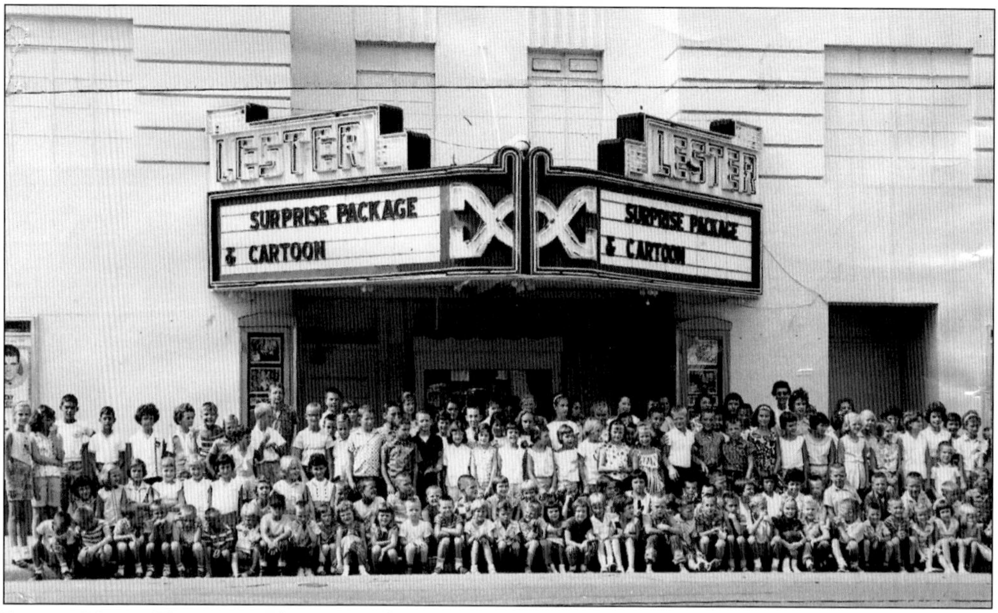

Lester Movie Theater. There was also at one time the Strand Movie Theater and even a drive-in movie theater, but the Lester Theater continued to be the site for moviegoers in Cherryville and the surrounding area for many years, even though the management changed many times through the years. Mrs. Maurice (Nell) Beam was the longtime cashier and secretary for the Carolina and the Strand Theater.

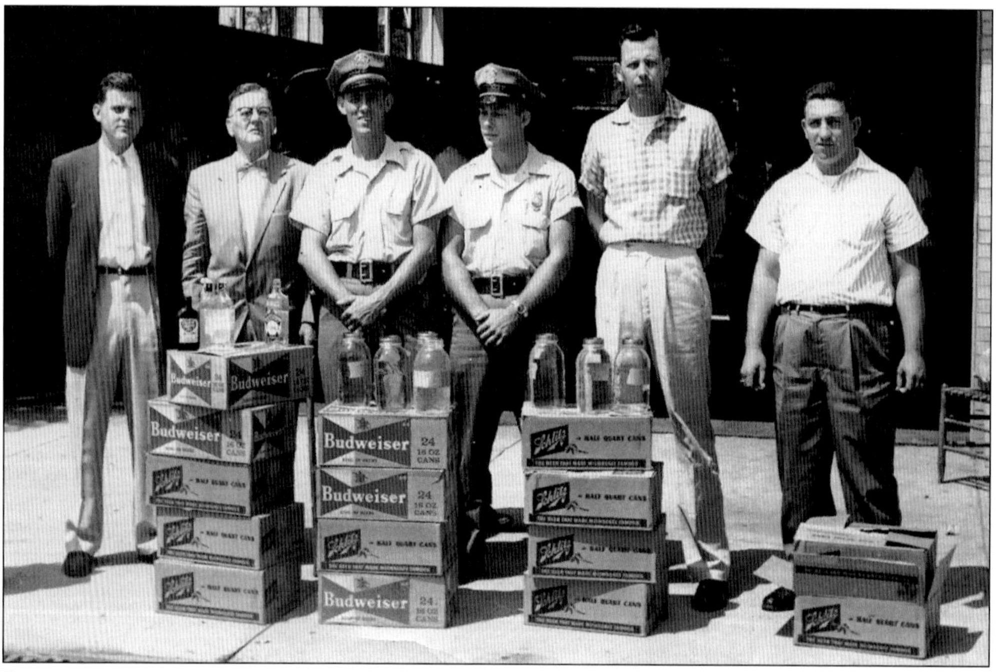

Revenuers and White Lightning. The Cherryville Police Department and revenuers broke up many stills in the 1950s. Seen here, ready to destroy cases of beer and mason jars of white lightning, are, from left to right, two unidentified, Yates McGinnis, Larry Thornburg, Bill Hovis, and Harold "Dag" Blackwood.

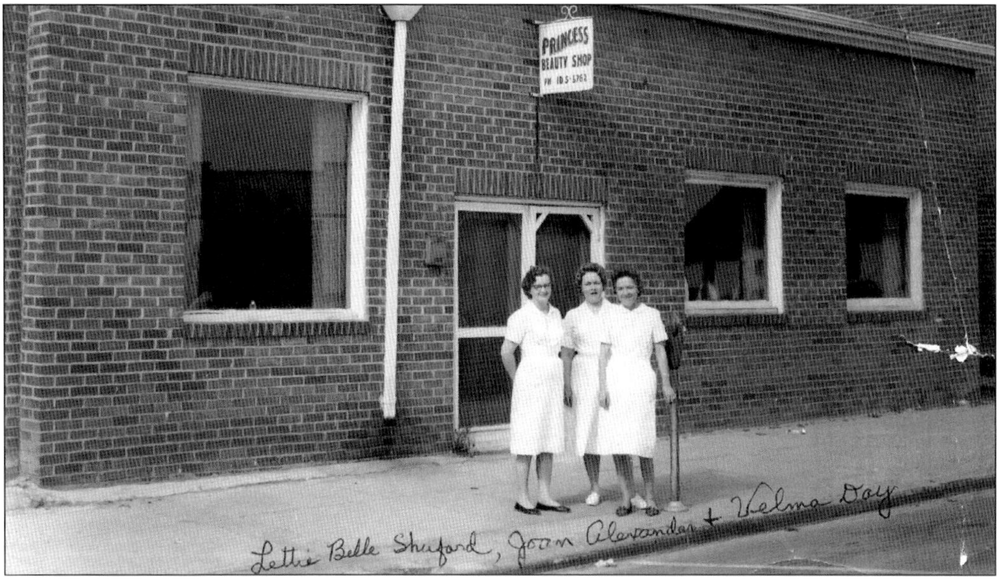

PRINCESS BEAUTY SHOP. In the 1950s, all one had to do was call Idlewood-5-5762 to reach one of these beauticians. Pictured from left to right are Lettie Belle Shuford, Joan Alexander, and Velma Day. Other beauticians in Cherryville were Helen Murphy and Mary George at the Deluxe Beauty Shop and the beauticians at the Modernette Beauty Salon in the 1930s. Later Thelma Sellers and Sue Johnson were at the Elite Beauty Shop (from 1941 to 1989).

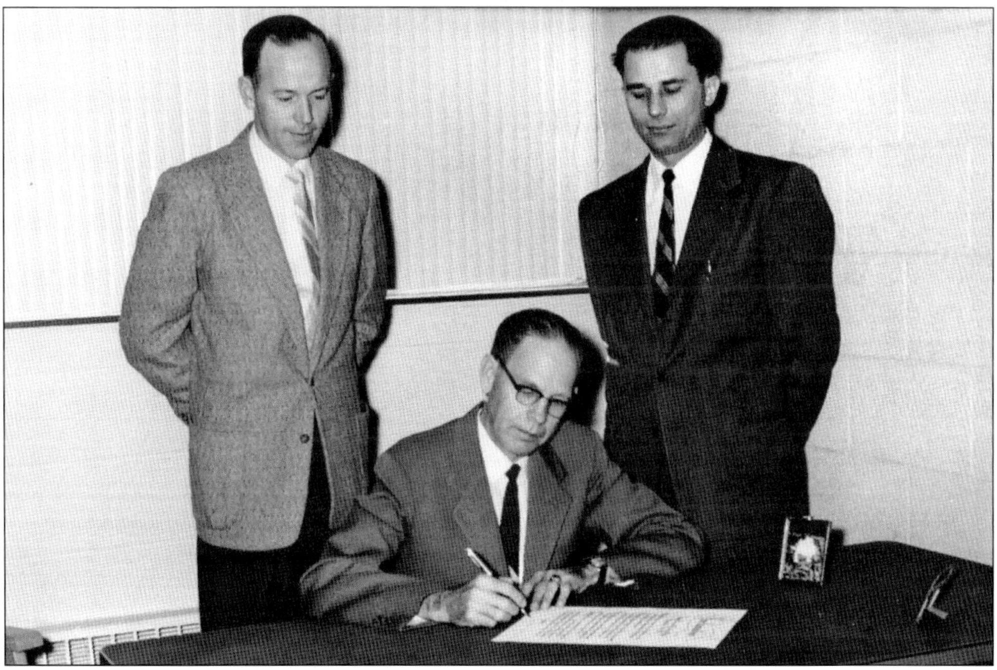

DR. CHARLES METCALF, W. T. ROBINSON, AND DR. TED PAIGE. Affectionately known as "Dub," W. T. Robinson (seated) was assistant secretary, assistant treasurer, and controller of Carolina Freight Carriers Corporation. As mayor of Cherryville, his administration was responsible for Cherryville's economic growth during the late 1950s and 1960s. He was a local historian and was married to Ethel Mae "Teeny" Boggs.

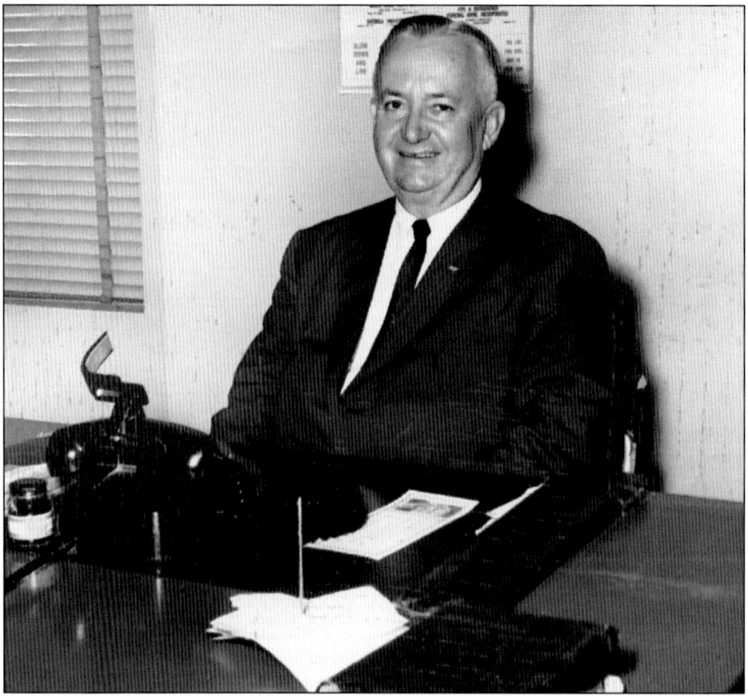

Sheriff Dwight Luther Beam (1911–1979). Sheriff of Gaston County for 20 years, Luther spent 40 years in law enforcement, from 1930 until his death. While Beam was sheriff, the county commissioners created the Gaston County Rural Police, known as "the Rurals." They drove black-and-orange patrol cars and were responsible for criminal police work, while the sheriff's office retained the jail and other responsibilities.

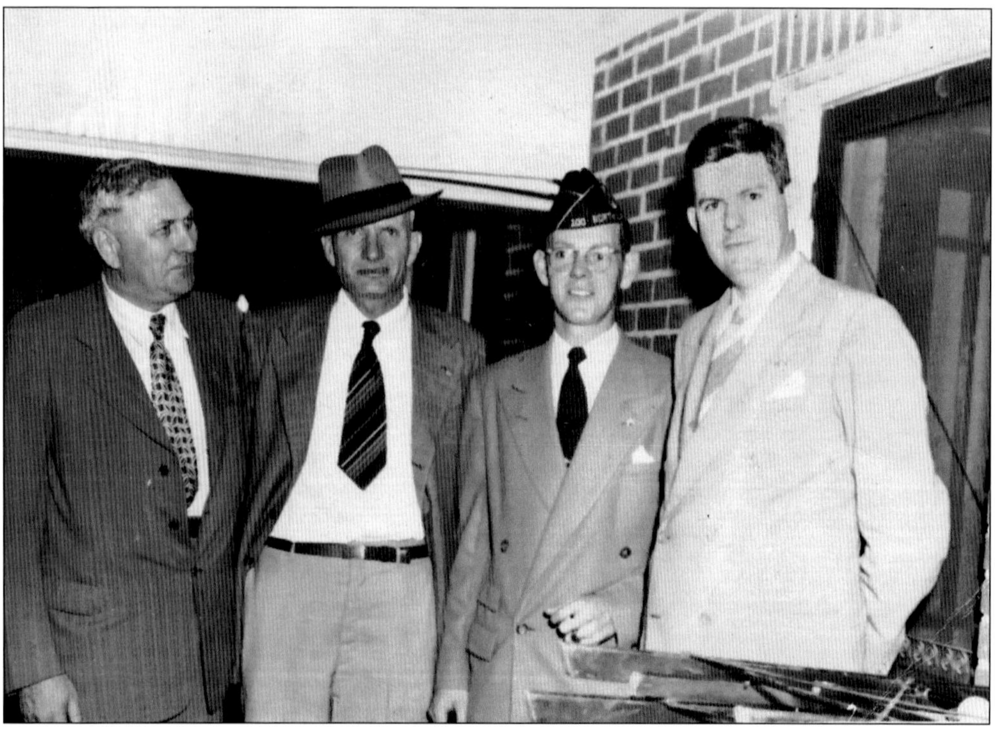

Big Days in Cherryville, 1949. W. Blaine Beam was host at his home, along with John L. ("Buck") Fraley, to Gov. R. Gregg Cherry and state representative Basil L. Whitener in August 1949 during one of Cherryville's "Big Day" Celebrations. Pictured from left to right are Gov. R. Gregg Cherry, W. Blaine Beam, Buck Fraley, and state representative Basil L. Whitener.

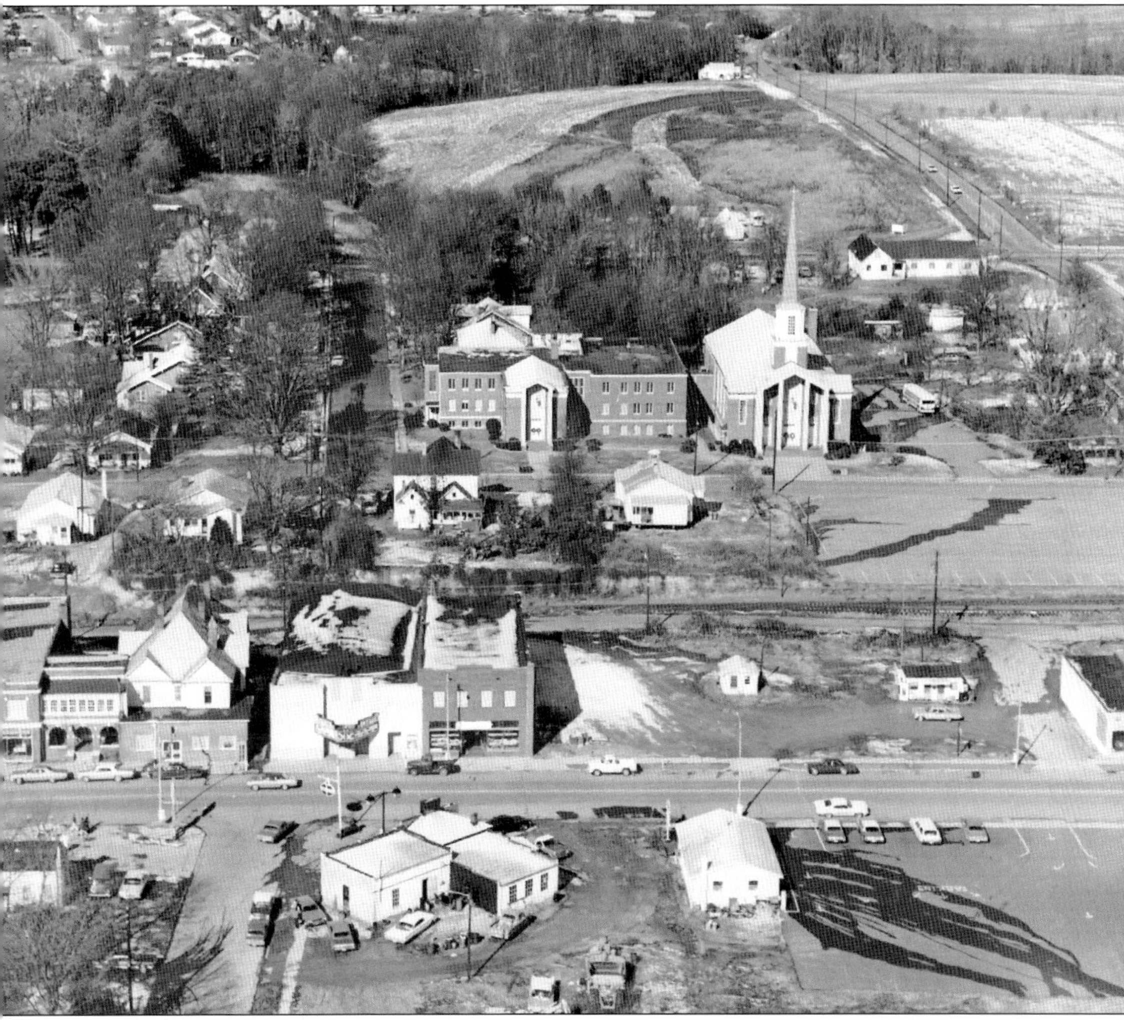

CHERRYVILLE AERIAL VIEW, 1960S. Look at this 1960s view of East Main Street with First Baptist Church on First Street in the background. Next door to the Lester Theater, Beam's Inn can be seen on East Main Street (the hotel was demolished to make room for the Mini-Park in the early 1970s). And in the distance can be seen the American Legion Building on Highway 150 and Cherryville City Memorial Cemetery.

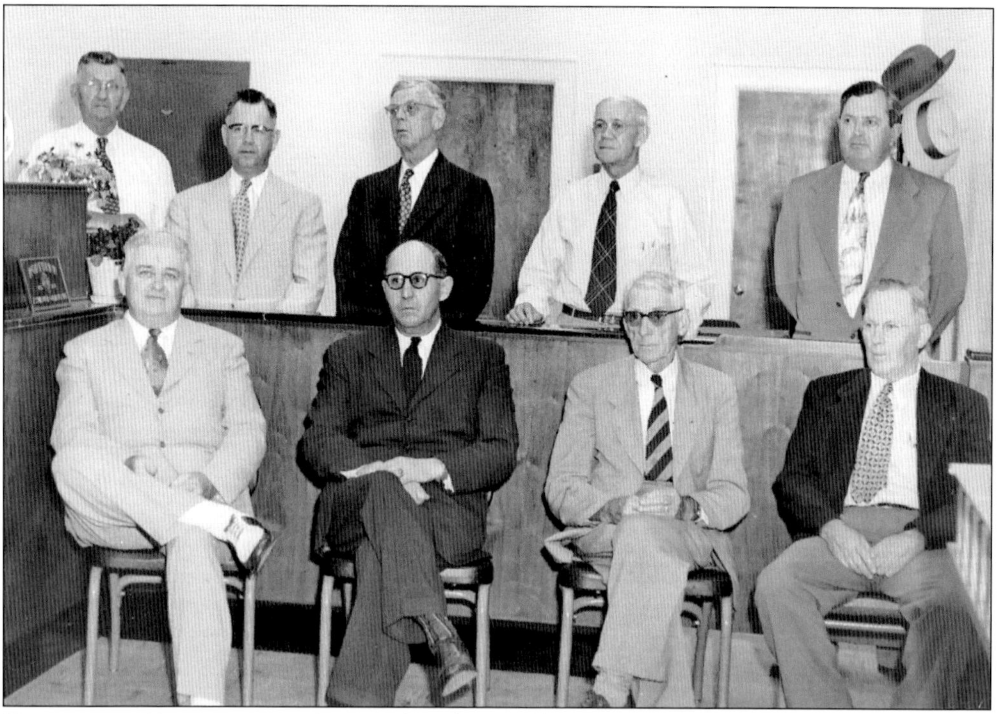

CHERRYVILLE BUILDING AND LOAN. The Cherryville Building and Loan Board of Directors is shown in this May 21, 1953, photograph. From left to right are (seated) T. C. Homesley, H. R. Harrelson, R. J. Morrison, and Claude C. Beam; (standing) Matthew Stroup, D. F. Beam, W. D. Brown, J. T. Allen, and Ezra Moss. In 1953, the association joined the Federal Home Loan Bank System. In 1960, its name was changed to Cherryville Savings and Loan Association.

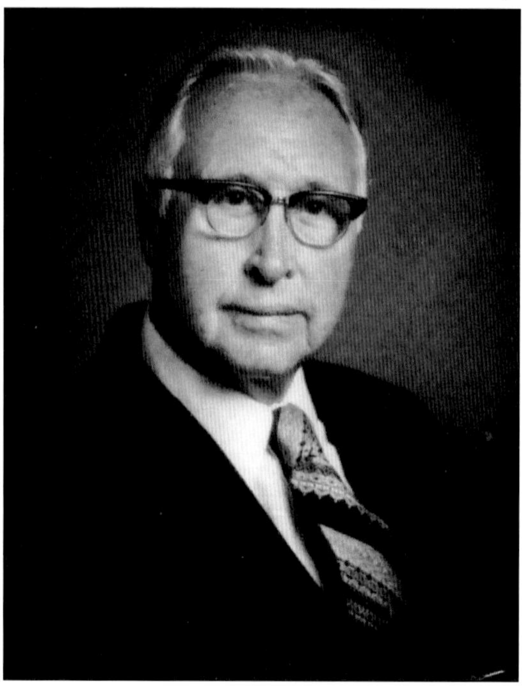

FOREST MELVILLE HOUSER, M.D. (1903–1998). The son of Dr. William Henry Houser and Mary Elizabeth Rudisill, Forest was a graduate of the University of North Carolina–Chapel Hill and the University of Pennsylvania in Philadelphia. He married Blanche Evangeline Duey and returned to Cherryville in 1929, where he practiced medicine until 1977. He was a lifetime member of St. John's Lutheran Church.

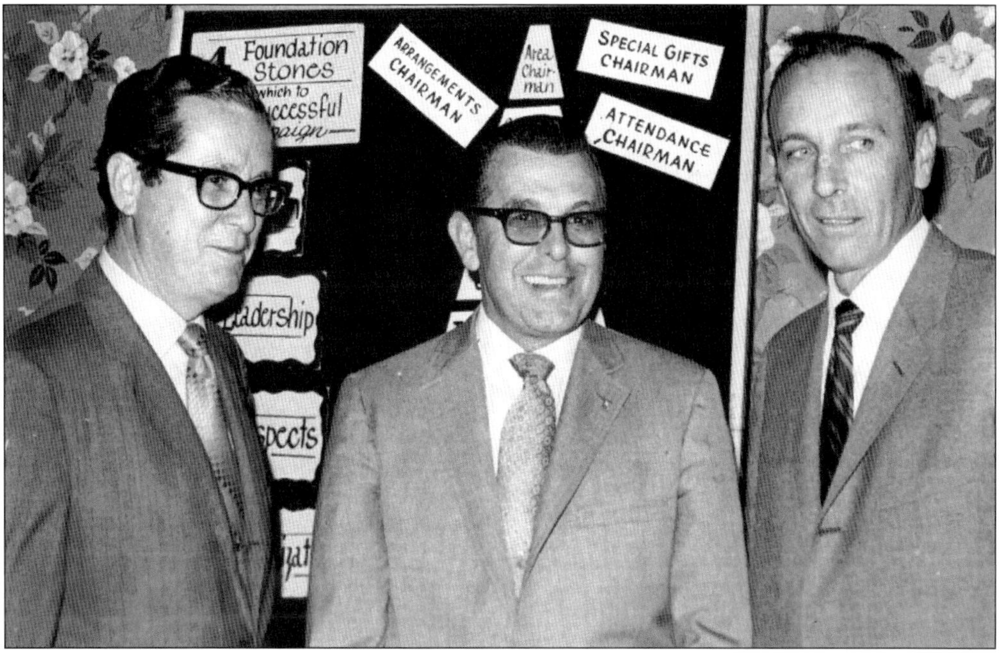

AARON B. MOSS. A retired Cherryville banker and son of E. V. Moss Sr., Moss (center) was president of Cherryville National Bank. He was mayor of Cherryville from 1965 until 1973 and is shown here at a fund-raiser held at Garner-Webb College in Boiling Springs. The Baptist-run college has always been attended by many Cherryville residents.

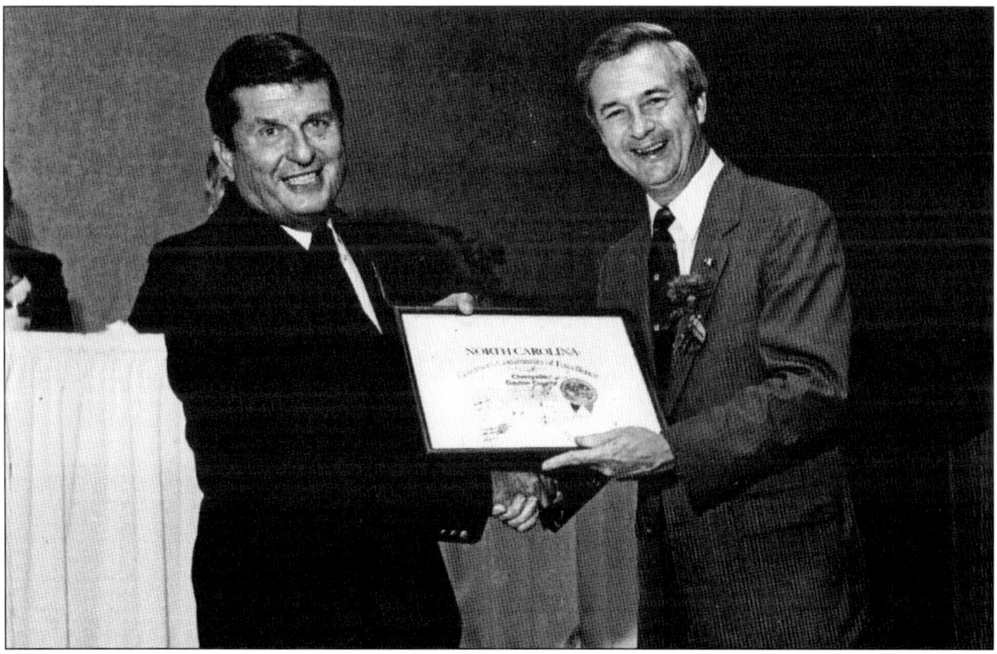

MAYOR WILLIAM O. UPCHURCH. Cherryville mayor W. O. "Bill" Upchurch (left) is shown here accepting the Governor's Community of Excellence Award for the city of Cherryville from Gov. Jim Hunt. The city of Cherryville was incorporated in 1872, and since that time, the citizens have continued to take pride in their town.

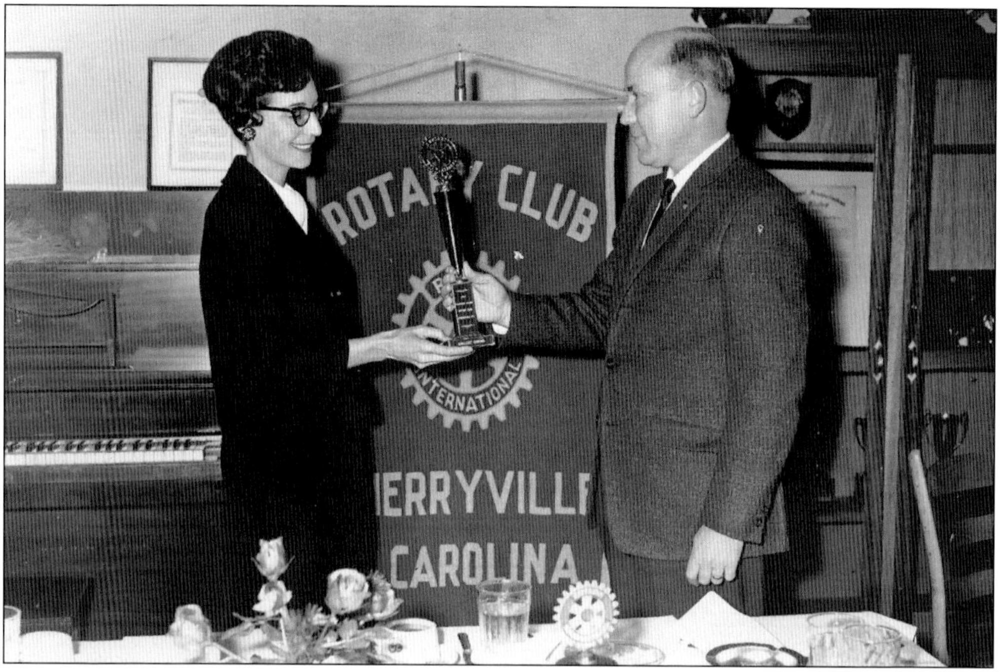

CHERRYVILLE ROTARY CLUB. Popular Cherryville librarian Margaret Ledford is seen receiving an award from the Cherryville Rotary Club presented by William "Bill" Allen, a Cherryville pharmacist, in this undated photograph.

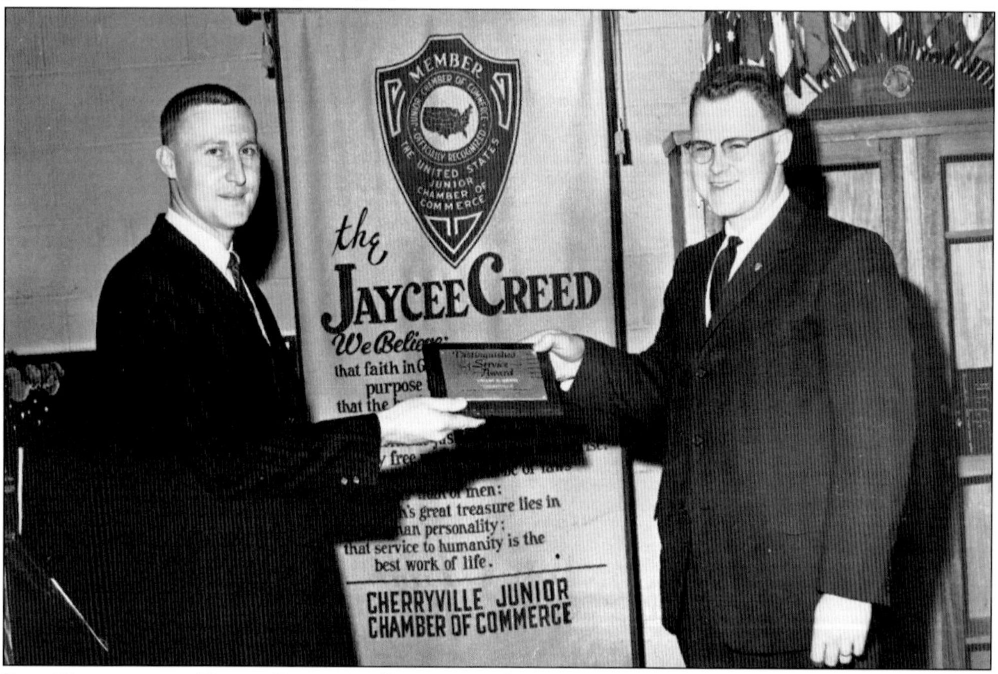

BILL HOUSER AND DAVID BEAM. William E. "Bill" Houser (left), a local pharmacist and son of Dr. Forest M. Houser, receives the Jaycees 1961 Young Man of the Year Award from Jaycees president David Carlyle Beam, with the Cherryville Savings and Loan. Beam is the son of Claude C. Beam and Mable Farnsworth Beam.

C. Grier Beam and John L. Fraley. C. Grier Beam (left), a trucking pioneer, was inducted posthumously into the North Carolina Transportation Hall of Fame in 2007. Fresh out of college but unemployed, he started Carolina Freight Carriers Corporation in 1932 in a Shell Station on Mountain Street in Cherryville. Today that building is listed on the National Register of Historic Places and houses a first-rate truck museum. The C. Grier Beam Truck Museum is located at 111 North Mountain Street. In the photograph at right is John L. "Buck" Fraley (right), who started selling produce for Grier Beam on the streets of Cherryville when he was 12 years old. Fraley retired in 1985 as chief executive officer of Carolina Freight Carrier Corporation. Fraley is shown here presenting Beam with a 40-year service pin. Shown below is the Carolina Freight Carrier Corporation's general offices and terminal in Cherryville in the 1960s.

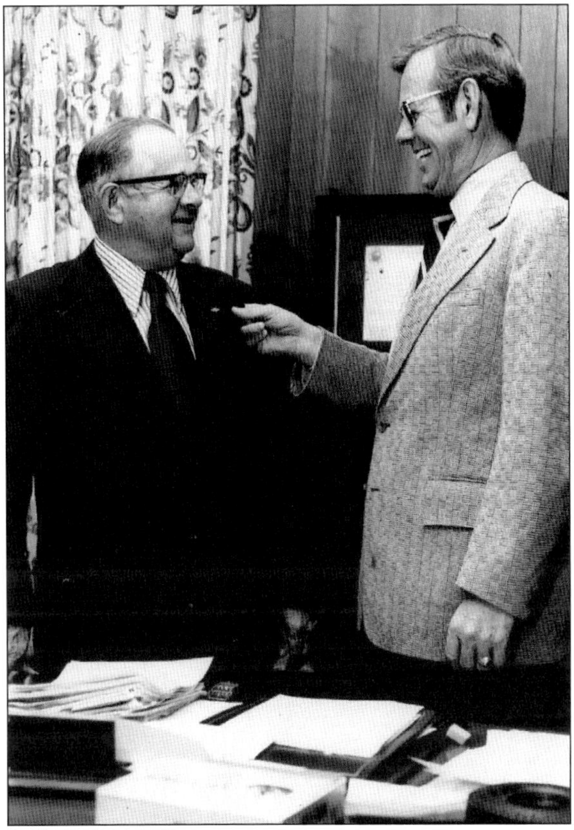

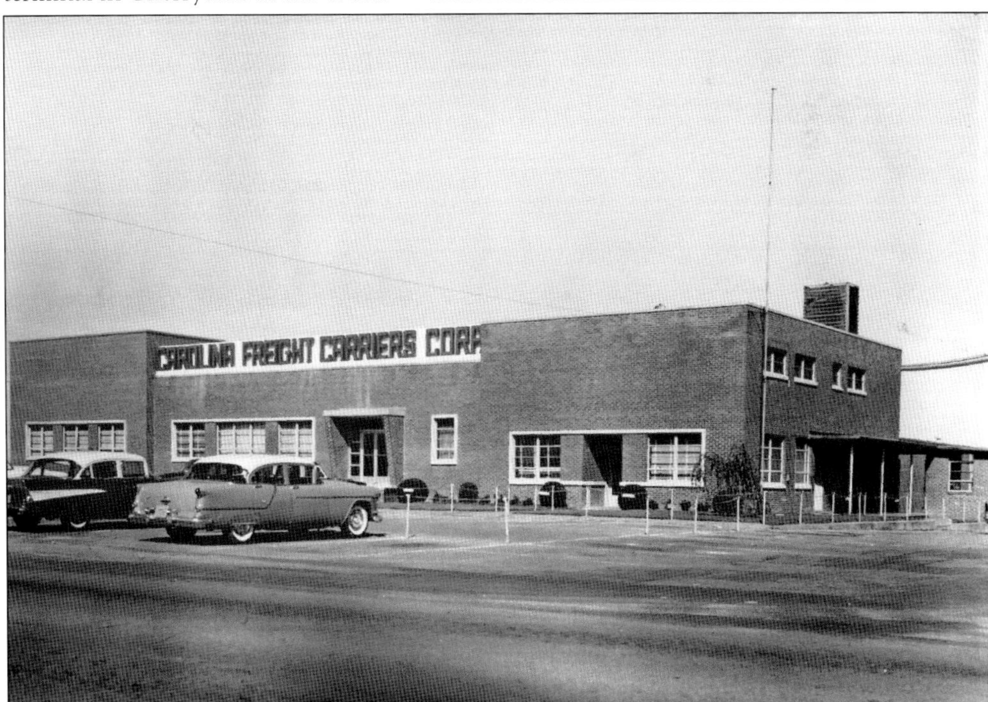

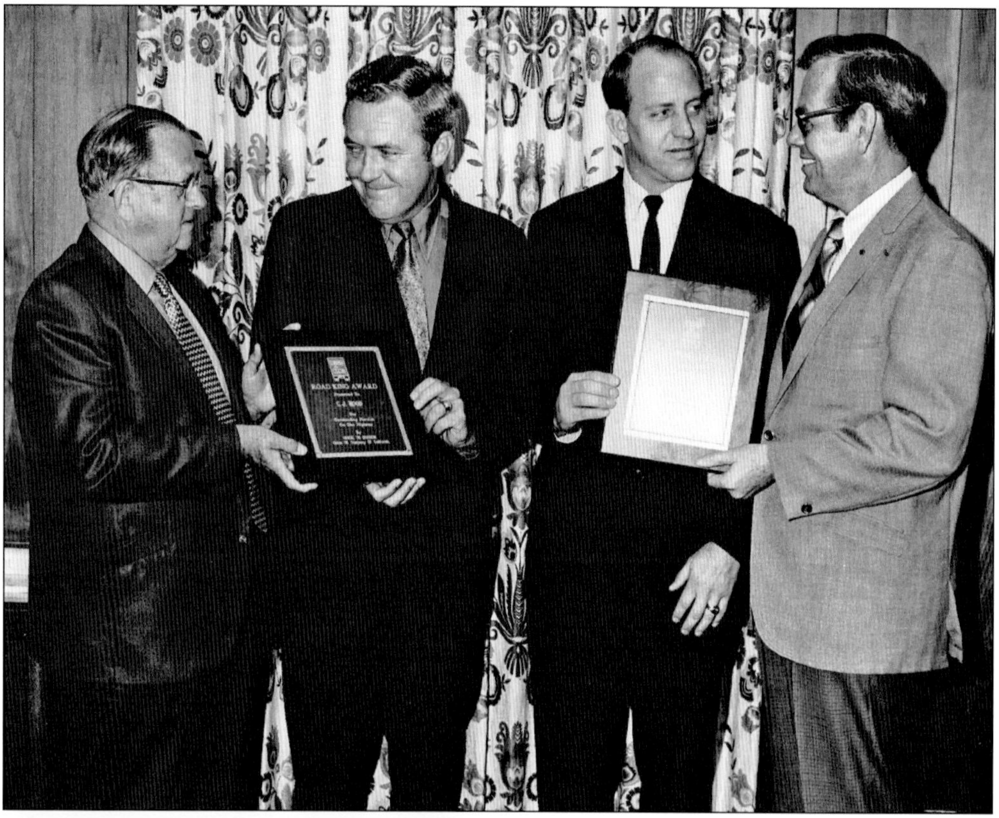

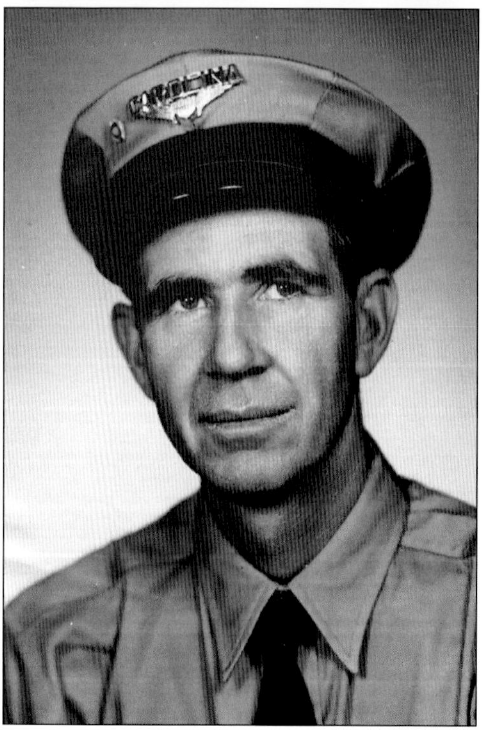

Carolina Freight Drivers, 1960s. C. J. Hood and Don Kester were surprised to see a whirlwind of money as they drove across a bridge in Virginia. They recovered $647, which was returned to the owner, a cab driver. They were each awarded a plaque and a $50 U.S. Savings Bond by Union 76 Division of Union Oil Company for heroism. Hood and Kester agreed, "There was never any question that we would return the money." Pictured above from left to right are C. Grier Beam, C. J. Hood, Don Kester, and John Fraley.

Ralph T. Self. The North Carolina "Driver of the Year" Governor's Gold Cup was presented posthumously to Ralph T. Self in 1967 in Raleigh and was accepted by his wife, Blanche Self, and his daughter, Nell Griggs. Self was a longtime driver for Carolina Freight Carriers Corporation. He had a 30-year safe-driving record of more than 2,200,000 miles without a chargeable accident.

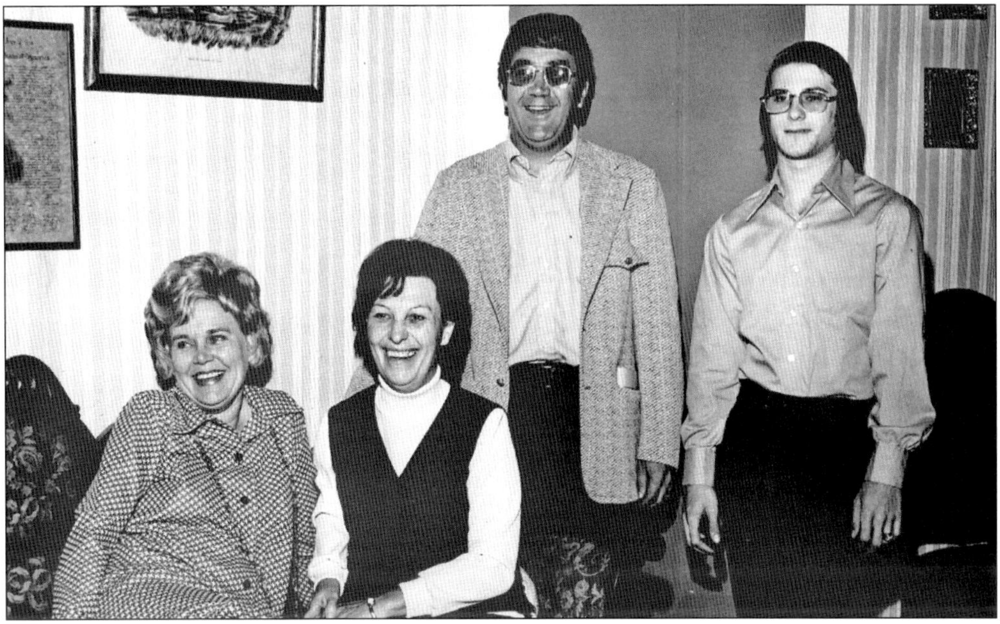

CHERRYVILLE LITTLE THEATRE. In 1972, the Cherryville Little Theatre was founded. Its first president was Ann Warlick, and the first play was *Barefoot in the Park*, directed by John David Kennedy. In 1993, *Barefoot in the Park* was presented again to celebrate the first 20 years of the theater. Seen here from left to right are actors Marvetta McGinnis, Pansy Dellinger, Burma Carpenter, and Doug Byers.

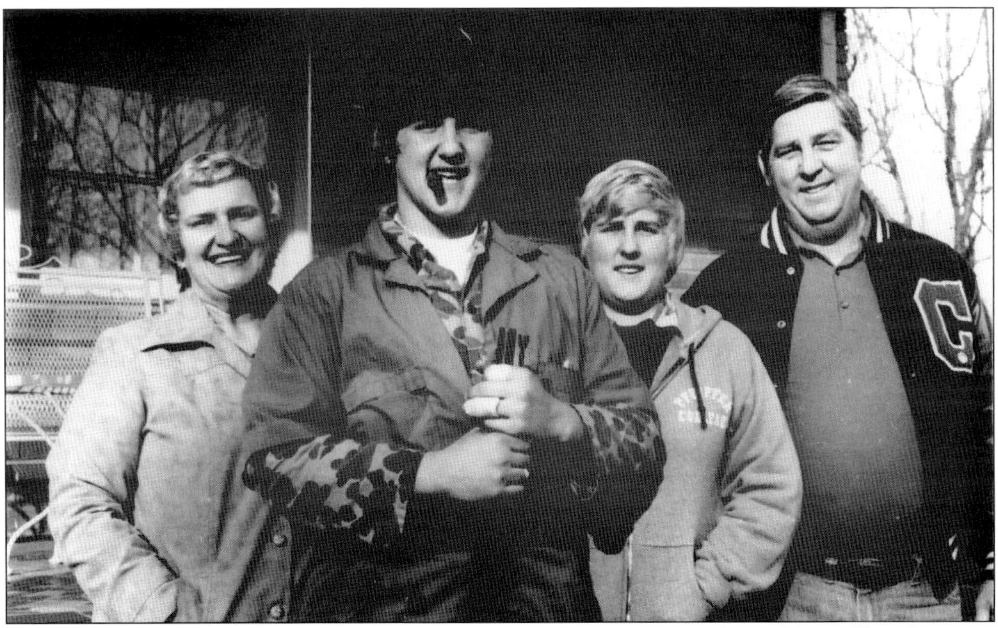

C. V. THORNBURG FAMILY. Few traditions last more than a century, but Cherryville is home to one that has lasted more than 250 years. Here Jerry and C. V. Thornburg (far left and far right, respectively) and their two children, Vee Thornburg and Bess Thornburg, help the Cherryville New Year Shooters celebrate the New Year. A well-known and loved family in Cherryville, the Thornburgs have always been involved in every aspect of the community.

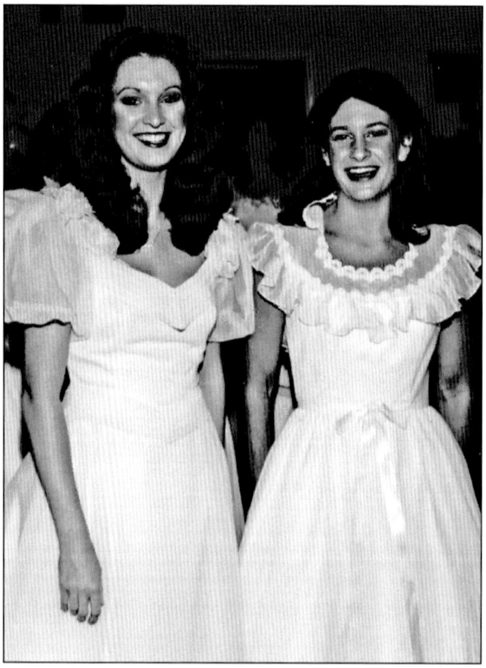

AVA ROXANNE BLACK AND MERRI MELANIE HOUSER. These girls were presented on June 12, 1982, at the 37th Annual Debutante Ball of the Junior Charity League in Shelby, North Carolina. Black (left) is a descendant of Thomas Black (1792–1880), John Wehunt (1798–1886), and Ben Alexander (1883–1933). Houser (right) is a descendant of John L. Beam and is the granddaughter of Dr. Forest M. Houser and Howard Ford. Today Roxanne Black Stritt is an accountant and financial analyst in Atlanta, and Melanie Houser Gentile is a pharmacist.

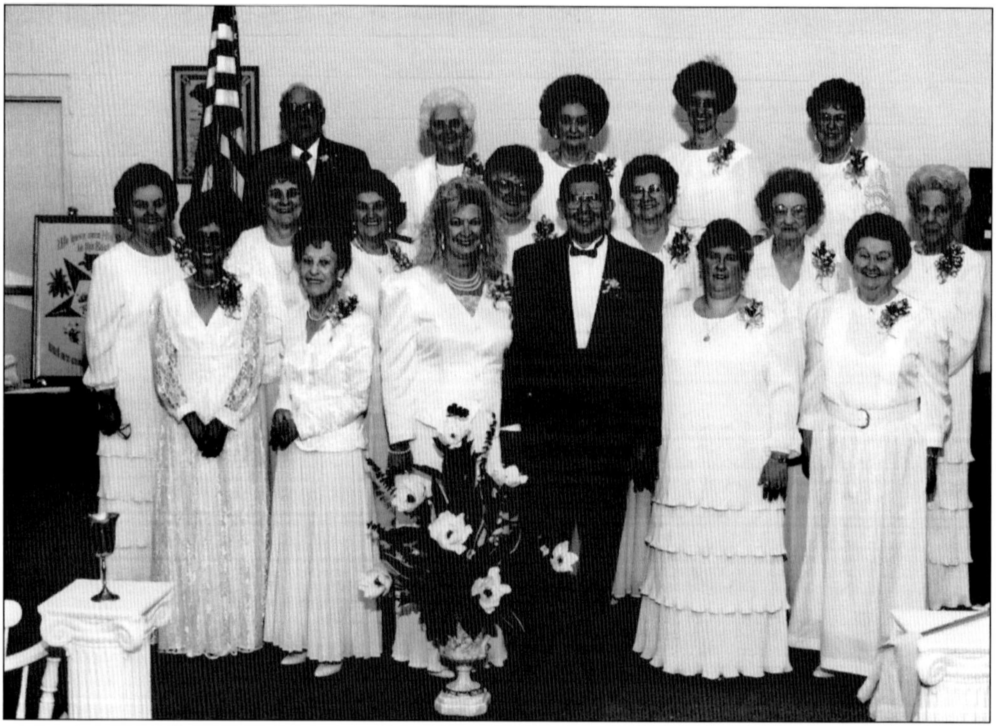

THE EASTERN STAR. Pictured here in 1996, the Cherryville Order (No. 156) of the Eastern Star included, from left to right, (first row) Katherine Moss, Pansy Dellinger, Debbie Brown, Cone Carpenter Jr., Bess Thornburg, and Carye A. Brown; (second row) Teny Mosteller, Betty Black, Frankie B. Brown, Cathy Reid, Evelyn Heavner, Maude Carter, and Margie Hallman; (third row) A. B. Beam, Blanche Stroupe, Patricia Beam, Juanita Fraley, and Jackie Bingham.

Three

The Cherryville Schools

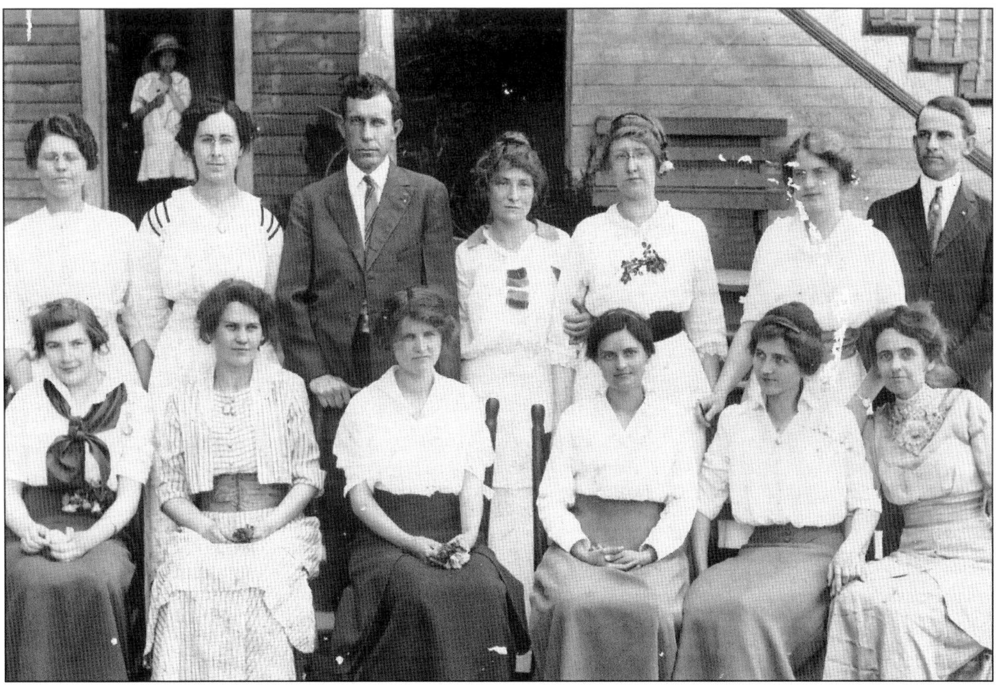

Academy Faculty, c. 1905. Members of the Cherryville Academy faculty in the first decade of the 20th century were, from left to right, (first row) Nell Dellinger, Mae Baber, Minnie Beam, Zona Stroup Falls, ? Pruden, and unidentified; (second row) Carrie Ballard, Mae Cline, superintendent Joe R. Nixon, Letha Lancaster, Mattie Camp, unidentified, and W. J. Allran Sr.

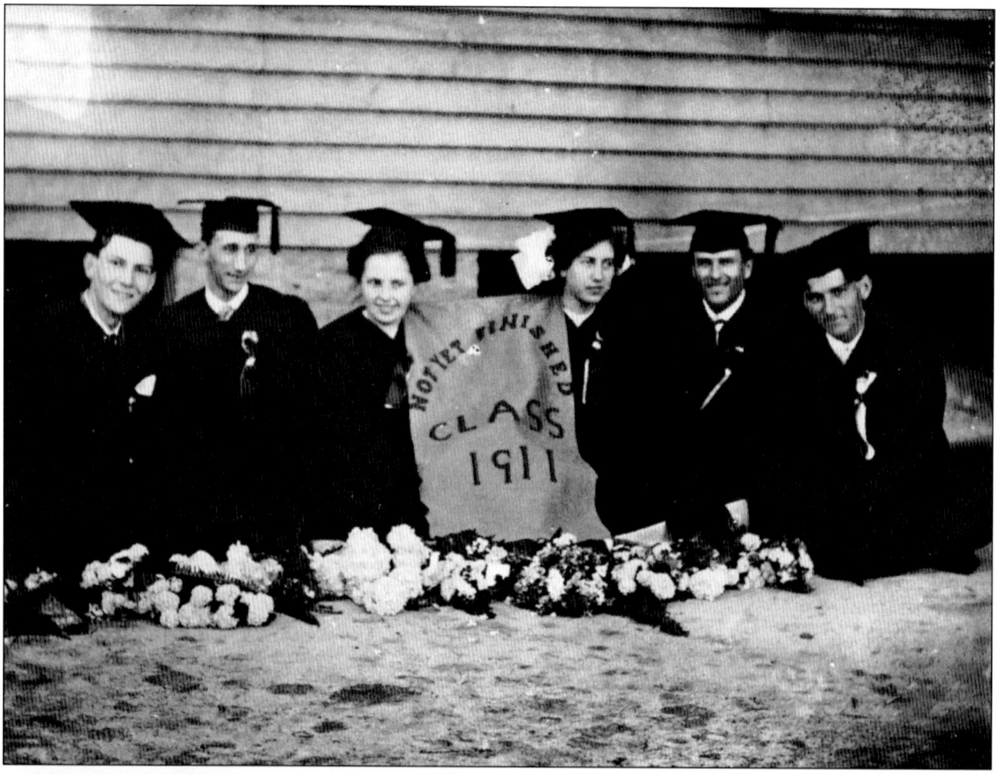

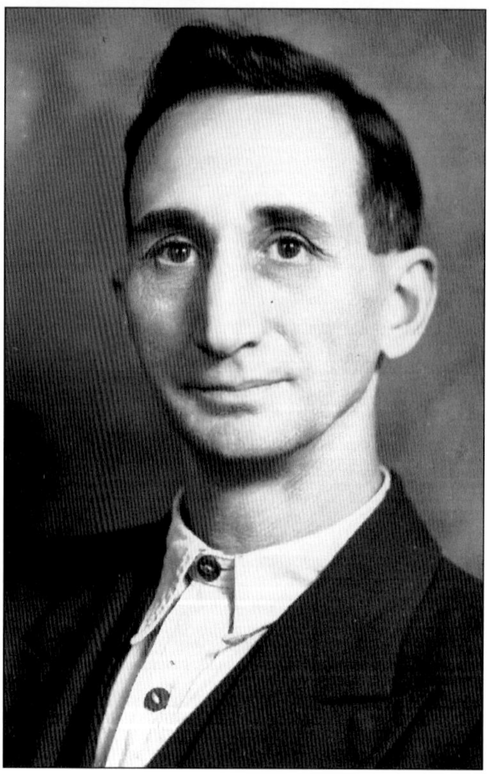

CHERRYVILLE ACADEMY CLASS OF 1911. The first graduating class from the old Cherryville Academy was awarded diplomas in 1911. The six students were Pantha Harrelson (Houser), Elsie Roberts (McCorkle), William W. Black, Lewis I. Mauney, W. Caldwell Howell, and Rex Eaker. The banner reads, "Not Yet Finished, Class of 1911."

L. REX EAKER. A member the class of 1911, Rex Eaker was the son of C. M. and Matilda Heavner Eaker. He attended Lenoir-Rhyne College and later became a teacher. He married Vacie Stroup, and during World War I, he was stationed in France with the American Expeditionary Forces as a machine gunner. In 1923, Eaker accepted a position with the Farmer's Union Supply Company as a bookkeeper and later became manager.

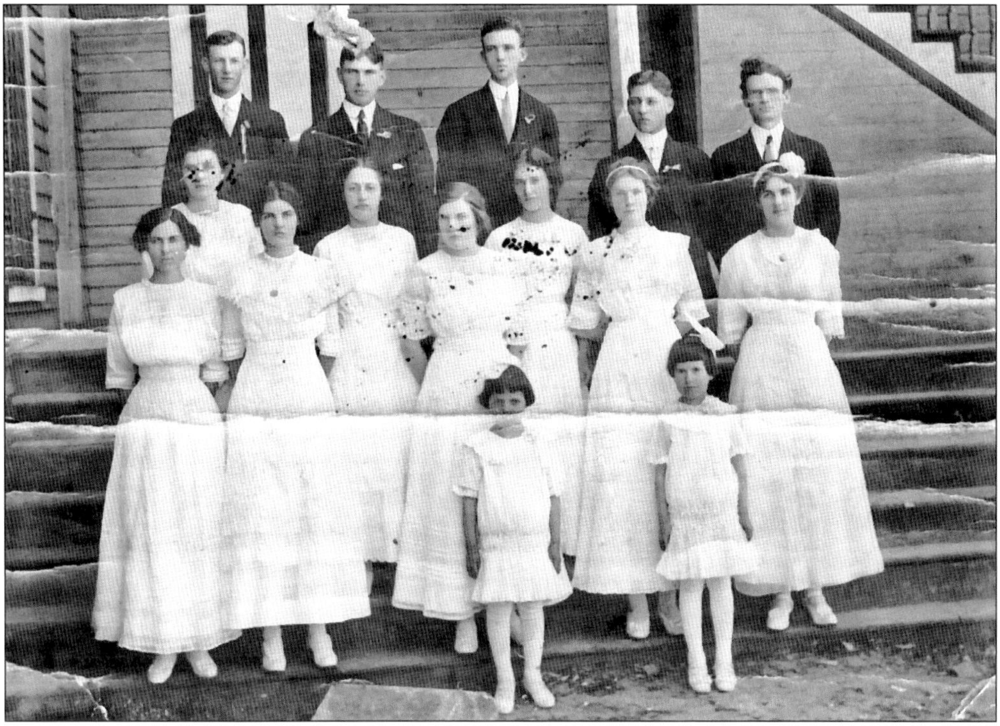

Cherryville Academy Graduating Class, 1913. The graduating class of 1913 held commencement exercises on Friday afternoon, April 25, 1913, at 2:30 in the academy auditorium. The high school chorus sang "Springtime," and a vocal duet was performed by Zona Stroup and Mattie Kendrick. Zona Falls also sang a solo with Margaret Hall on the piano. Those graduating were David Webb Beam, Lela Brae Black, Jessie Burgoyne Caldwell, Bertha Clyda Caldwell, Clisby Augustus Clark, Jewell Dellinger, Ethel Pearl Houser, Mary Virginia Kerr, Susan Margaret Ledford, Melvin Sipe, and Nellie Mae Summers. Superintendent was H. S. Moseby, and the principal was Katherine Whitener. Early faculty members at the academy included John J. George, W. T. R. Bell, L. H. J. Houser, Frank Harrelson, Prof. S. P. Wilson, J. W. Strassell., John Rudisill, Pearl Harrelson, David P. Dellinger, W. J. Allran Sr., Dora McDowell, D. R. Mauney Sr., and Verner Dellinger Rudisill.

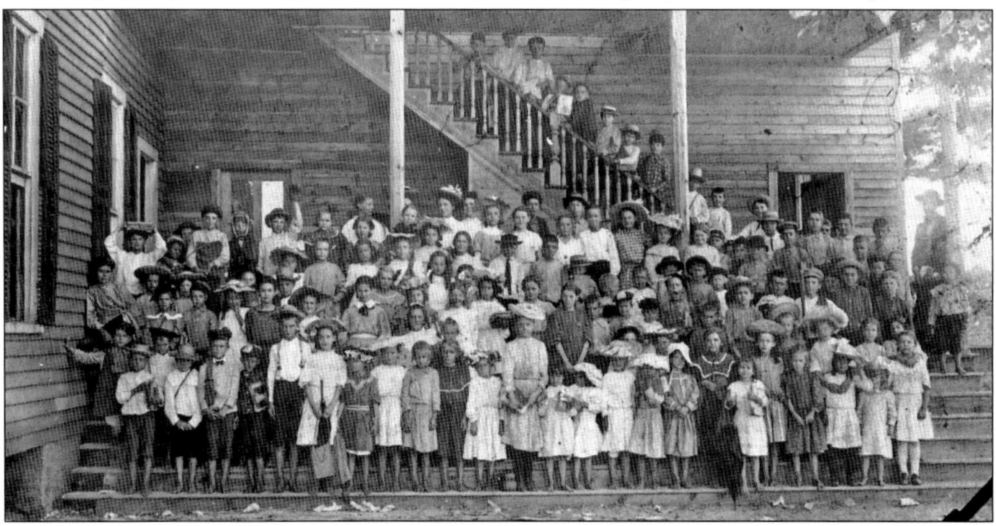

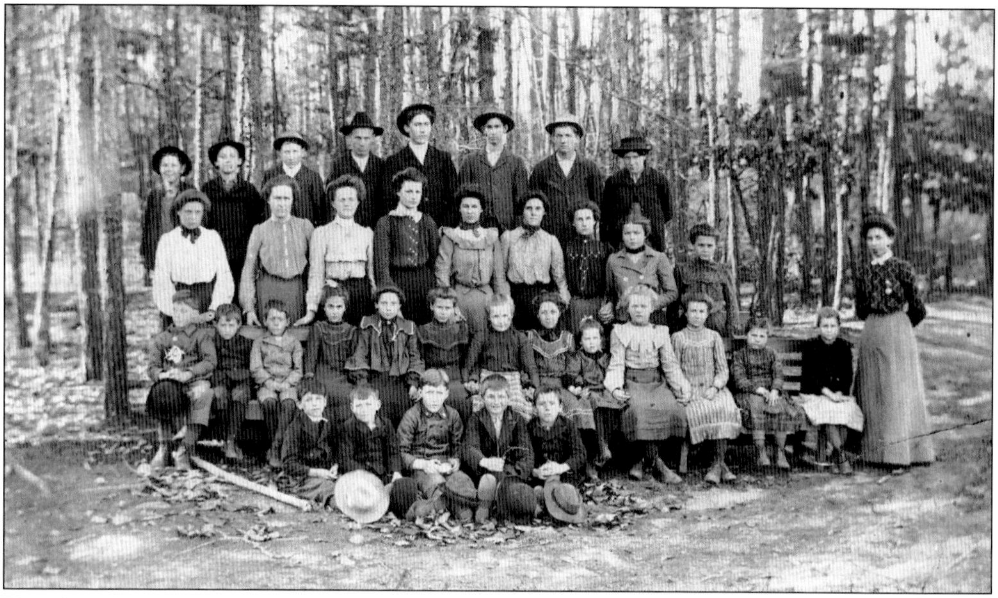

The Old Cherryville Academy, 1892–1915. Originally in what was known as the Morrison School District, Cherryville was made a separate school district in 1881. By 1892, the first permanent school building was erected on land donated by W. R. Carroll and M. L. Dellinger. The school faced east and was situated almost in the middle of what is today Academy Street. The building was a two-story frame building with a tower in front and a stairway on the right. Additions to the north, south, and rear were later added to the original structure around 1911. The academy housed all grade levels, and it was a special day (below) when the photographer came to take photographs. All wore their "Sunday best" for the occasion. Another earlier group of students (shown above) gathers for a photograph near the pines.

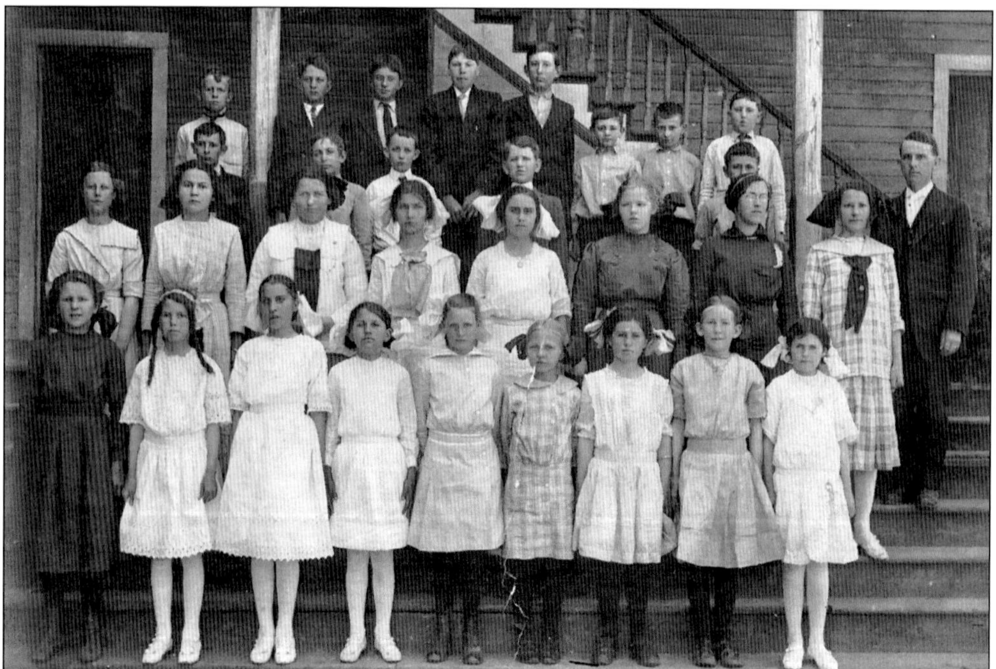

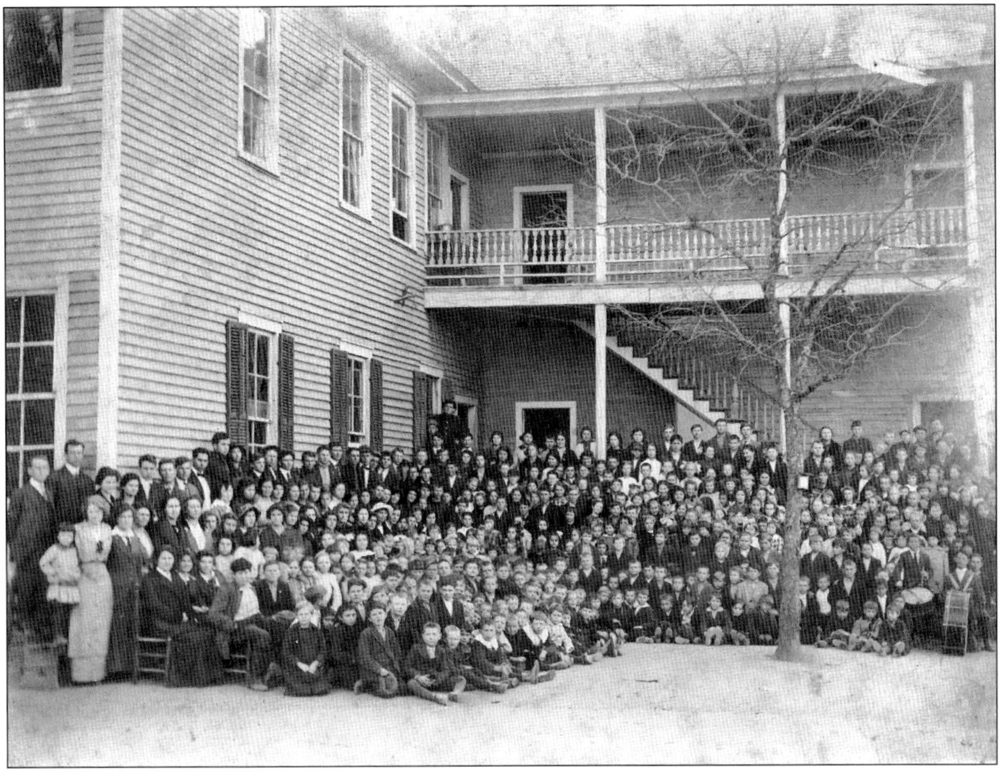

J. Frank Harrelson. Born in 1884, J. Frank Harrelson taught at the academy during the early 1900s. The son of Joseph M. Harrelson and his wife, Fannie, Frank is listed on the 1910 census as a "preacher" living in Gastonia. His wife, Nora, died early in their marriage, and in 1920, he and his son were living with Vernon Harrelson on South Mountain Street. At one time, he was a bookkeeper for the First National Bank in Cherryville. Around 1900, on commencement night at the academy, a tragedy was prevented by Deputy Sheriff E. Lee McGinnis. The building was crowded with people when a large swinging oil lamp fell to the floor and started a blaze in the midst of the crowd. McGinnis seized the blazing oil lamp and threw it out the second-story window, doubtless saving many lives.

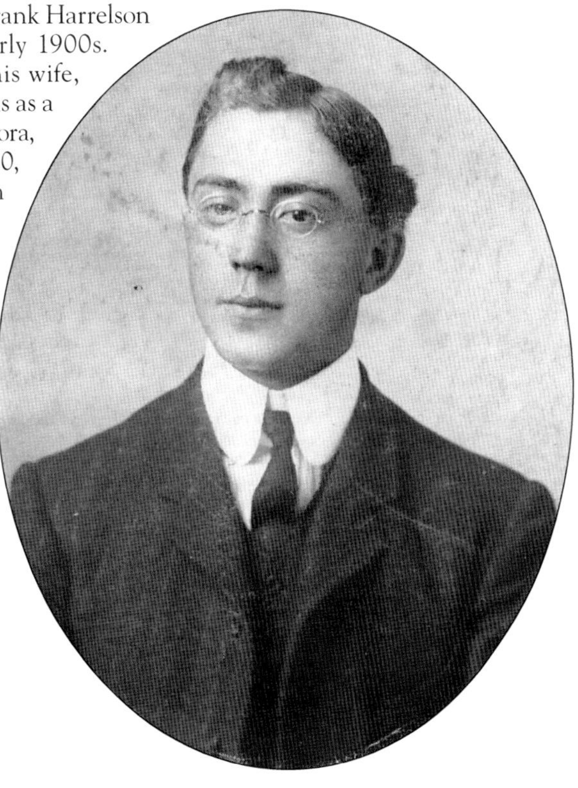

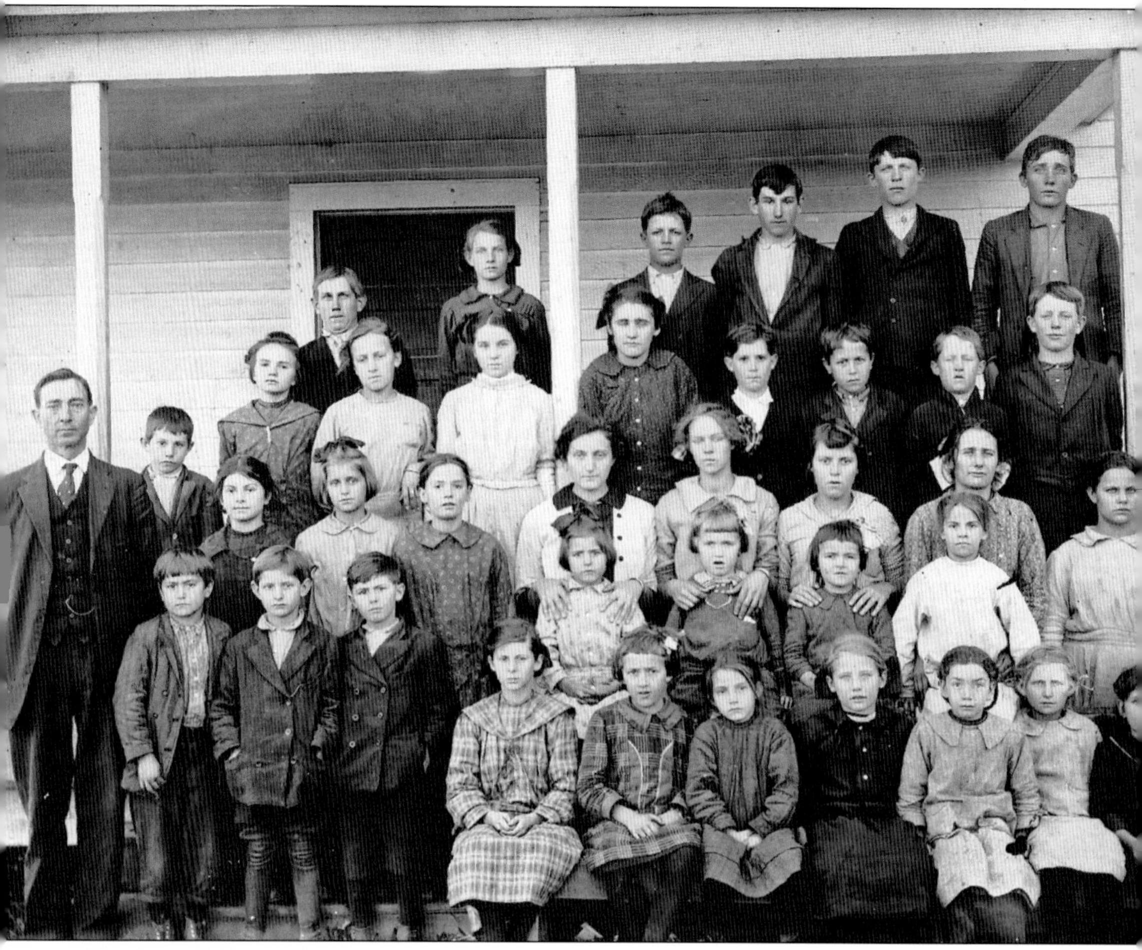

The John F. Black School, 1916. Located two miles north of Cherryville, the original school was built by John Franklin Black's father, Thomas Black (1792–1880). That first structure of logs, built around 1846, was destroyed by fire. The second school, built in 1898 by John F. Black, was a two-room school. This frame building was used until 1912, when a larger structure replaced it. The John F. Black School can be seen at the J. Ralph Beam Jr. Heritage Park. From left to right are (first row) Roy Anthony, Hugh Helms, Star Black, Mary Florence Black, Attie Shuford, Jesse White, Bertha Simpson, Ollie Mae Black, Ethel Morrison, and Tex Black; (second row) Rev. Charles Robinson (teacher), Marshall White, Virgie Whitworth, Edna Helms, Essie Mitchem, Emma Black, Stella Shuford, Pauline Shuford, and Reva Whitworth; (third row) Junie Black, Mary Dellinger, Lee Shuford, Mollie Simpson, and Bryte Morrison; (fourth row) Ocie Mitchem, Bryte Shuford, Bryte White, Pearl Simpson, Ernest Helms, Doris Anthony, Theodore Shuford, and John Trammel; (fifth row) Ruffin White, Barbara White, Clyde Helms, James White, Andrew Trammel, and John Simpson.

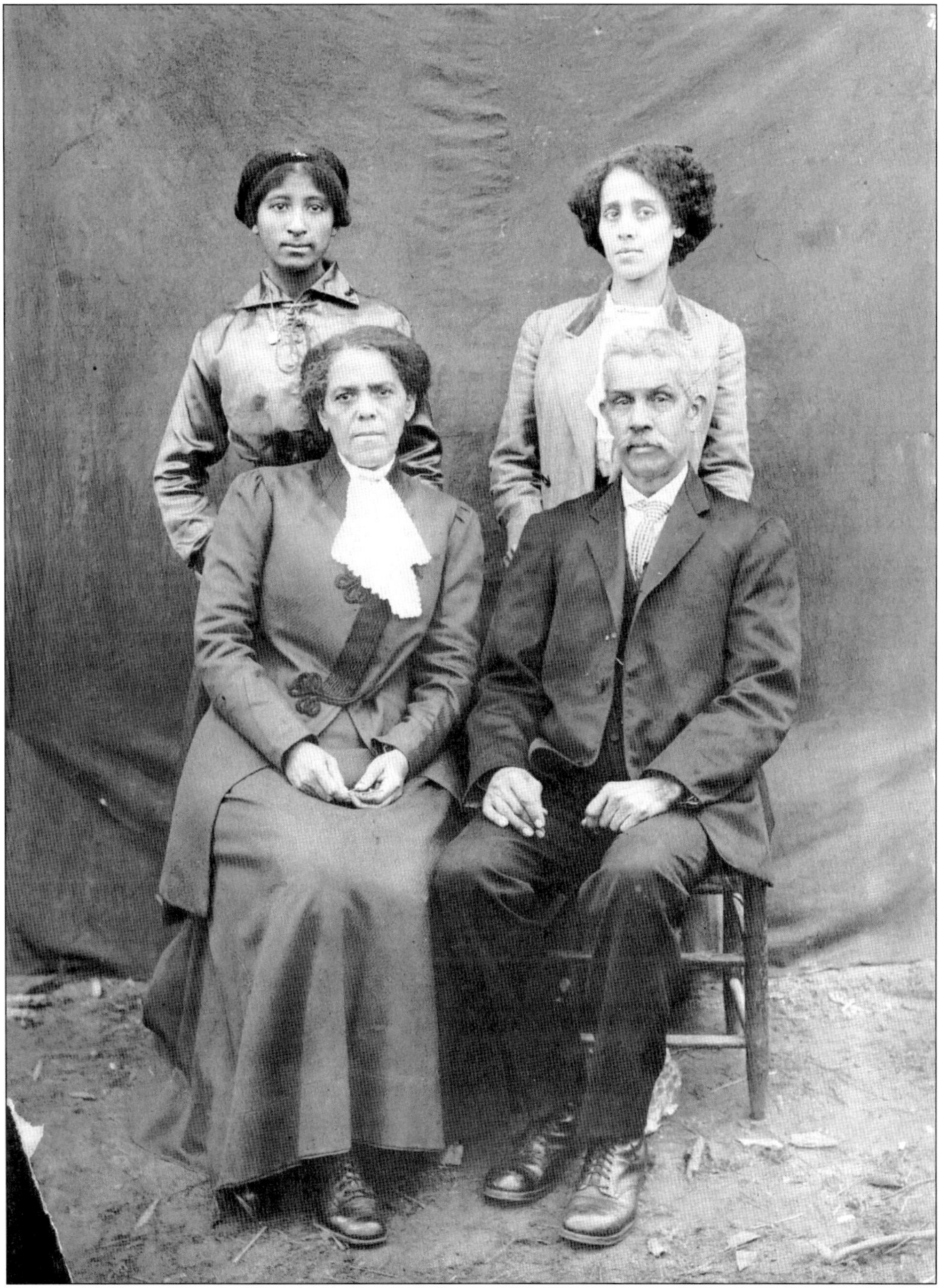

The Rosenwald Schools for African Americans. Mr. and Mrs. P. L. Lacour, Mrs. A. L. Mauney, and S. A. Sadguiar came to Gaston County around 1910 to teach in the Rosenwald Schools for African Americans. The Rosenwald Schools were started by Sears and Roebuck executive Julius Rosenwald. Matching grants were offered to build schools for black students, but half the money had to be raised by local citizens. There were 813 Rosenwald Schools in North Carolina, the most of any state. Many of these schools were located in Gaston, Lincoln, and Cleveland Counties.

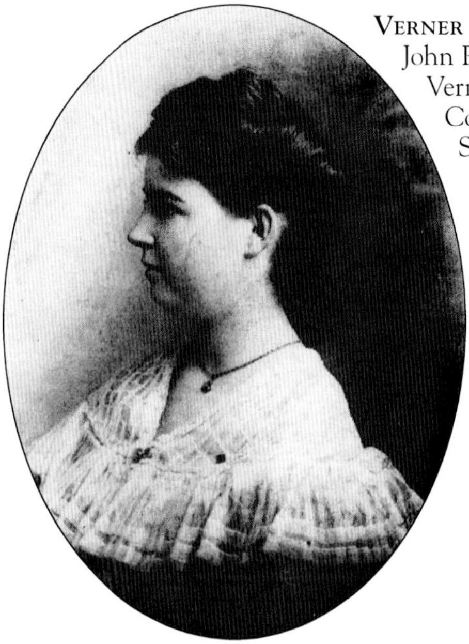

VERNER LEE DELLINGER (1886–1977). The daughter of John Pinkney Dellinger and Margaret Paulina Carpenter, Verner is shown here while an art student at Elizabeth College (later Queens College) in Charlotte in 1907. She was a popular and well-liked student. She later married Carl A. Rudisill and spent the rest of her life in Cherryville.

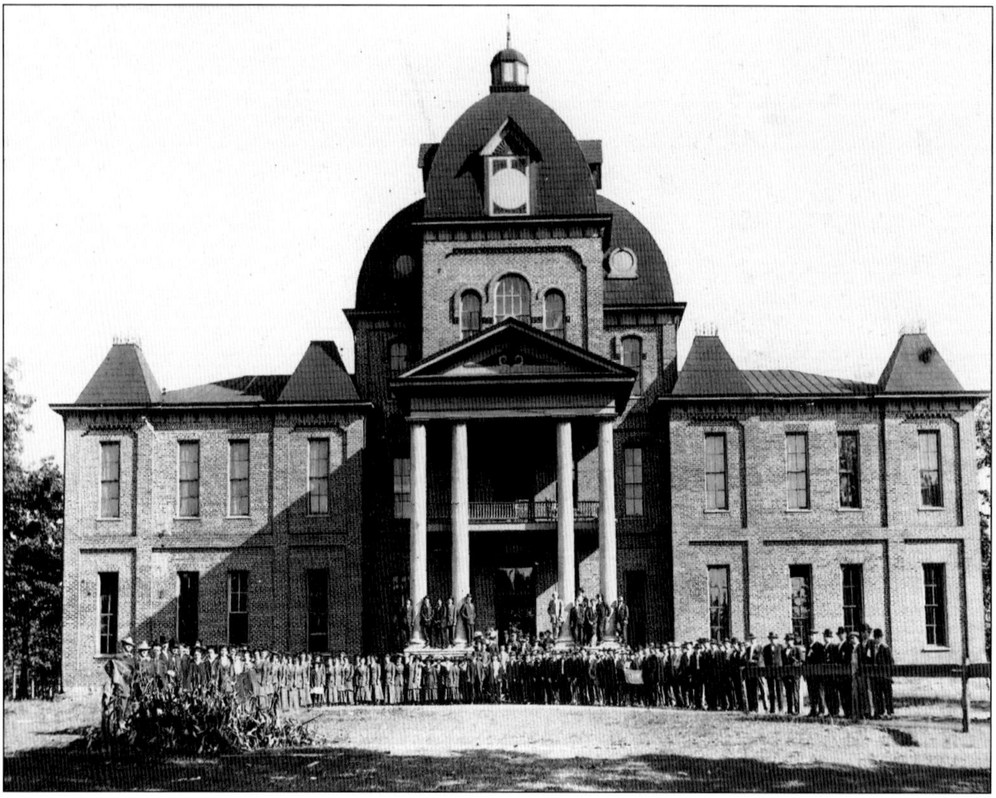

LENOIR-RHYNE COLLEGE. Many Cherryville students attended the Lutheran college in Hickory known first as Lenoir College, named for W. W. Lenoir. Later the name was changed to Lenoir-Rhyne College in honor of D. E. Rhyne because of his philanthropic gifts to the college. Cherryville students are among these graduating students in this undated photograph.

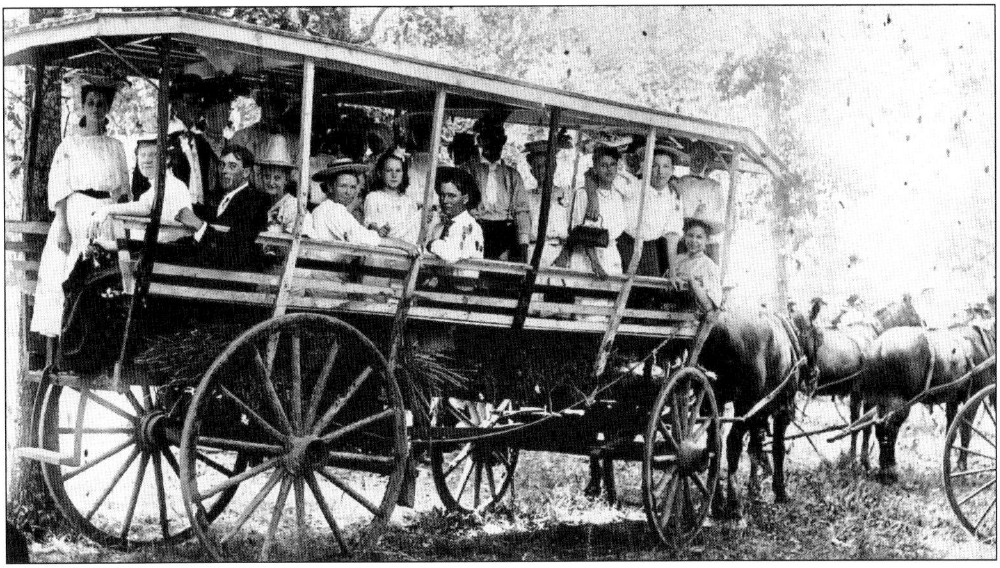

THE PIEDMONT BUS. In the early 1900s, many Cherryville families sent their children to Piedmont High School in Lawndale; many students boarded at the school. Music, drama, and voice were taught, in addition to the usual academics. Gardner-Webb College in Boiling Springs is said to have sprung from "Old Piedmont." Dr. Evan Wehunt and his sister Blanche Wehunt (Hoyle) were students. The Falls family also sent its children there, and Zeb Grigg, the evangelist, attended Piedmont.

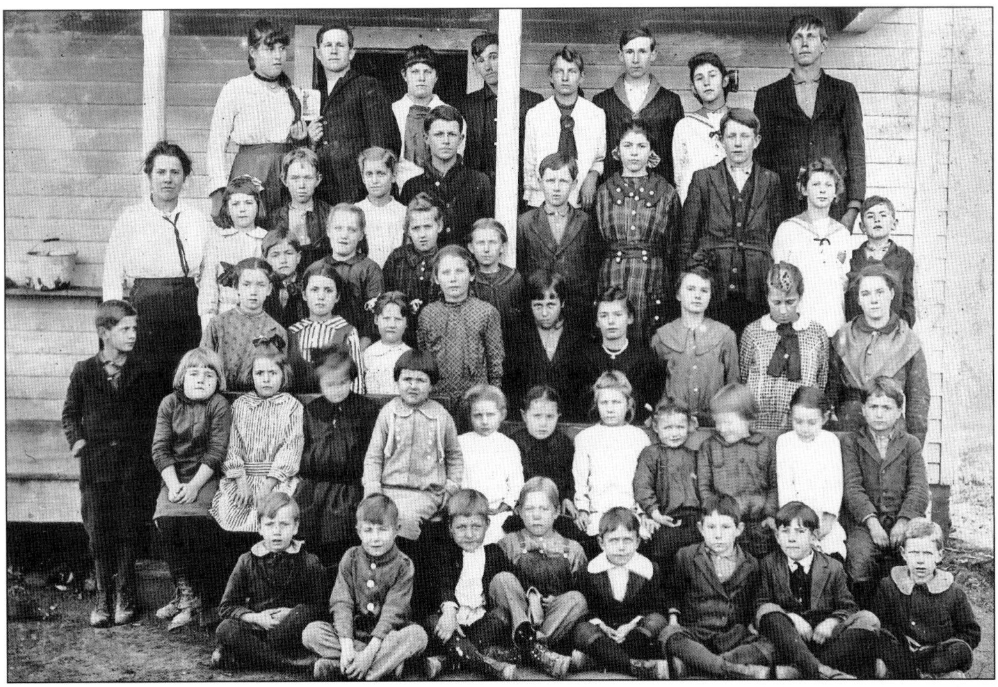

JOHN F. BLACK SCHOOL, 1917. John F. Black (1848–1940) lived in the Panhandle area north of Cherryville. The John F. Black School seen in this photograph was built around 1912, replacing an earlier two-room school that had been built in 1898. The 1912 school was used until the early 1920s. The 1898 John F. Black School can be seen at the J. Ralph Beam Heritage Park.

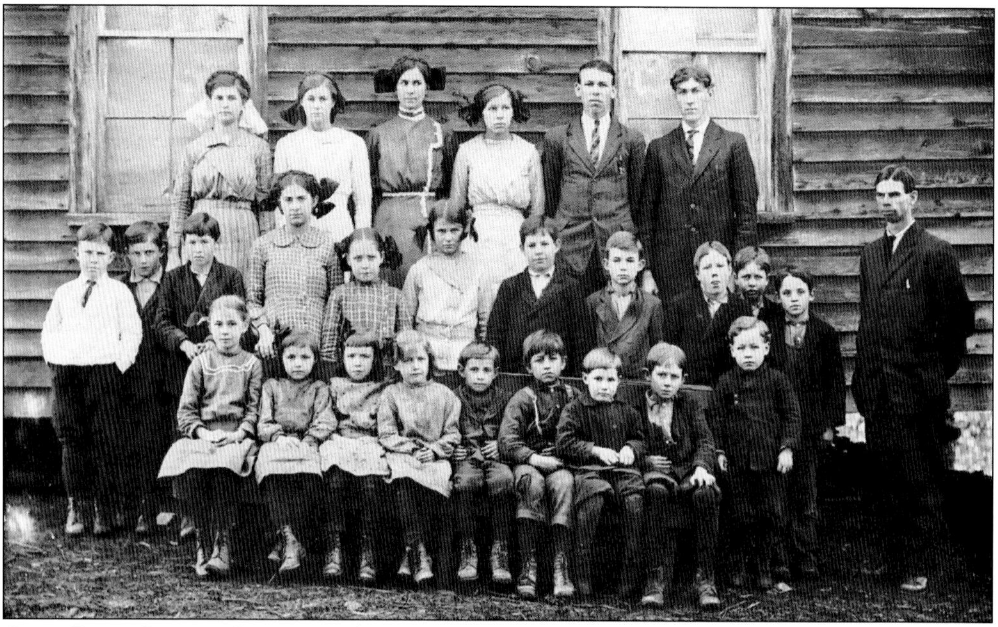

Gray Rock School (1874–1921). One-room schools were common in rural areas of North Carolina from the 1880s until the 1920s. Gray Rock School (1874–1921) was one of several one-room schools located north of Cherryville in the Panhandle area. Gray Rock began operating in 1874 and closed in 1921. Those above are, from left to right, (first row) Madeline Dellinger, Ethel Henry and Edith Henry (twins), Laura Wright, Blaine Dellinger, Perry Carpenter, Tew Dellinger, George Kiser, and John William Putnam; (second row) Clyde Reynolds, Alvin Dellinger, Hollifield Houser, Mae Dellinger, Mary Reynolds, Evelyn Dellinger, Charlie Dellinger, Conley Kiser, Andy Wright, Ben Wright, Jenkins Henry, and Dow Putnam (teacher); (third row) Jane Dellinger, Rosa Dellinger, Addie Dellinger, Vada Putnam, Henry Putnam, and Caris Dellinger. The group of patriotic students seen below is also from the Panhandle area.

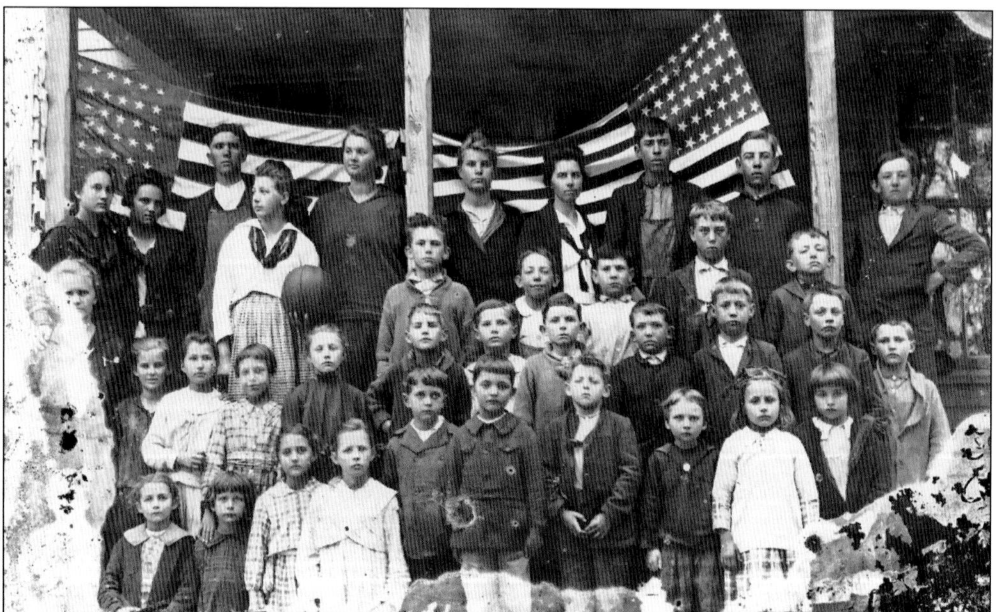

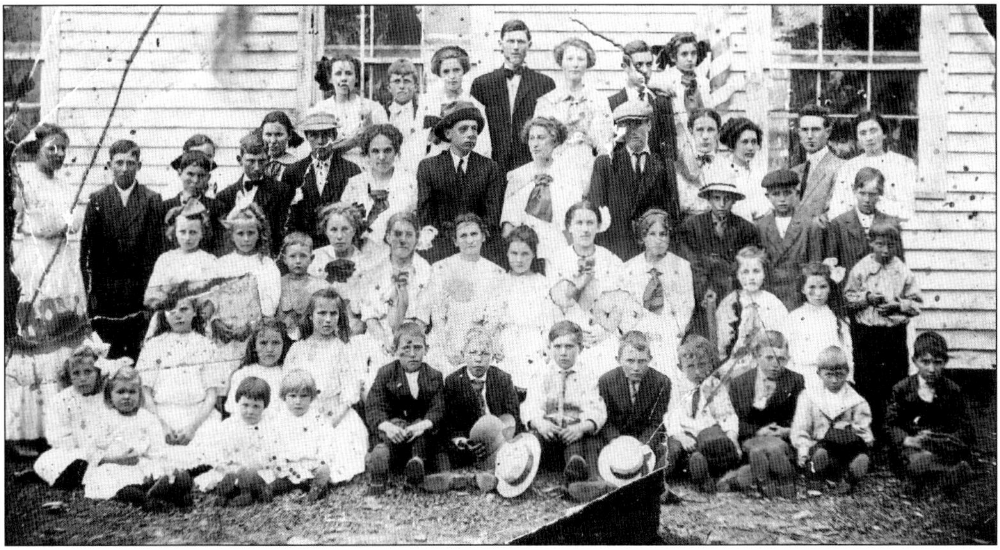

HALLMAN SCHOOL, C. 1910. The Hallman School was located near Indian Creek, close to where the Wal-Mart stands today. Some of the families who sent children to the Hallman School were Wyant, Carpenter, Hovis, McGinnis, Baker, Dellinger, Black, Sigman, Aderholt, Costner, Blackwood, Eaker, Jenkins, Sellers, Brown, Anthony, Mauney, Hinkle, Biggerstaff, Heavner, Hallman, Beam, Pendleton, and Blakely.

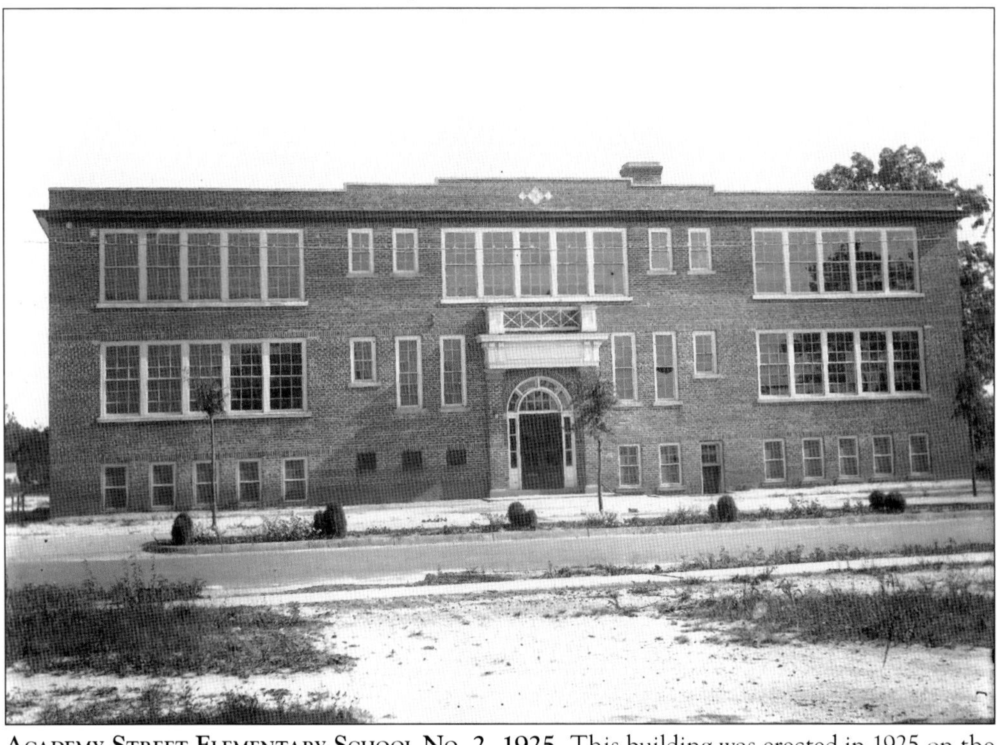

ACADEMY STREET ELEMENTARY SCHOOL NO. 2, 1925. This building was erected in 1925 on the south side of Academy Street, west of Elm Street, as an elementary school to house the first five grades. It was built on part of the old academy grounds. It contained an auditorium, a boiler room, toilets, two offices, and 12 classrooms. When it closed in 1973, it was known as West School.

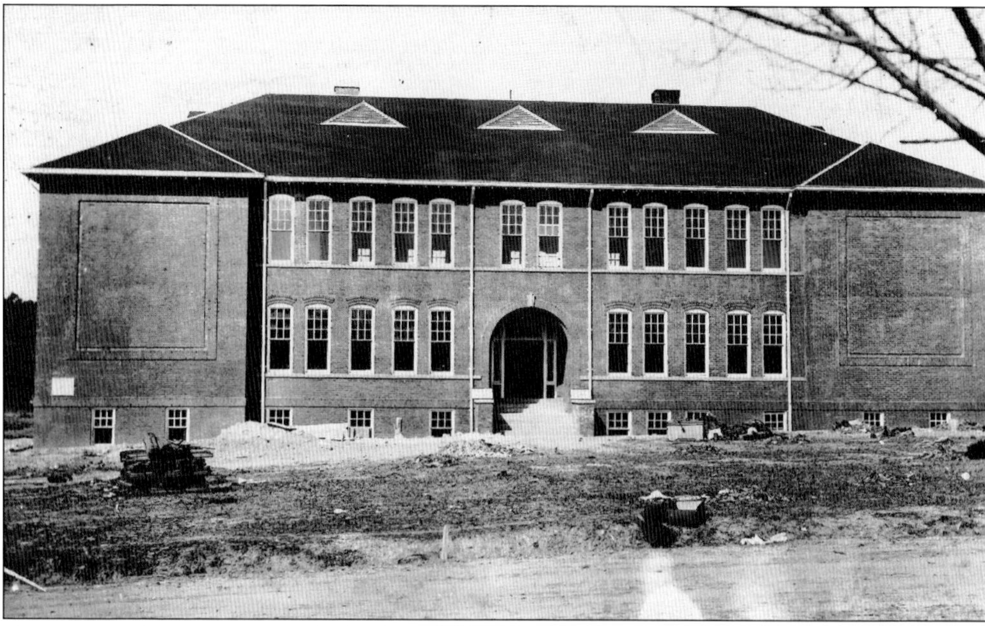

Cherryville High School, 1915. The old Cherryville High School building on East First Street was completed in the latter part of 1915 at a cost of approximately $30,000. A gymnasium building was erected in 1929 on the right side, and a ball park and playground were located in the back. The building contained 19 recitation rooms (classrooms), offices, and music rooms. On the second floor were eight classrooms and offices. On the first floor, there were seven classrooms, a boiler room, and two toilets. On the top floor were four classrooms and the auditorium. During the Christmas holidays in 1919, this building was almost destroyed by fire and soon was rebuilt. Much controversy arose over the location of this school. Some wanted it to be located near the old academy, and a court injunction stopped the construction for a while. The Masonic Lodge, who had been asked to lay the cornerstone, withdrew, and the Junior Order of United American Mechanics at Flay laid the cornerstone. This building would later be used as an elementary school.

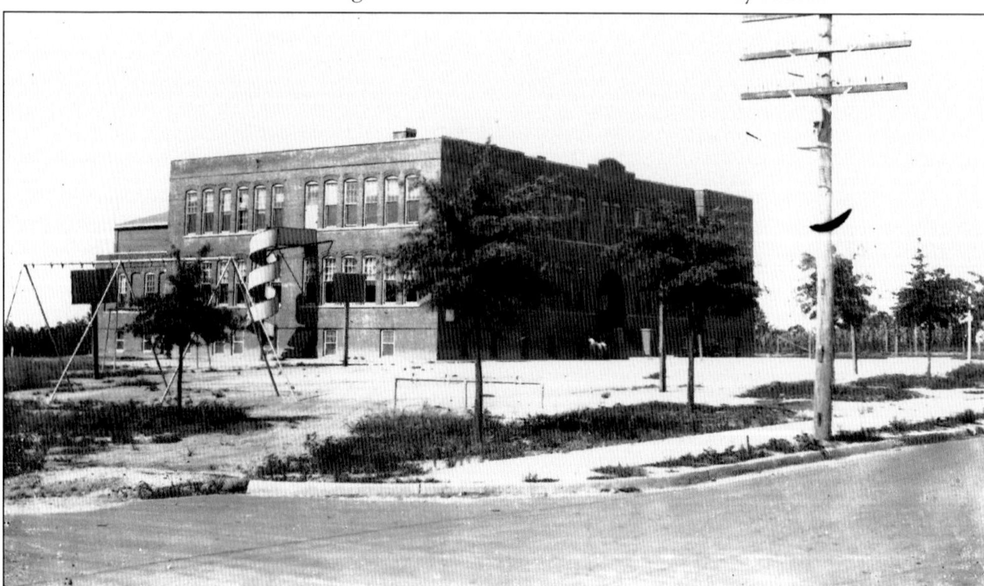

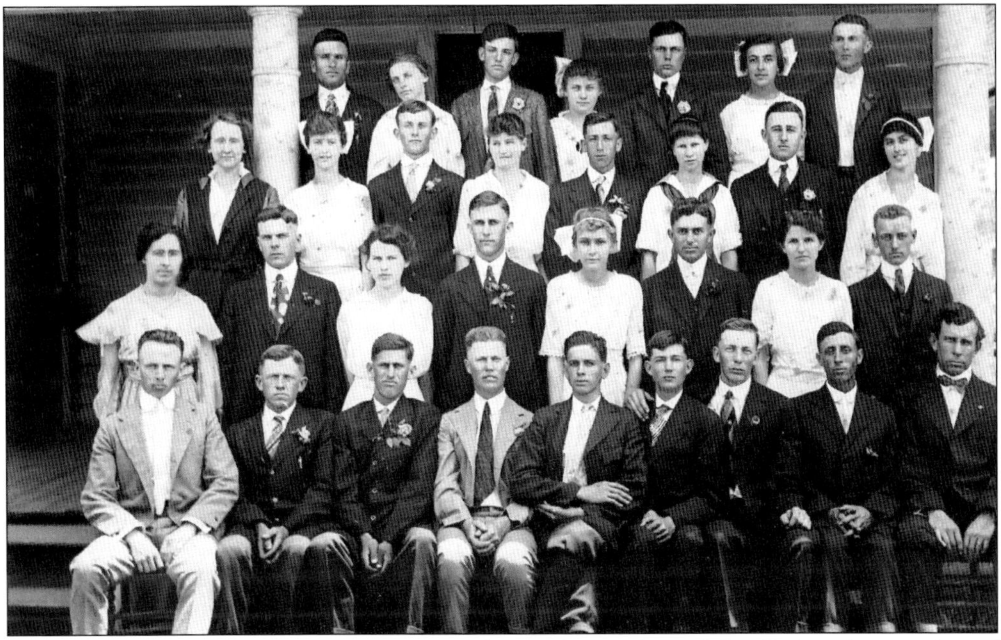

Class of 1916 (Above) and Class of 1918 (Below). Members of the 1916 graduating class of Cherryville High School pose with principal F. W. Orr (far left): from left to right are (first row) Vance Sellers, Cletus Carpenter, Paul Stroup, Brice Gates, Dewey Dellinger, Hunter Carroll, Graydon Harrelson, and Joe Nixon; (second row) Mae Cline Stroup, Thomas Stroupe, Edna Roberts, Henry Dellinger, Connie Ballard, E. V. Moss, Lela Kendrick, and Guy Sipe; (third row) Mattie Camp, Jennie Harvey, Yates Beam, Pearl Beam, Charlie Warlick, Carrie Howell, Lester Sipe, and Margaret Harvey; (fourth row) Floyd Mauney, Vinnie Ford, Hunter Rudisill, Hettie Homesley, Victor Stroup, Pauline Harrelson, and Lloyd Beam. The 1918 graduating class is below. From left to right are (first row) Haywood Kendrick, Ruth Dellinger (Sherrill), Lee Stroup, Annie Howell, Rush Stroup, Mae Strutt, and Leslie Black; (second row) Joe R. Nixon (teacher), Edna Dellinger, ? Sellers, Addie Carpenter, Lowell Beatty, and Kern George Farris.

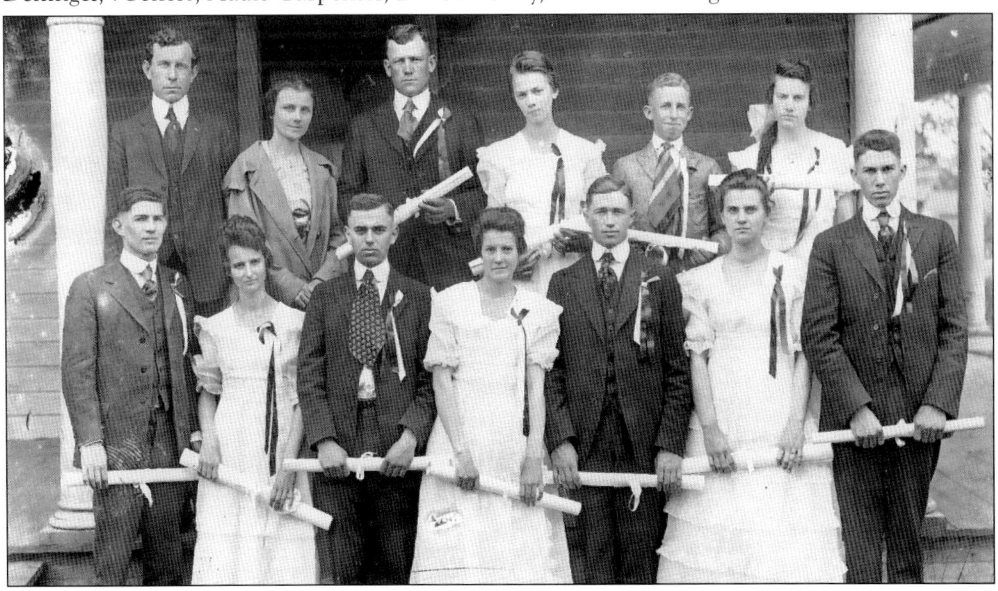

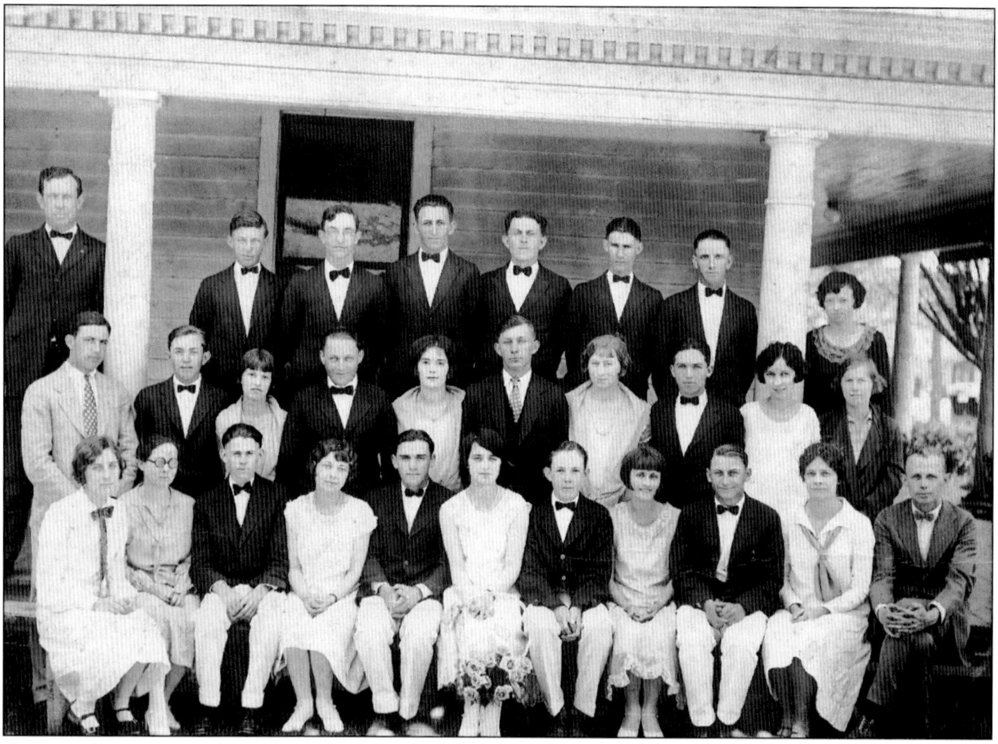

CHERRYVILLE HIGH SCHOOL (CHS) CLASS OF 1926. On graduation day are, from left to right, (first row) teacher Ruth Higgins, teacher Dora McDowell, William Brown, Florence Ford (Stiles), Edwin Rudisill, Lorene Mauney, Gary Kendrick, Pansy Witherspoon (Pharr), Gene Sipe, teacher Margaret Newell, and teacher Hunter Huss; (second row) teacher Fred Brown, Pratt Quinn, Geraldine Mullinax, Edward Osborne Hill, Essie Mitchem, David Farris, Nora Dellinger, Dewey Melton, Leta Bell Beam, and teacher Sarah Kirby; (third row) Supt. Joe R. Nixon, Ambrose Hendricks, Blake Ford, Perry Carpenter, Kelly Huss, Tew Dellinger, Carl Helms, and teacher Rebecca McClain Stroupe. A new Cherryville High School building, shown below, was built in the summer of 1936, during the time Hunter Huss was superintendent.

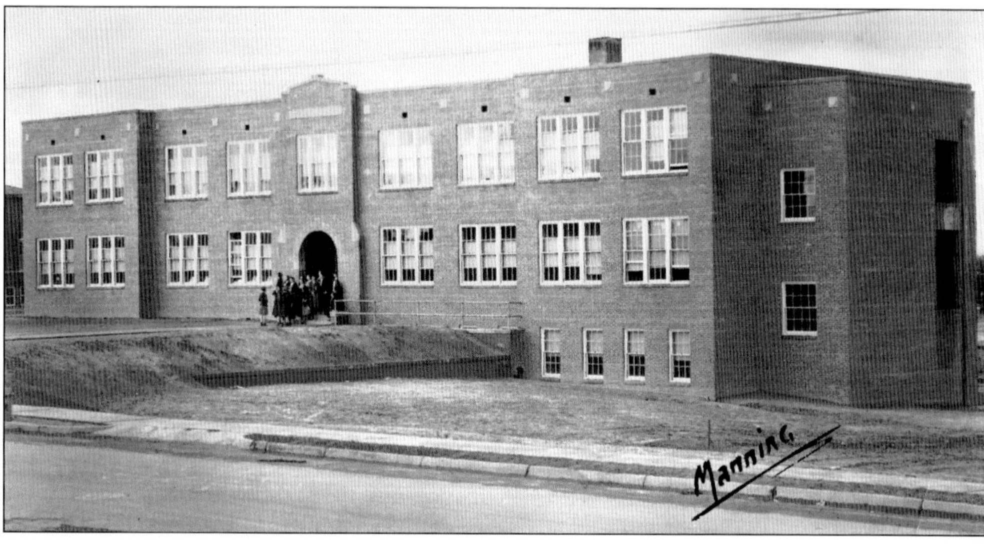

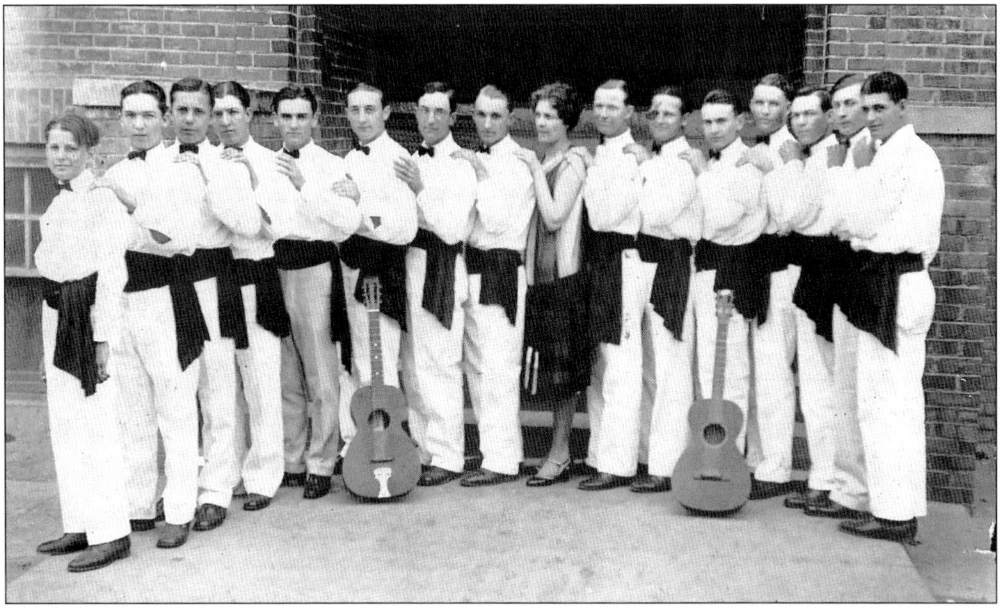

The Cherryville High School Glee Club, 1925. The members of the Cherryville High School Glee Club, under the direction of Margaret Newell, a popular music teacher, are, from left to right, Charles Morrison, Dewey Melton, Floyd "Dink" Dellinger, Dewey Craft, Edwin Rudisill, Howard Houser, Blake Ford, Lawrence Self, Margaret Newell, John Beach, Russell Boggs, unidentified, Lewis McCurry, Boyce Short, David Farris, and Parham Henderson. Below is a music class from the Cherryville Schools made up of young girls dressed in their finest for the photographer with their beloved music teacher, Margaret Newell.

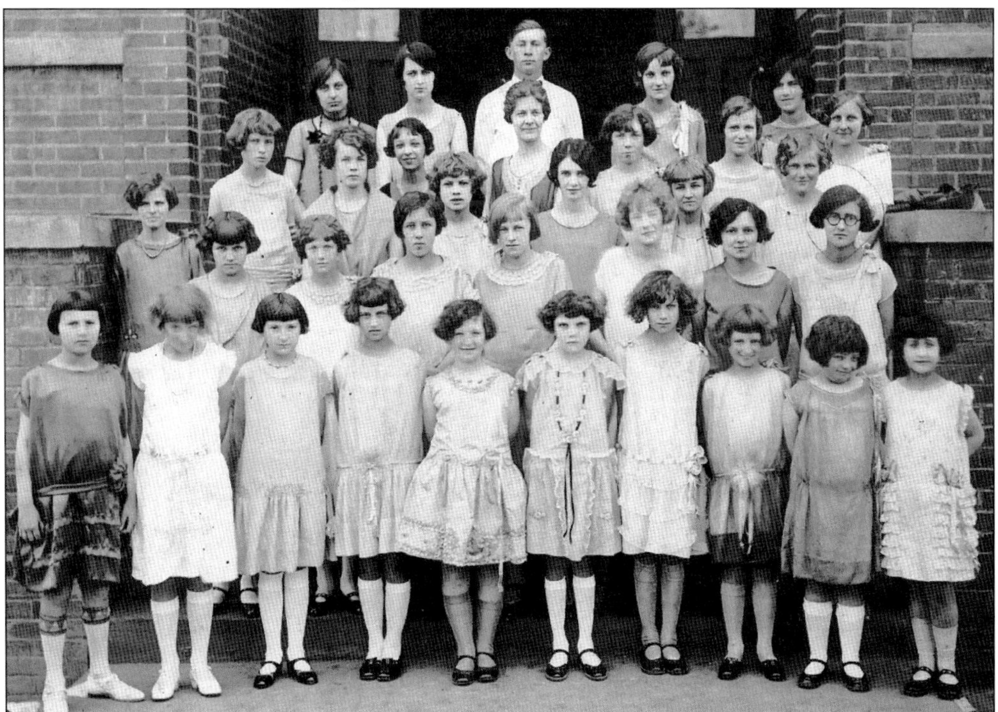

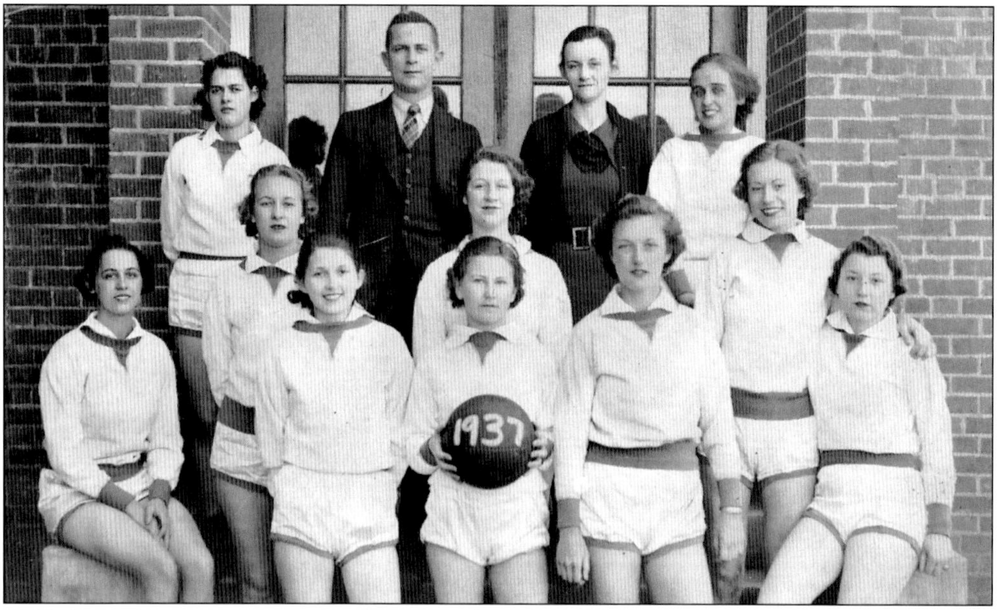

CHS Girls' Basketball Team. This 1937 Cherryville girls' basketball team is made up of the following athletes: from left to right, (first row) Kate Eaker Smith, Rebecca Harrelson Rhyne, Billy Beam, Ruth Friday Camp, and Ruth George Roberts; (second row) unidentified, Ruby Stroup Duffy, and Mildred Hayes Wease; (third row) Ruth Craft, coach Galen Bennett Jr., coach Vera Black Hoyle, and Margaret Moss Buff.

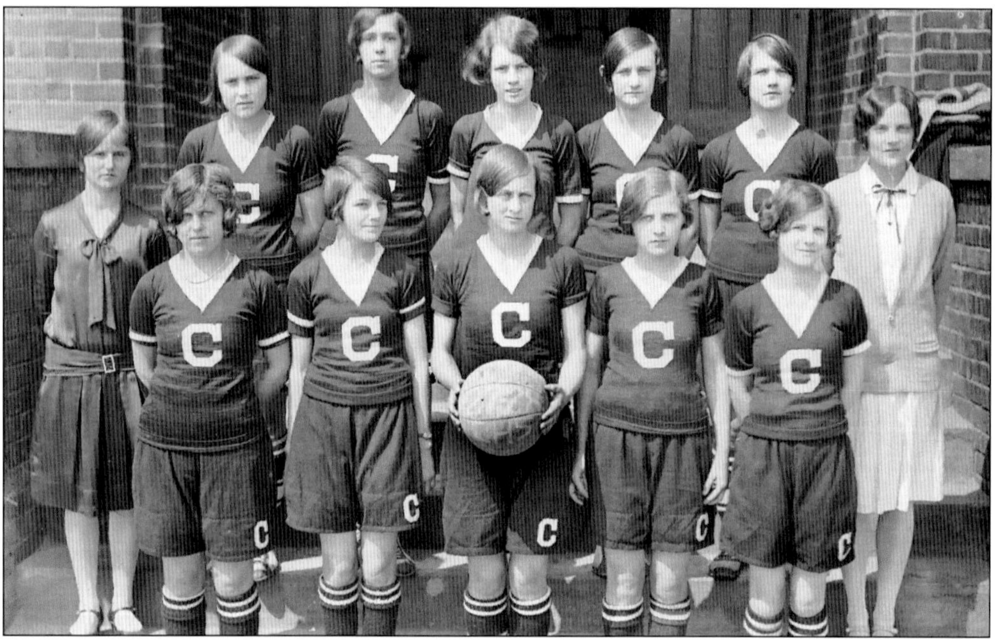

CHS Girls' Basketball Team, 1920s. Winning Cherryville athletes are, from left to right, (first row) Alma Witherspoon, Marietta Huffstetler, Daisy Witherspoon, Katherine Eaker, and Mariland McClurd; (second row) teacher Faith Beam, Mable Helms, Mozelle Eaker, Tulla McCurry, Vera Black Hoyle, unidentified, and coach Elizabeth Byers. Vera Black Hoyle later coached basketball at Cherryville High School in 1937 (see above).

FUTURE FARMERS OF AMERICA. Around 1939, Cherryville High School students entered the Future Farmers of America (FFA) State Seed Judging Contest. They were state winners, and two are seen sporting prize ribbons. In the Cherryville area in the 1930s, this was quite a popular event. Pictured from left to right are Harry Halstead, Everett Harrelson, Bruce Eaker, and R. C. Sharpe, teacher.

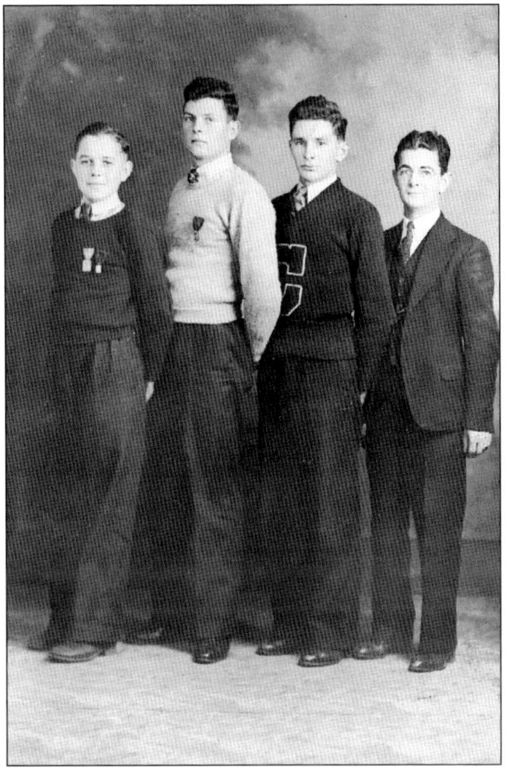

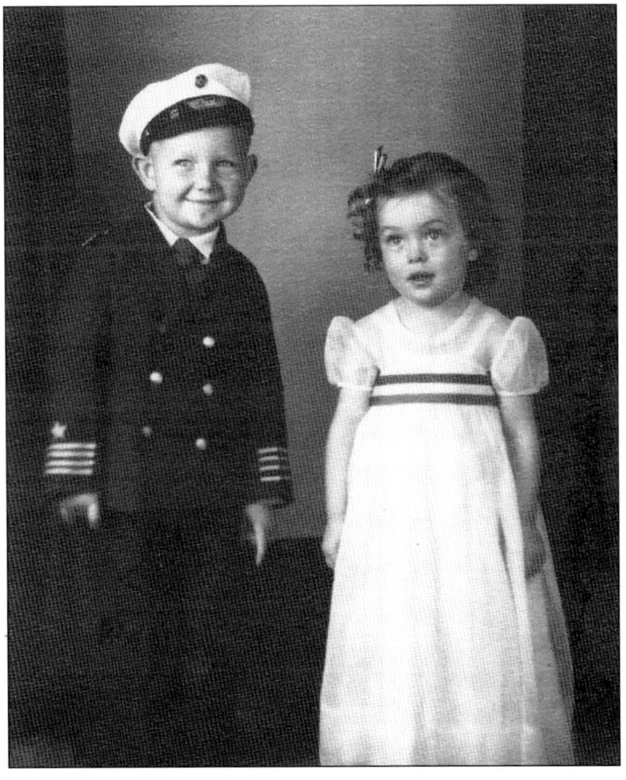

CLASS OF 1943 MASCOTS. The Cherryville High School class of 1943 graduated as World War II raged in Europe. Many students would join the armed forces, and some would not return. That year, they chose Anne Hunter Sharpe and John Crain as their mascots. They pose for the camera on April 19, 1943, and they are nothing short of adorable. The military dress was quite appropriate for the times.

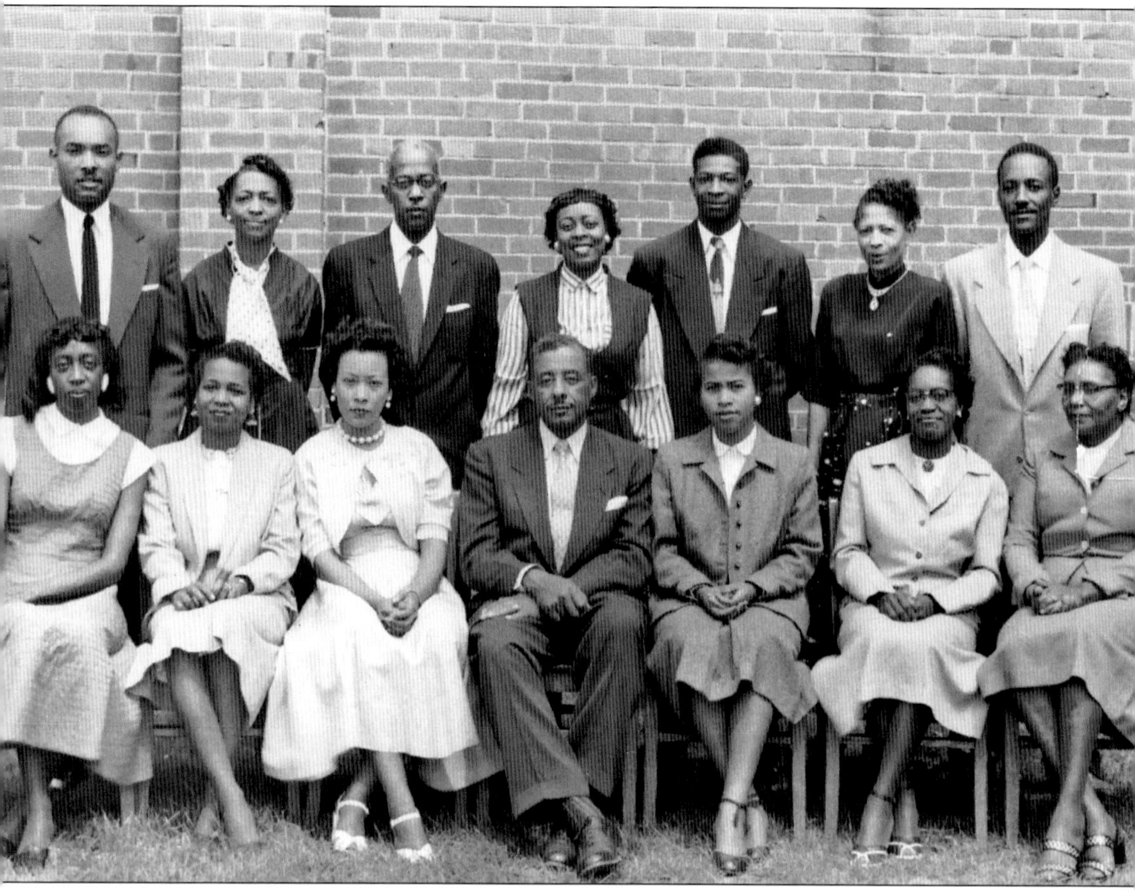

JOHN CHAVIS HIGH SCHOOL FACULTY, 1955. From left to right are (first row) Anna L. Lutz, eighth grade and music, J. C. Smith University graduate; Wilma Imogene Taylor, third grade, Bennett College graduate; Mrs. E. E. Foster, home economics, North Carolina College graduate; J. T. Twitty, principal, A&T College graduate; Shirley Harrison, fourth grade, Elizabeth City Teachers' College graduate; Genevieve Van Catledge, seventh grade, Livingston College graduate; and Charlotte Byers, third grade, J. C. Smith University graduate; (second row) W. M. "Bill" Edwards, agriculture, A&T College graduate; Missouri Morgan, first grade, Winston-Salem Teachers' College graduate; Frederick L. Smith, social science, North Carolina College graduate; Ann Patterson, second grade, Knoxville College graduate; Charles L. Crump, sixth grade and band director, Winston-Salem Teachers' College graduate; Berta Simmons, English and drama, A&T College graduate; and J. L. Bowers, mathematics, science, and coach, Shaw University graduate.

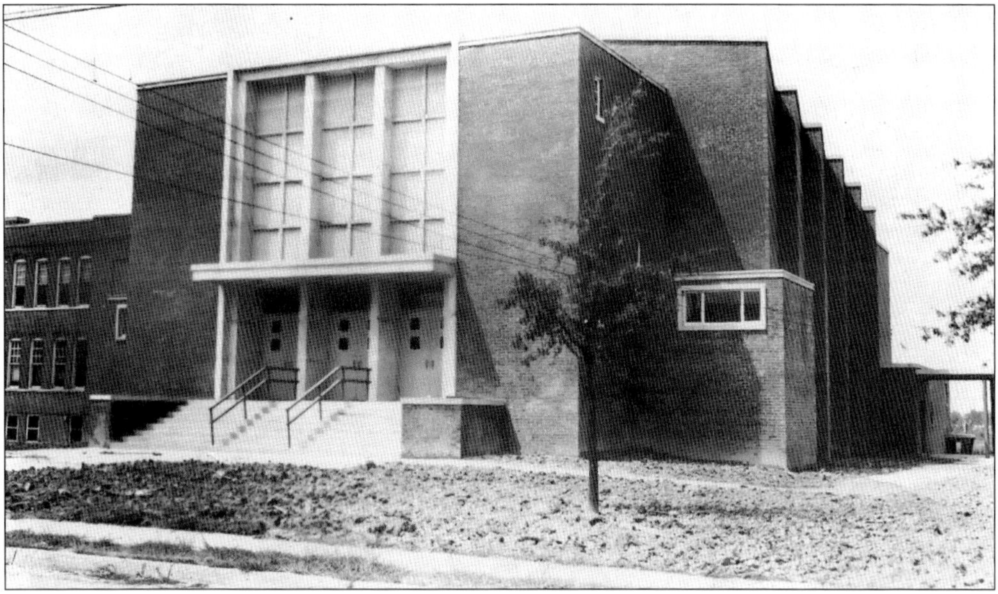

CHS Class of 1950. The first class to graduate in Starnes Auditorium, built in 1949 and named for W. F. Starnes, included, below, from left to right, (first row) mascots Bobby Armstrong and Drenda Alexander; (second row) Adean Murphy, Betty Bookout, Bobbie Carswell, Catherine Mayhue, Gayle Mendel, Mirian Allen, Audrey Britton, Shirley Homesley, Peggy Hayes, Betty Saine, Sue Carpenter, Patsy Coggins, and Joan Alexander; (third row) Norma Putnam, Betty Daggerhart, Jane Beam, Margaret Smith, Julia Stroup, Sara Froneberger, Mary Farris, Frances Stroup, Peggy Upton, Daphine Dale, Neva Harrelson, Betty Smith, Dora McDowell, and Pauline Sneed; (fourth row) Herman Dellinger, E. V. Moss, Wayne Froneberger, John Harrelson, C. J. Hood, R. B. Robbs, Alton Newton, Bill Carpenter, Bill Beam, Forest Allran, Bill Sneed, and Frank Goins; (fifth row) Burl Hartman, Joe Bill Homesley, Junior White, Howard Crane, Charles Carpenter, Max Beam, G. B. Beam, Ben Quinn, Stanley Bumgarner, Cecil Seals, Wayne Allran, Thomas Kiser, and Donald Fawnsworth.

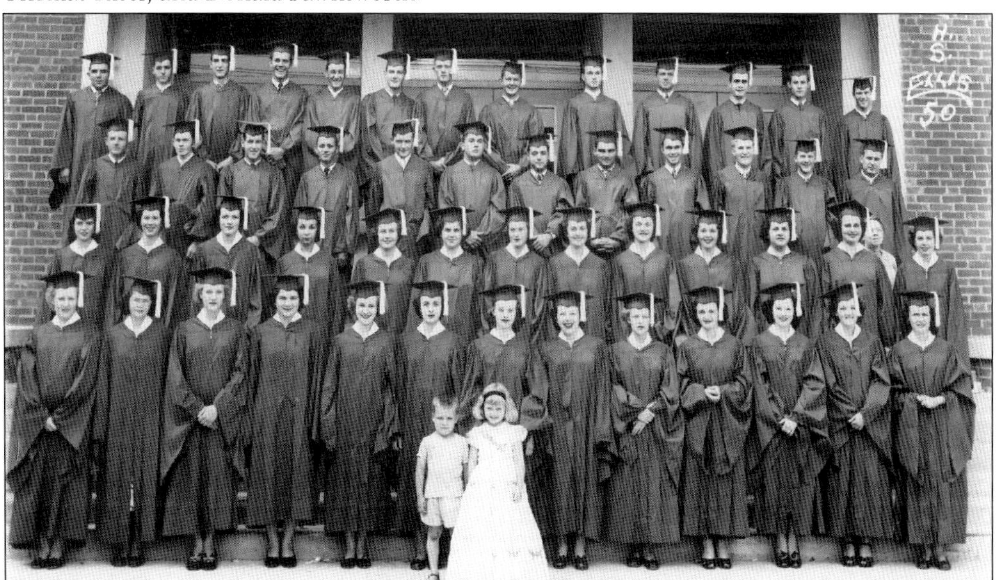

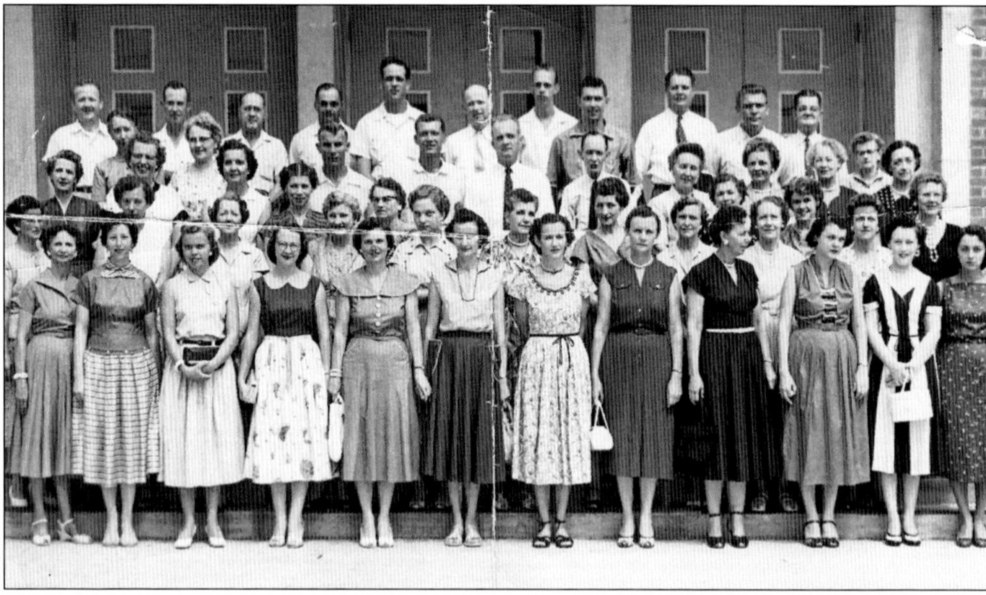

CHERRYVILLE TEACHERS, 1955–1956. Preparing for the start of a new school, Cherryville teachers gather on the steps of Starnes Auditorium in the fall of 1955. Some in the group are Ruth Sherrill, Von Eva Allran, Vera Black Hoyle, Ruth B. Anthony, Margaret Dixon, and Reid Parker.

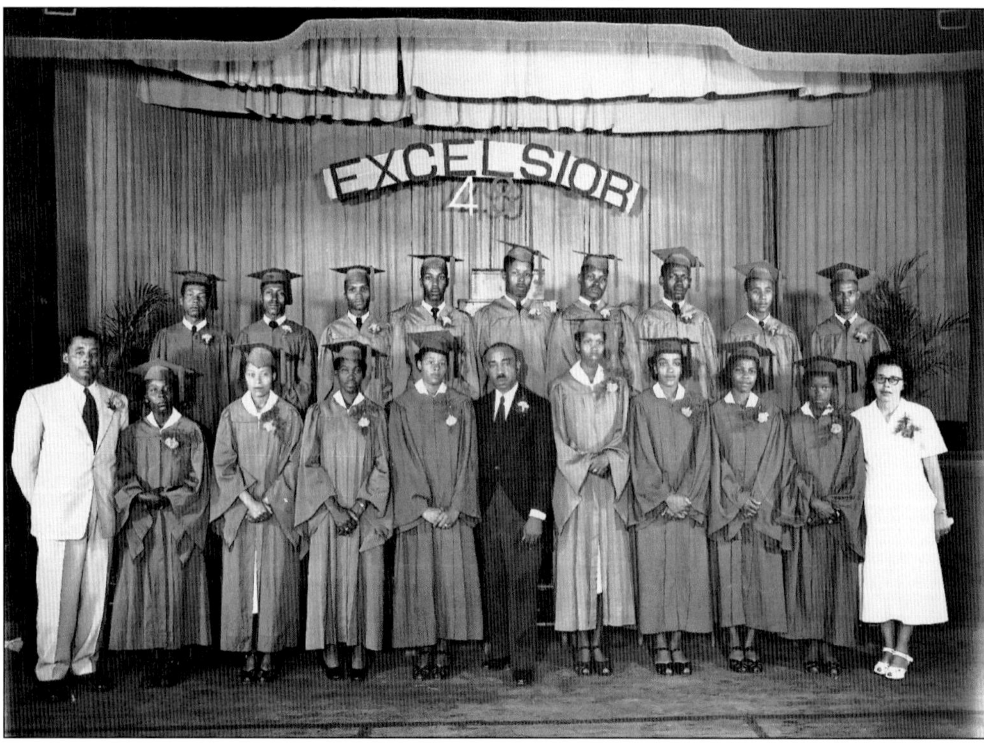

JOHN CHAVIS HIGH SCHOOL. Eighteen students were in the 1949 John Chavis High School graduating class. At left, their beloved principal, James T. Twitty, was well known in the community. He looks on with pride as they dream of their futures. The school was opened in 1937, and the first graduating class was in 1938. The school burned in 1964, and a new school was built.

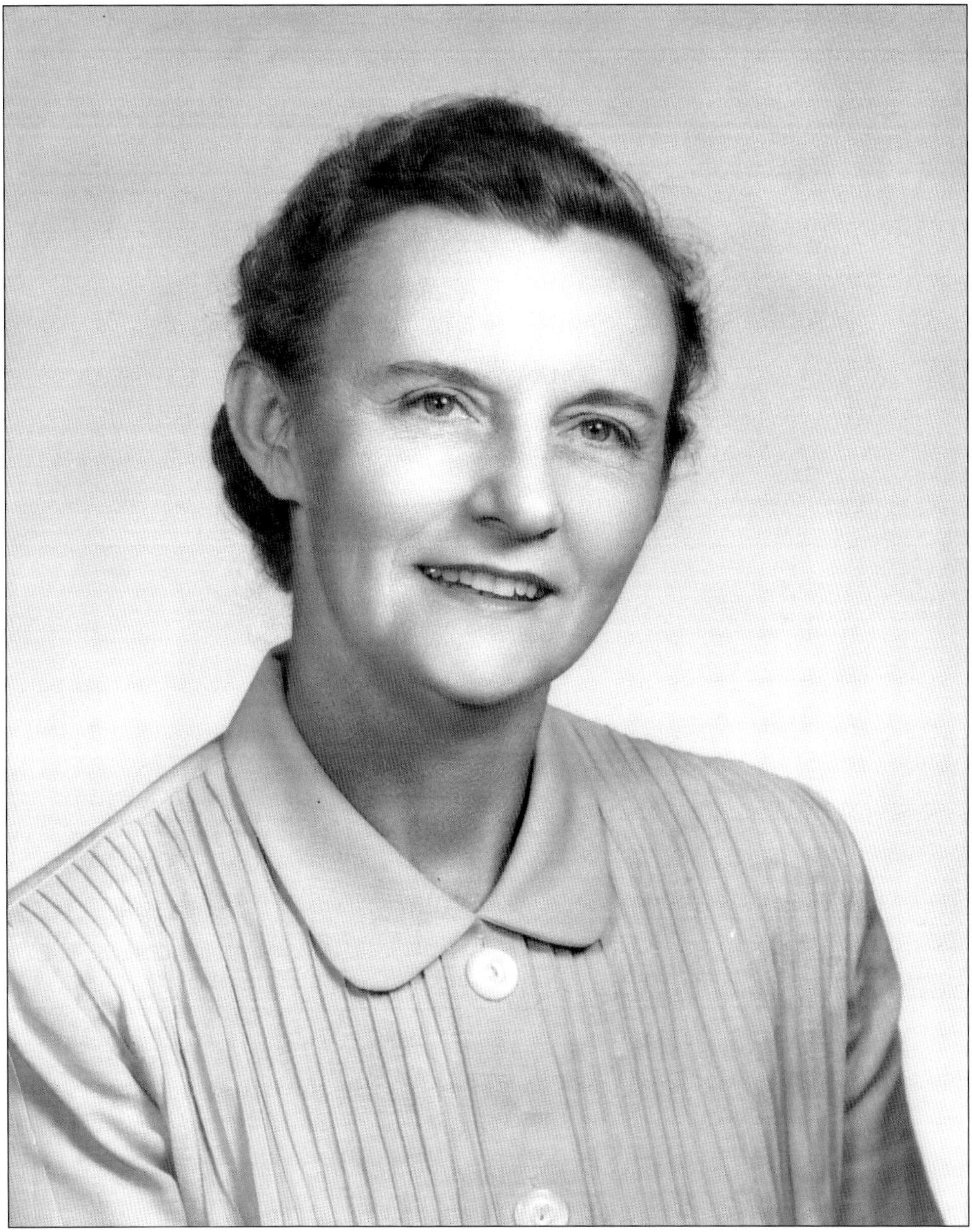

VERA B. HOYLE. Daughter of Ben and Jane Whitworth Black, Vera graduated in 1929 from Cherryville High School. She was a graduate of the University of North Carolina–Greensboro Women's College and taught English for more than 40 years. Her sisters Von Eva Black Allran and Ruth Black Anthony were also teachers in Cherryville for many years. Her older sister, Elsie Black Deaton, taught school before becoming a dietician.

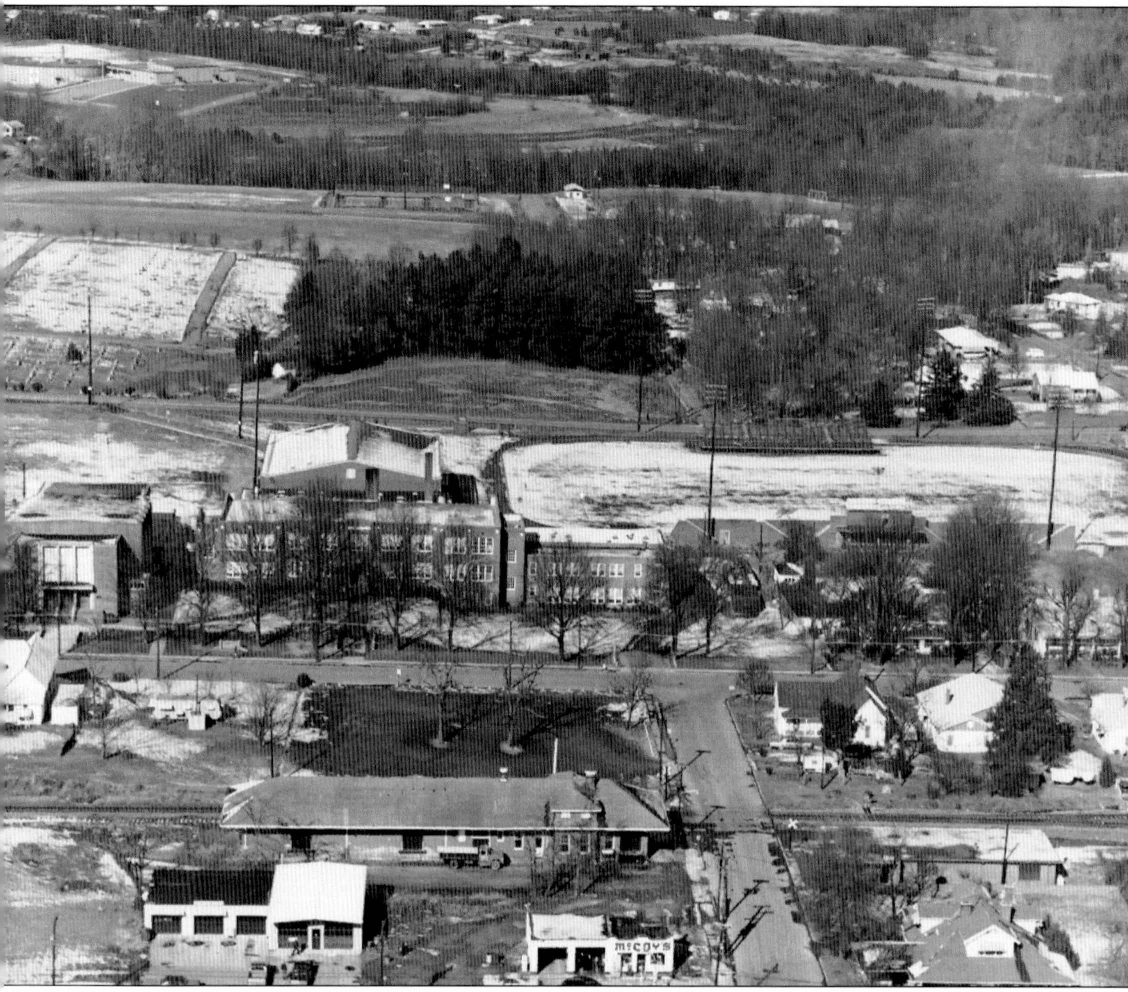

CHERRYVILLE HIGH SCHOOL, 1960S. In a late-1960s aerial view, Cherryville High School, built in 1936, can be seen, along with Starnes Auditorium, built in 1949, on the left. Rudisill Stadium and Nixon Gymnasium are in the background. In the foreground are the Cherryville Train Depot and McCoy's Service Station. In the upper left-hand corner is the circular Cherryville Junior High School, completed in 1966.

The Cherryville Ironman. Mascots Cathy Summer and Tadd Huffstetler trudge along at Rudisill Stadium as they pull the Cherryville High School's "Ironman" onto the field. Hunter Huss is credited with giving the football team the unique nickname "the Ironmen." Rudisill Stadium was completed as a citywide project in 1963.

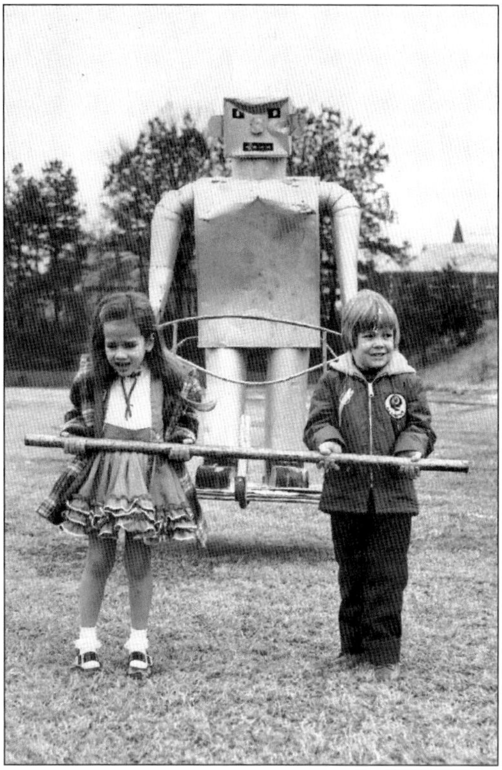

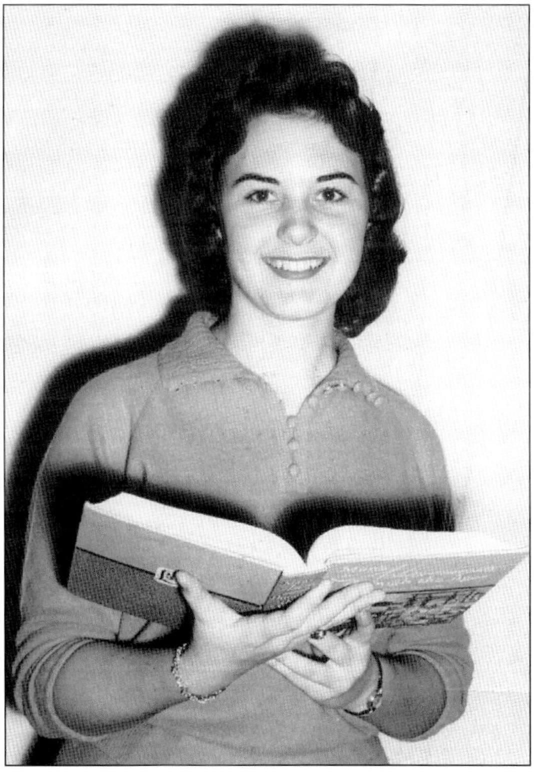

Shirley Black Starling. Descended from early Scots-Irish immigrants, Shirley graduated for Cherryville High School in 1958. At Cherryville High School, she was a cheerleader and athlete, and was voted prettiest in her class. She married Don Starling and remained in Cherryville.

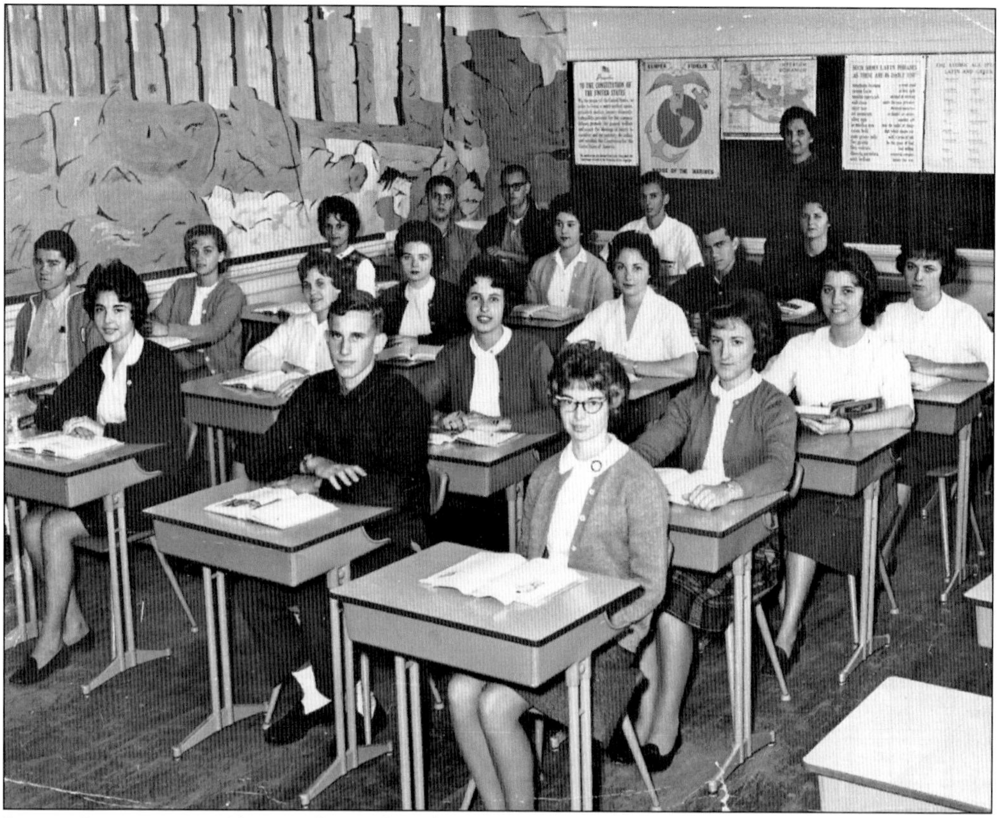

LATIN CLASS, 1963. Cherryville High School Latin students and their teacher prepare for class in the early 1960s. Among the students are Glen Link, Doris Beam, Alice Rudisill, Kenny Beam, Marsha Gurley, Judy Pow, Pat Crocker, Vickie Carpenter, Nancella Harden, Nona Dayberry, Patty Brown, Bill Eaker, Kay Homesley, Harold Lee Bare, and Bobby Hoyle.

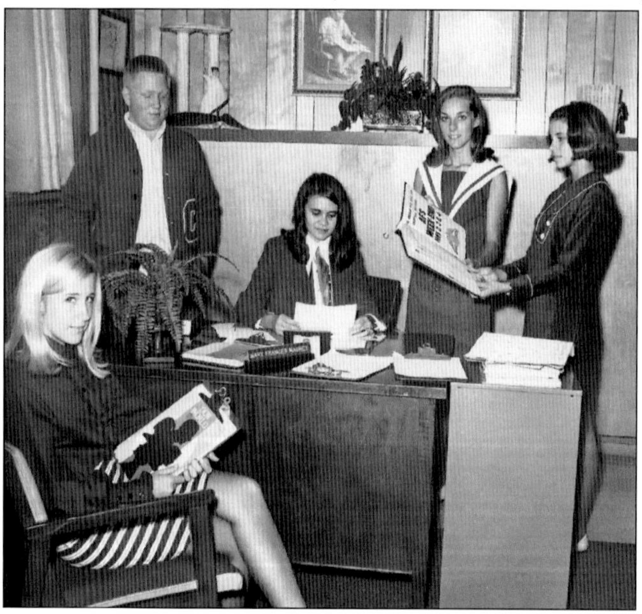

AMERICAN FIELD SERVICE CLUB. American Field Service (AFS) Club officers at Cherryville High School are shown making plans in April 1970 to host 13 students from foreign countries as special guests of the school. Shown from left to right are Cathy Doggett, AFS vice president; Keith Kiser, treasurer; Becky Leonhardt, president; Ann Dellinger, historian; and Sadie Allran, secretary. The club's sponsor was Mary Frances Mauney. The foreign students were housed in private homes, and the Cherryville Rotary Club gave financial assistance.

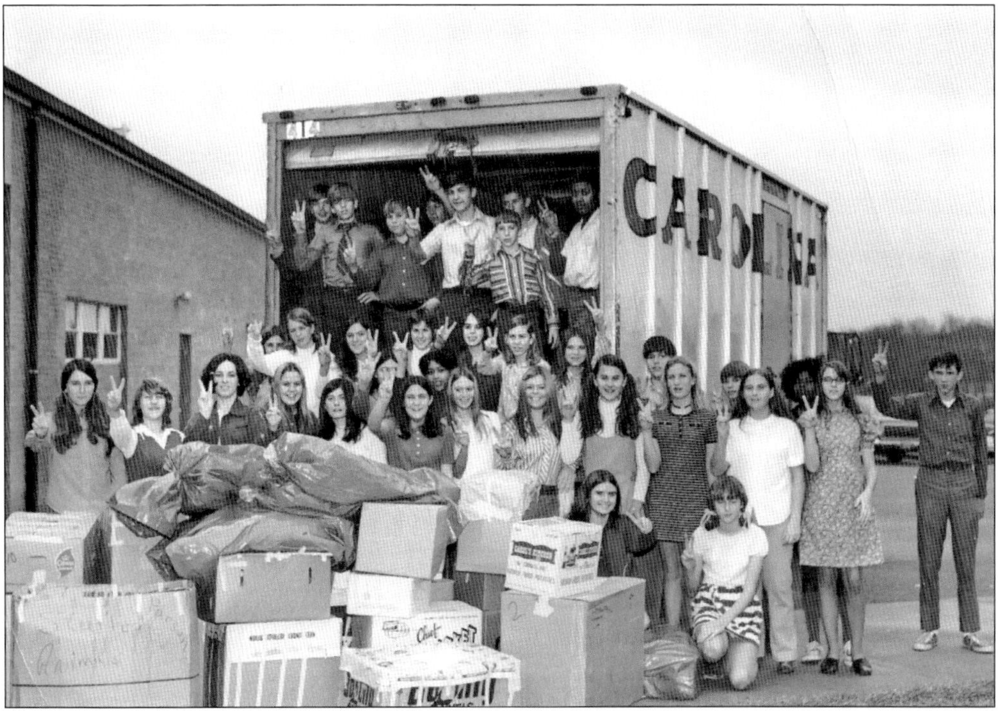

Parson of the Hills. The city of Cherryville came together in December 1971 when the residents participated in the Parson of the Hills Project, a program to help the poor families in the Appalachian Mountains. Margaret Harrelson at H&W Cleaner sent a huge assortment of dry-cleaned and laundered clothes, and H&H, Harris-Teeter, and Roy and Troy's grocery stores sent boxes of food. Money was also collected, and Grier Beam at Carolina Freight Carriers Corporation donated a load of oranges direct from Florida. These Cherryville Junior High students sorted, sized, packed, labeled, and wrapped gifts.

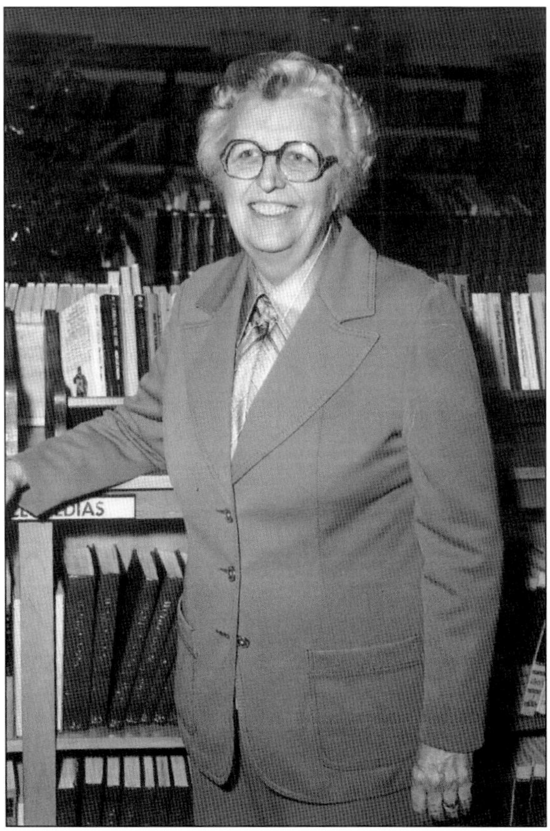

Julia Renfro. A school librarian, Renfro was an adored member of the Cherryville High School faculty for many years. She was loved by students and parents alike. She was a graduate of Appalachian State Teachers' College, today known as Appalachian State University, in Boone, North Carolina.

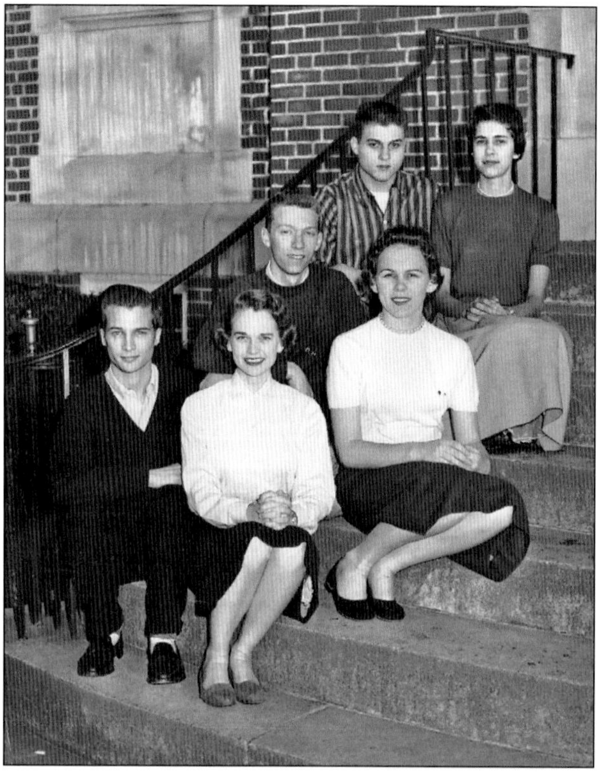

EDUCATOR DR. JUDITH FORD HOUSER. Daughter of Grady Howard Ford and Aldena Parker, Dr. Houser (shown here, first row, right) graduated from Lenoir-Rhyne College. In 1957, she became the first female to be elected to the presidency of the Luther League of America. She met two presidents, Eisenhower and Kennedy, in her travels. In 1958, she was sent by the Lutheran World Federation and the Luther League of America as a delegate to a worldwide assembly in Copenhagen, Denmark.

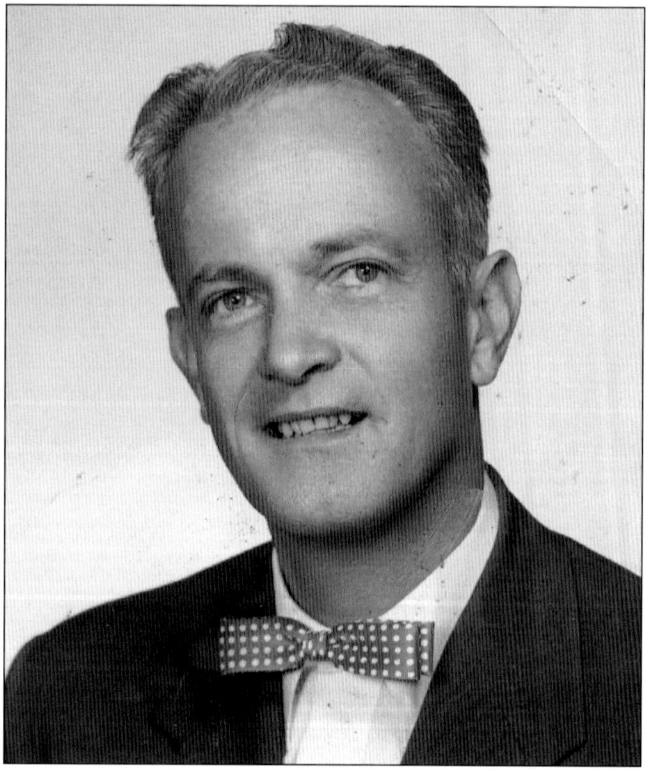

ERSKINE W. CARSON (1911–1968). A gifted educator and graduate of Erskine College, Carson was principal of Cherryville High School for many years. He was well known in the community and well liked by students and parents. He was also a popular athletic coach.

Four

PLAY BALL

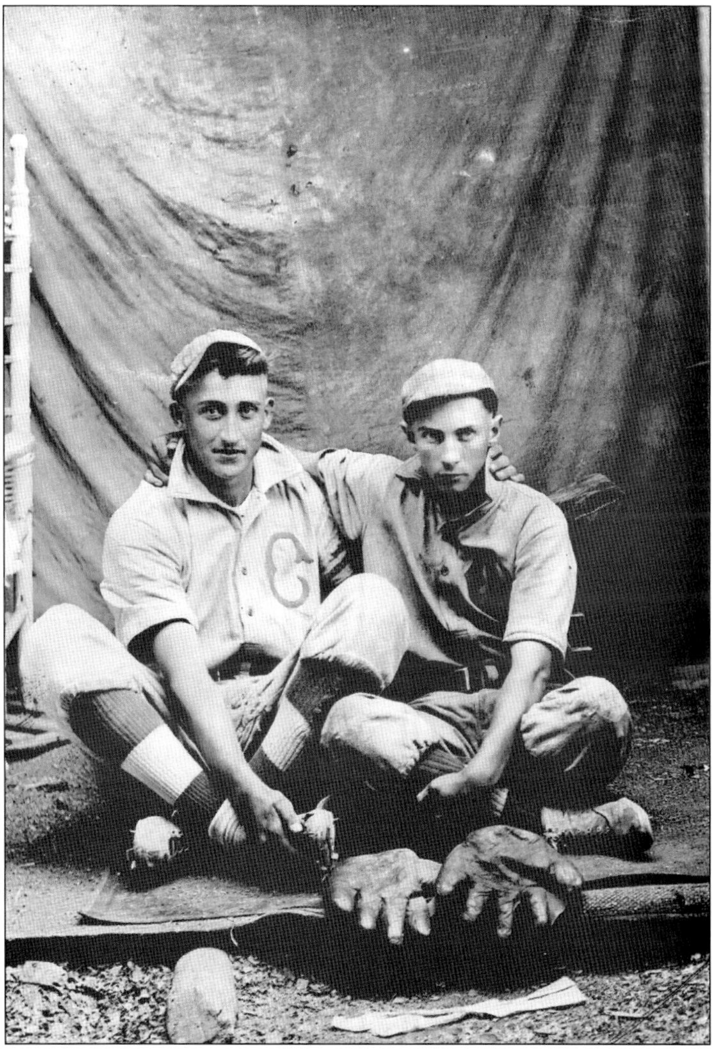

GRIER FRIDAY. Small-town boy Grier Friday pitched one of the best games of his career in 1917 with his "blazing fast ball" when Cherryville High School played Raleigh in Chapel Hill for the state championship. Some of the players would swing at the ball when it had already been caught by the catcher, Jay Boggs. Friday later pitched for Charlotte, Raleigh, and other South Atlantic teams. Later he played for the Washington Senators in the major league; in his first game playing for Washington, he broke a world record of walks, giving 13 men free passes. Pictured is Friday (right) with Bryan Sipe.

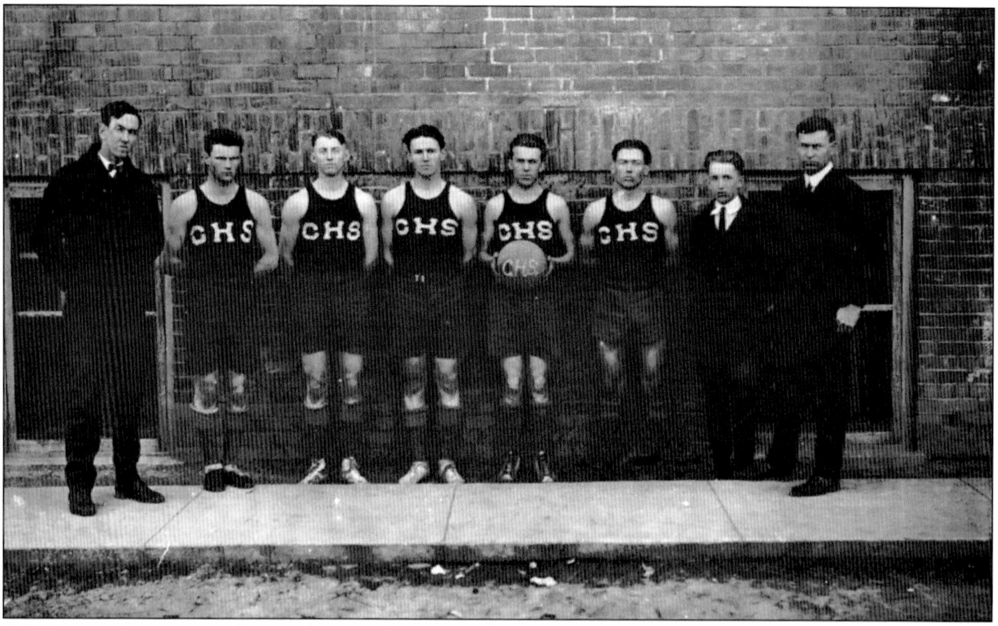

CHS 1920 IRONMEN. These Cherryville High School basketball players are, from left to right, John Barnette (coach), Alphonso Beam (forward), Jimmy Harris (guard), Wayne Howell (center), J. B. Houser (forward), Roy McGinnis (guard), Lucius Hall (manager), and A. C. Warlick (superintendent of Cherryville City Schools).

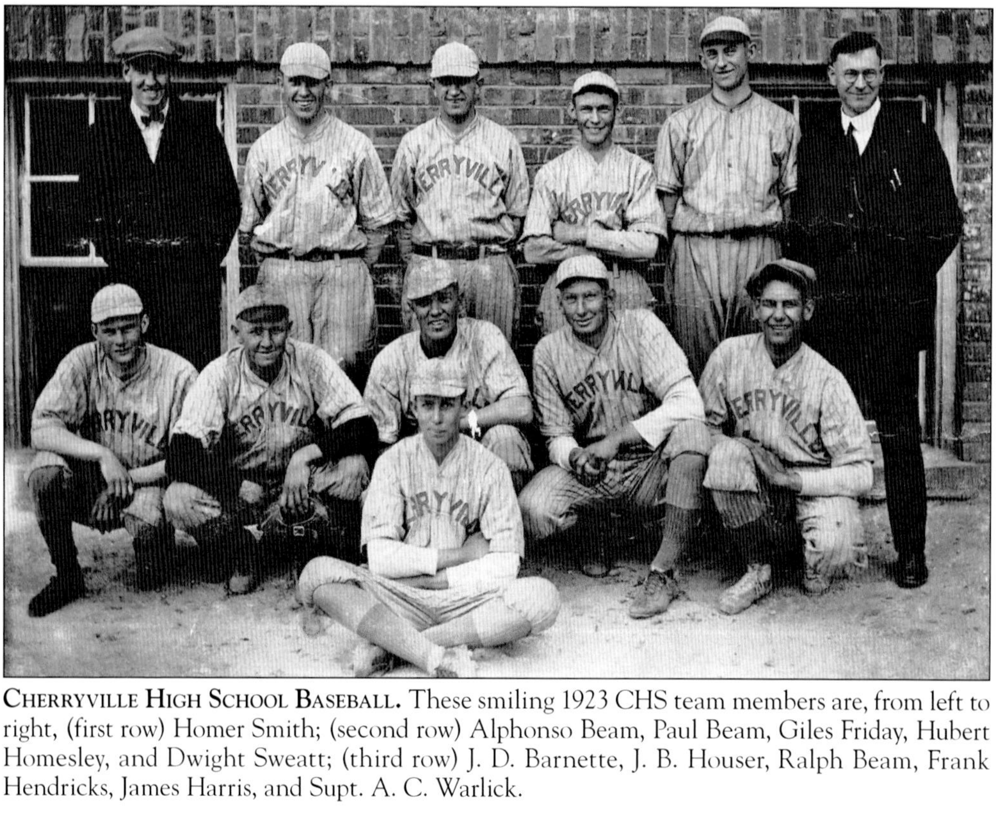

CHERRYVILLE HIGH SCHOOL BASEBALL. These smiling 1923 CHS team members are, from left to right, (first row) Homer Smith; (second row) Alphonso Beam, Paul Beam, Giles Friday, Hubert Homesley, and Dwight Sweatt; (third row) J. D. Barnette, J. B. Houser, Ralph Beam, Frank Hendricks, James Harris, and Supt. A. C. Warlick.

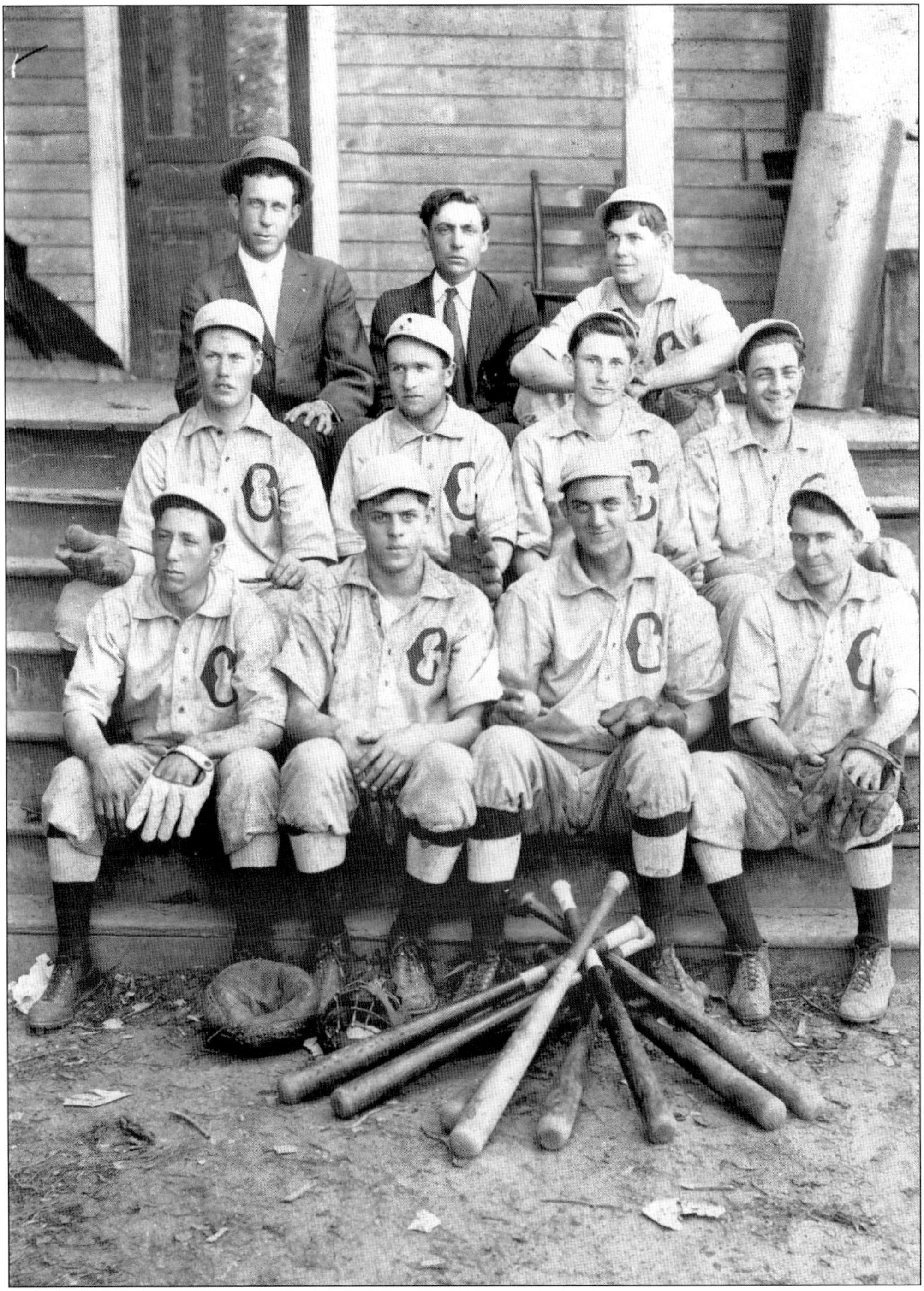

Baseball in Cherryville, 1915. One of Cherryville's first baseball teams was coached by Joe R. Nixon, seen here in the third row, far left. The team members are, from left to right, (first row) Charlie Warlick, Bryan Sipe, Grier Friday, and J. Ben Dellinger; (second row) Paul Stroup, Floyd Mauney, Click Beam, and Lloyd Summer; (third row) Nixon, Alfonso Mauney, and Clyde Kendrick.

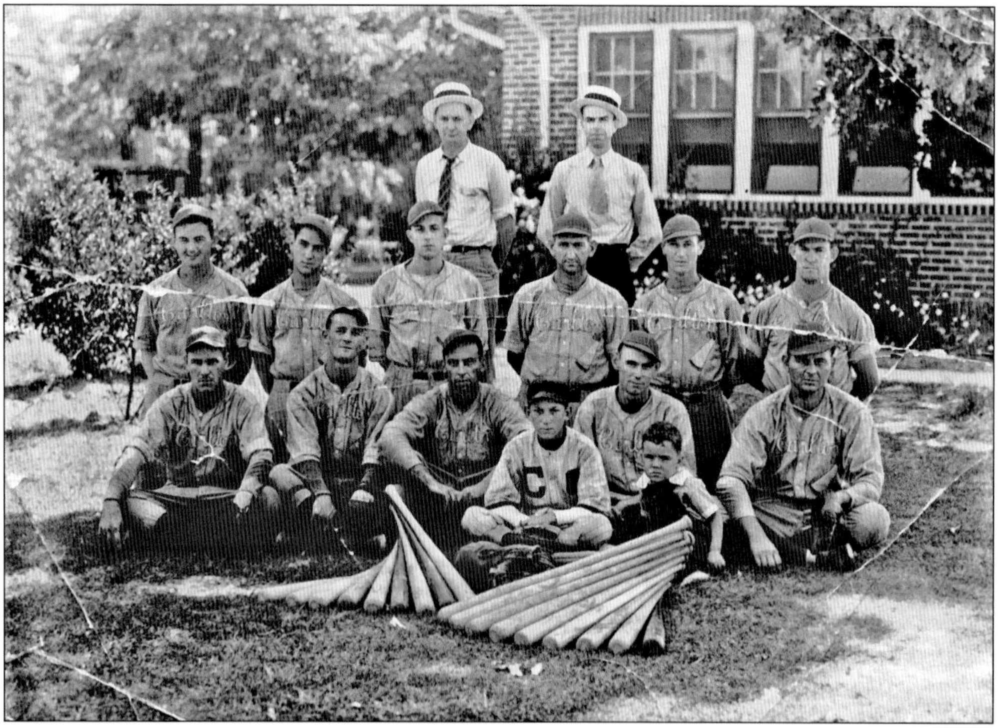

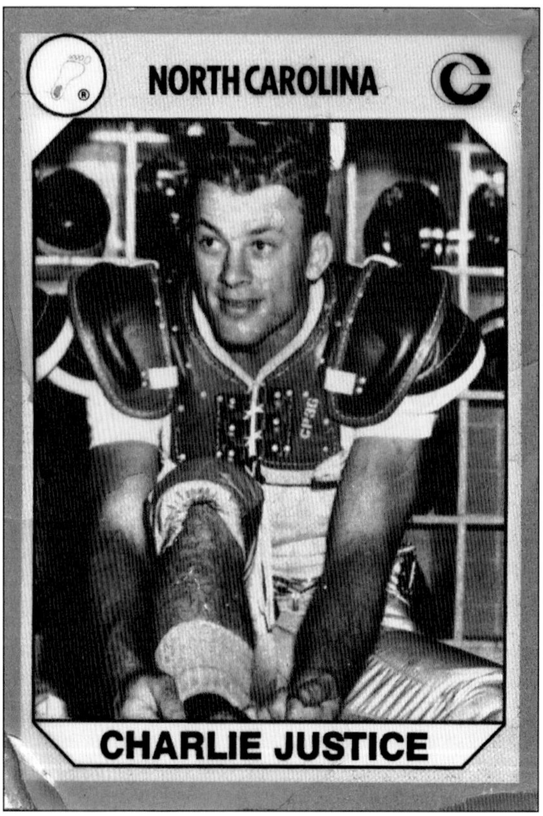

THE CARLTON YARNERS. The Carlton Yarn Mill baseball team, shown above in 1933, is identified only by last names. From left to right are (first row) batboy Beal and mascot Quinn; (second row) Crain, outfield; Quinn, shortstop; Short, outfield; "Lefty" Carpenter, outfield; and H. Quinn, pitcher; (third row) Quinn, first base and manager; Beal, catcher; Sisk, second base; L. Beal, catcher; Scism, pitcher; and Randall, outfield; (third row) W. B. Putnam and S. M. Butler, mill officials.

CHARLIE "CHOO-CHOO" JUSTICE (1924–2003). Born in Asheville, Justice is considered to be the most famous of all North Carolina athletes. A UNC–Chapel Hill standout in the 1940s, he led the Tar Heels to three major bowl games and two Southern Conference titles, was twice a Heisman Trophy runner-up, and ran and passed for 4,883 yards at UNC–Chapel Hill. He led the Tar Heels to four consecutive wins over Duke. He was pictured on *Life* magazine's cover on October 3, 1949.

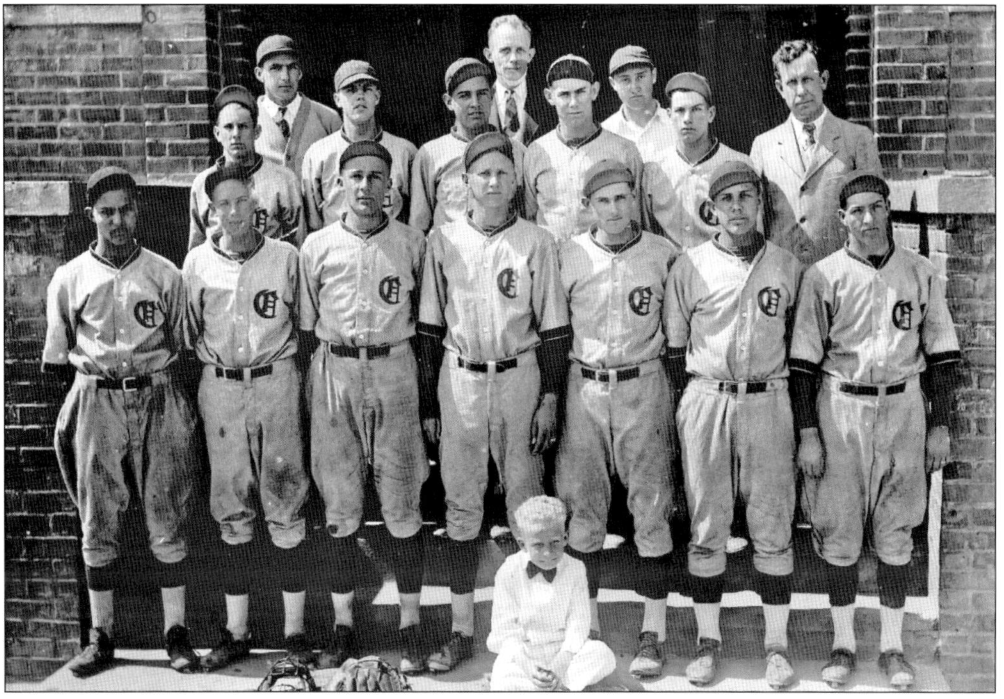

The 1928 Baseball Team. Hunter Huss and Joe R. Nixon coached this 1928 Cherryville High School baseball team. Pictured from left to right are (first row) John Ray Eaker, Hazel Self, Carl Thornburg, Bob Beam, Frank Seagle, Floyd "Dink" Dellinger, and Dewey Craft; (second row) Charles Morrison, Fred Brown (coach), Cecil Jarrett, Kenneth Van Dyke, Hunter Huss (coach), Everett Carpenter, Bill Houser, Ed George, and Joe Nixon (coach). The mascot or batboy in front is unidentified.

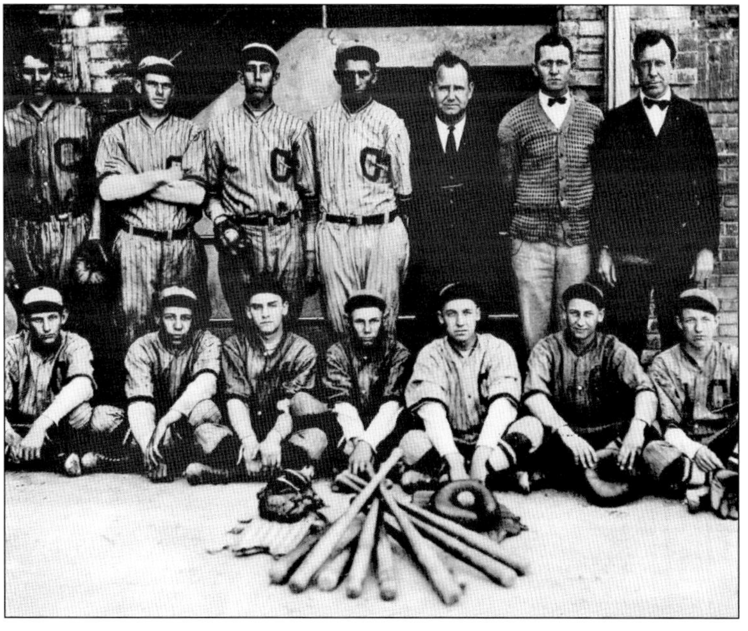

Batter Up. Joe R. Nixon coached this young-looking Cherryville High School baseball team around 1920. Pictured from left to right are (first row) Hugh Helms, Hugh Harrelson, Ed Rudisill, Everett Carpenter, unidentified, Gene Sipe, and John Beach; (second row) Stacy Harrelson, Alfonso Beam, "Curly" Smith, Perry Carpenter, Claude Moser (coach), Paul Beam, and Nixon.

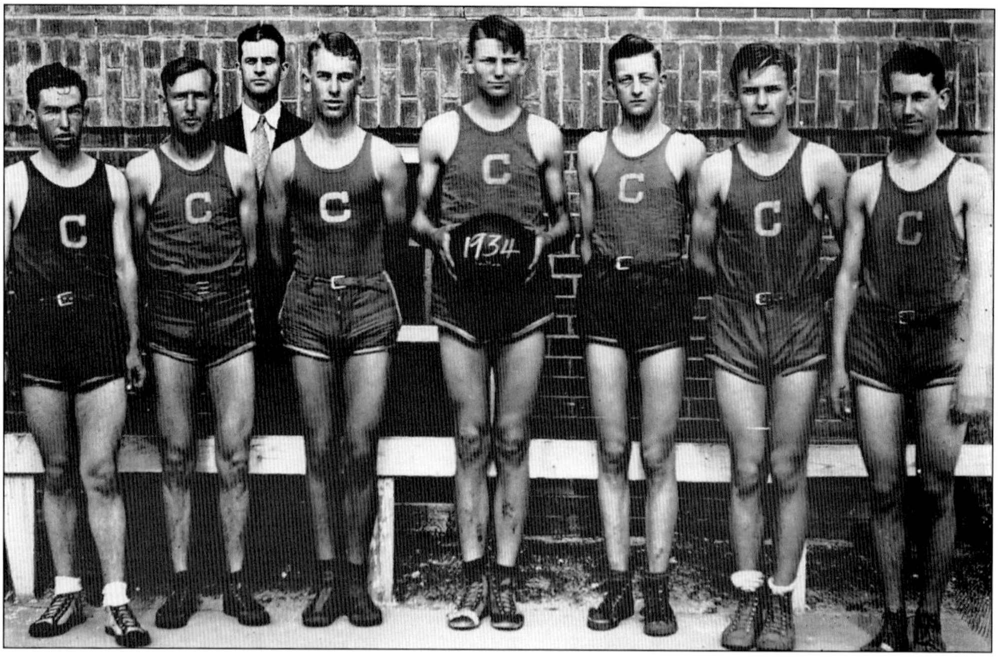

Cherryville High School Basketball, 1934. A young and handsome Jack Kiser (wearing a suit) coached this winning 1934 basketball team. Pictured from left to right are Bill Boggs, Jack Huss, Laverne Bowlin, Howell Stroup, T. A. Moss, unidentified, and Alf Black.

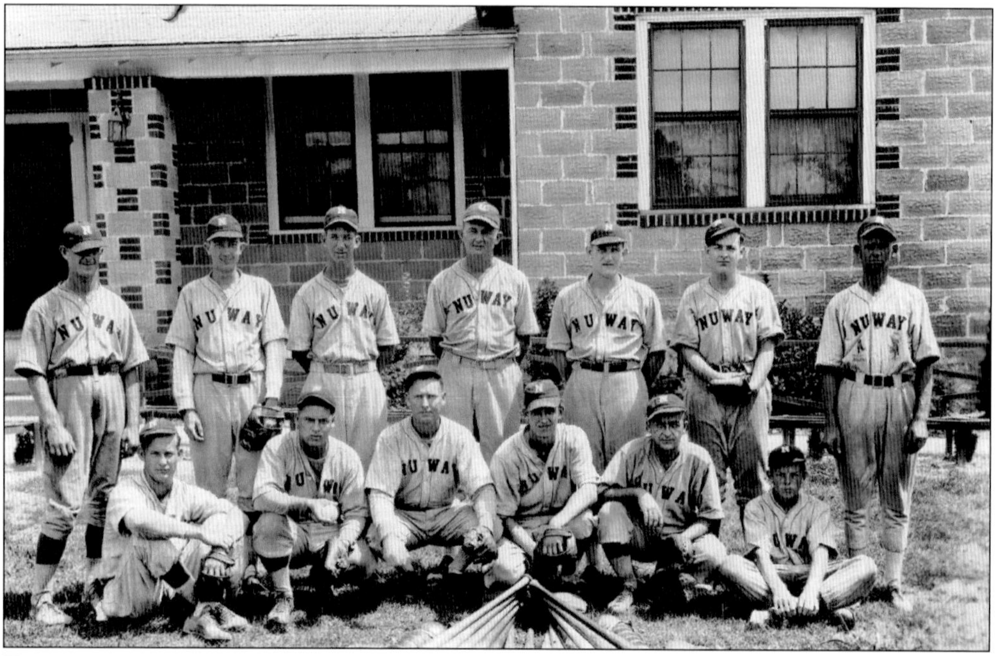

The Nu-Way Mill Ball Team. The Nu-Way Mill baseball team gathers in front of the Nu-Way Club House in 1938. The clubhouse was quite modern for its day and was used for many activities by the mill employees. The Nu-Way Spinning Company was originally the Vivian Cotton Mills. Established on March 6, 1900, by S. S. Mauney, D. W. Aderholt, and M. E. Rudisill, it was the third mill in Cherryville and the 26th in Gaston County.

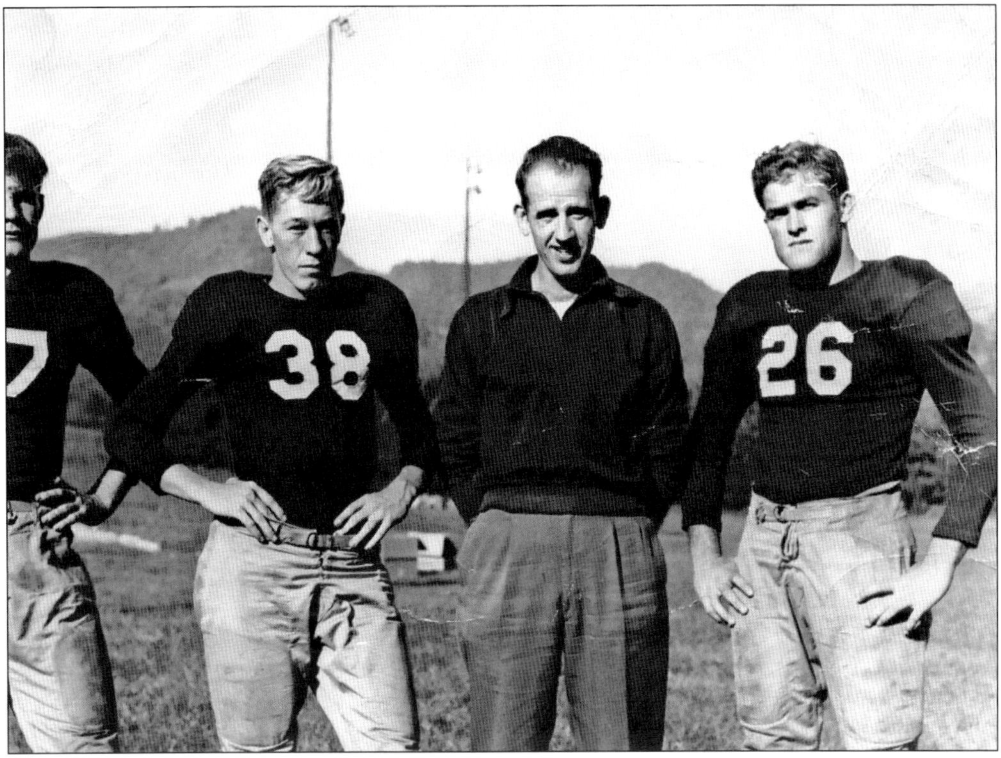

WESTERN CAROLINA CATAMOUNTS. From left to right, Cherryville's Max Beam (200-pound end) and Ovie Heavner (180-pound wingback), along with trainer ? Neill and right tackle ? Humphries (200 pounds), are at practice in Cullowhee as they prepare to play a homecoming game against a longtime rival of the Cats, Appalachian State Teachers' College. This game was going to be the first played with the Mountaineers since 1942.

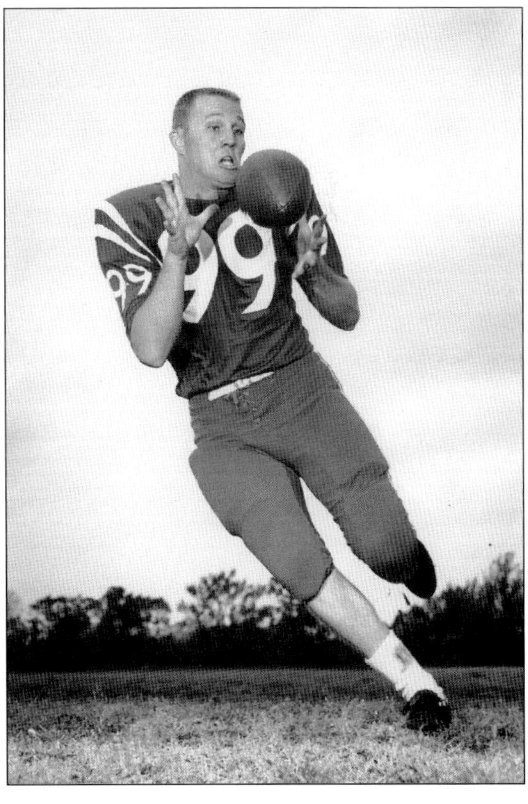

STAN CRISSON, 1960S. After a great collegiate career at Duke University, Crisson starred in the pro ranks in the Canadian league. At Lenoir-Rhyne, Crisson and Ronald Turner made all–South Western Conference in three major sports in one season. And don't forget Larry Helms, who played in the Shrine Bowl at Charlotte, the Lions' Bowl at Forest City, and the East-West game at Greensboro. He was a Bear cocaptain in 1967 at Lenoir-Rhyne College.

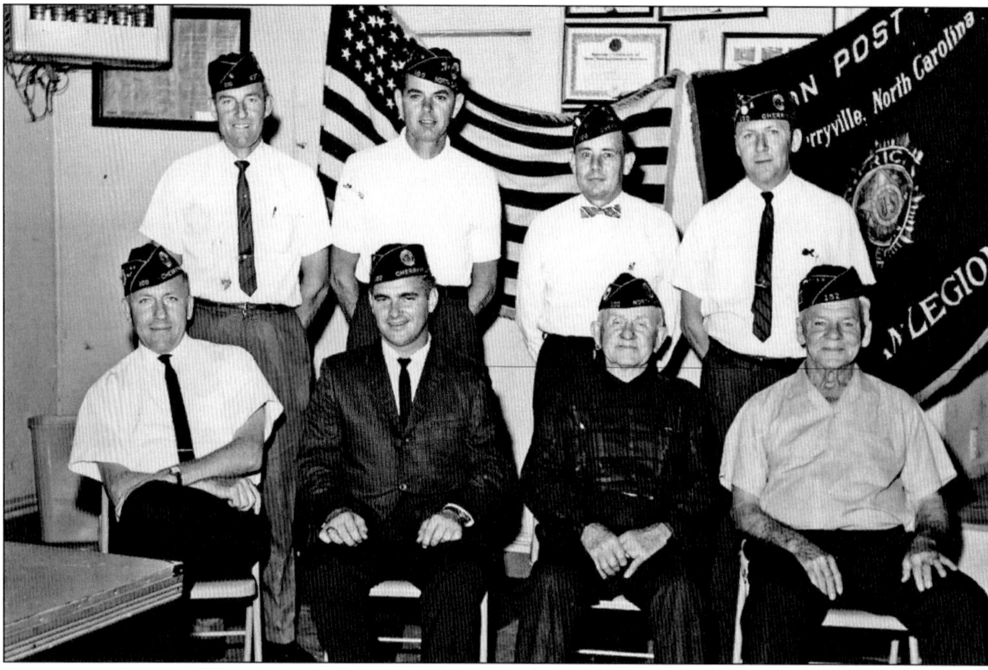

American Legion Post 100. Probably nowhere else in the United States is baseball loved as much as in Cherryville, and today baseball remains the favorite sport. Cherryville has long been noted for its baseball powerhouses and has copped many state titles since 1917. The 1953 Legion squad finished fourth in the national finals after capturing Post 100's first state and regional championships. Post 100 teams took Area Four crowns in 1953, 1960, 1961, 1962, 1981, 1982, 1997, and 1998. State crowns belong to the 1953, 1981, 1997, and 1998 clubs. In 1945, Shelby beat Cherryville's Post 100 in the area finals, and Shelby went on to take the national title. "Legion Ball" is just as popular today as it was in the 1930s, 1940s, and 1950s.

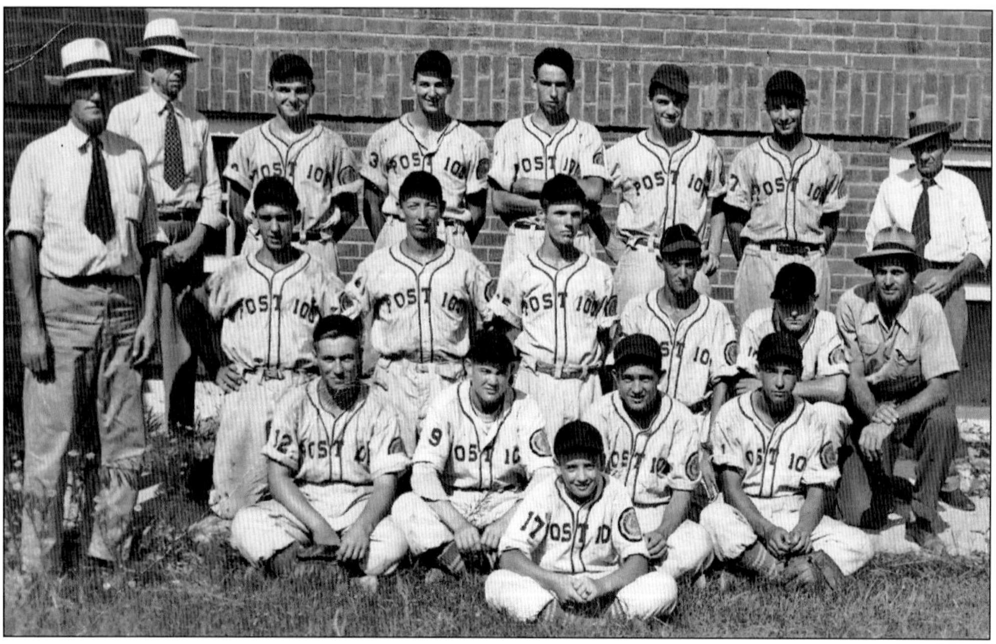

Five

Carolina Mill Town

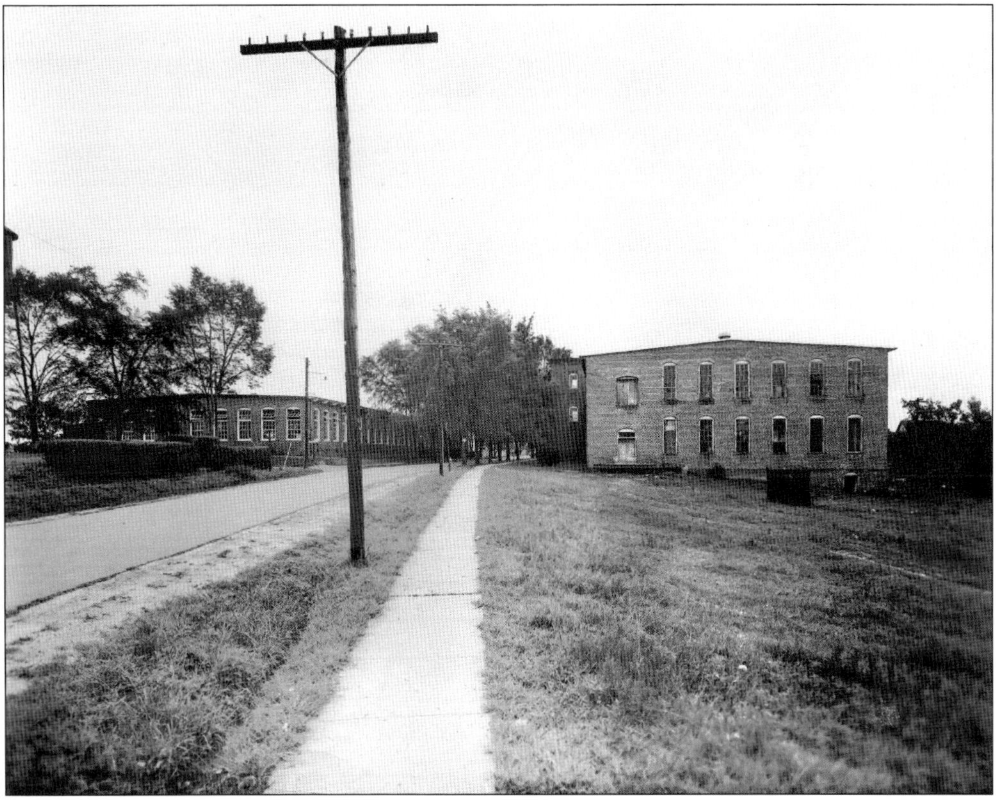

The Dora Mill. The second cotton mill established in Cherryville, north of town, was the Gaston Manufacturing Company. It received its charter on May 19, 1896, when J. M. Rhodes, D. P. Rhodes, David Mauney, J. J. George, H. S. Sellers, P. M. Houser, E. A. Mauney, T. C. Farris, J. B. Moore Jr., J. D. Rudisill, R. E. Pope, Dr. L. L. Self, D. W. Aderholt, and S. S. Mauney signed the papers to incorporate. Jacob Black, who was not one of the signers of the articles of incorporation, was elected president, an honorary position. John M. Rhodes was elected secretary, treasurer, and active manager. David P. Rhodes became the mill's first superintendent. J. H. Hull soon succeeded Jacob Black. Gaston Mill No. 2 was erected on the opposite side of Mountain Street in 1907. The property was purchased in 1938 and became Dora Yarn Mills. The mill closed permanently in 2000.

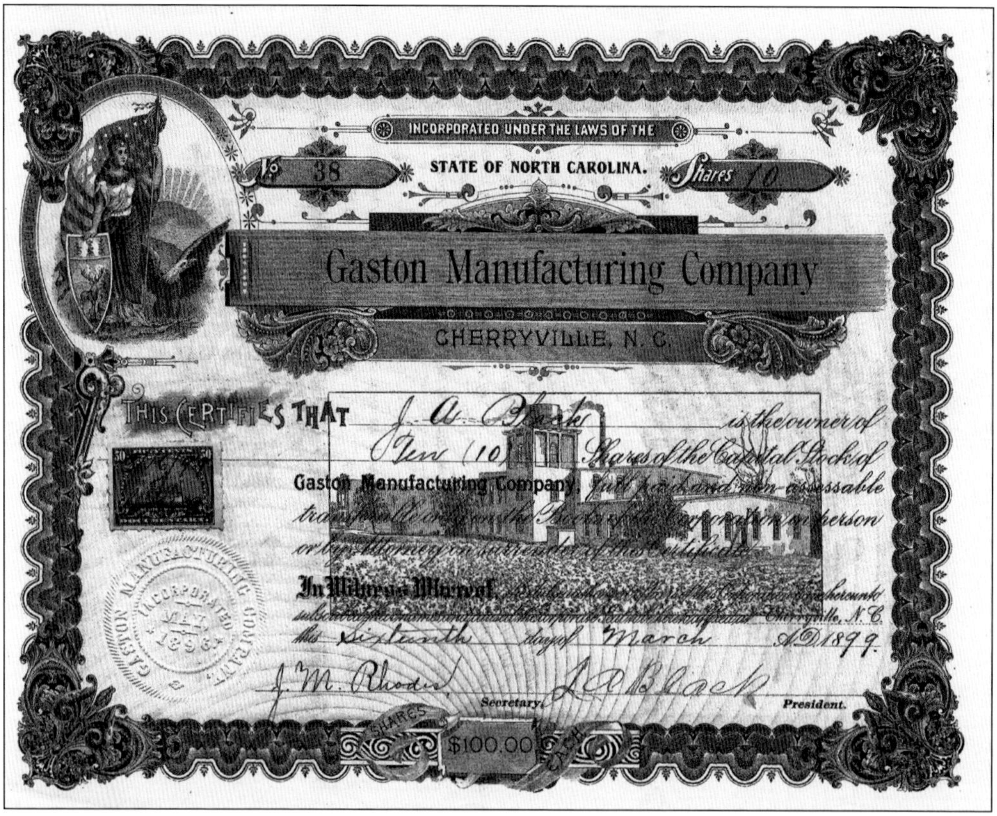

INCORPORATED UNDER THE LAWS OF THE
STATE OF NORTH CAROLINA.
No 38
Shares 10
Gaston Manufacturing Company
CHERRYVILLE, N. C.
THIS CERTIFIES THAT J. A. Black is the owner of Ten (10) Shares of the Capital Stock of Gaston Manufacturing Company, full paid and non-assessable transferable only on the Books of the Corporation in person or by Attorney on surrender of this Certificate.
In Witness Whereof, ... Cherryville, N.C.
this Sixteenth day of March A.D. 1899.
J. M. Rhodes Secretary.
J. A. Black President.
SHARES $100.00 EACH
GASTON MANUFACTURING COMPANY INCORPORATED MAY 1896

Gaston Manufacturing Company, 1896. The second cotton mill established in Cherryville was the Gaston Manufacturing Company. A two-story brick building and mill village was erected a short distance north of town on Mountain Street. It received its charter on May 19, 1896. The owners subscribed to 400 shares of $100 par value stock. The beginning capital stock was set at $40,000 with authority to increase to $200,000. Gaston Manufacturing Company erected Mill No. 2 in 1907 on the opposite side of North Mountain Street from Mill No. 1.

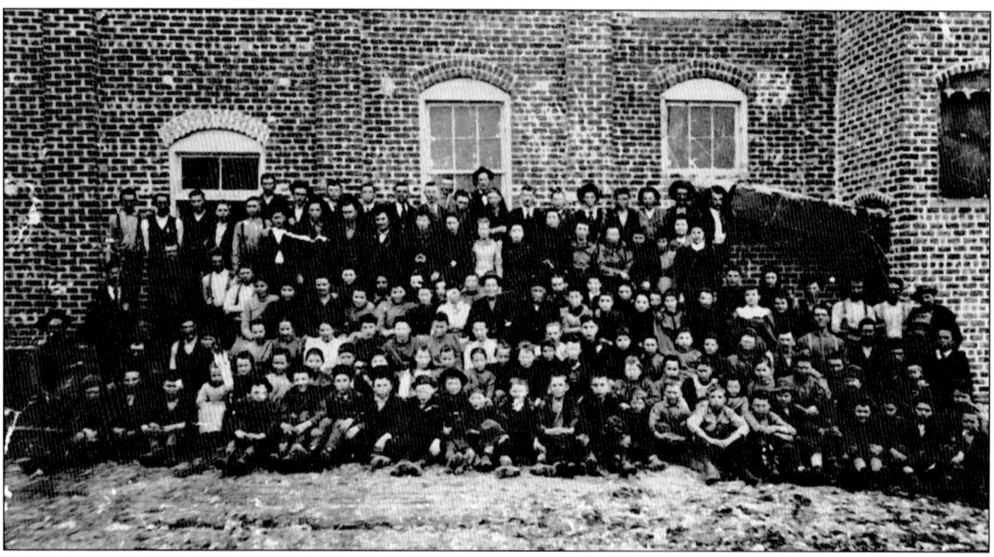

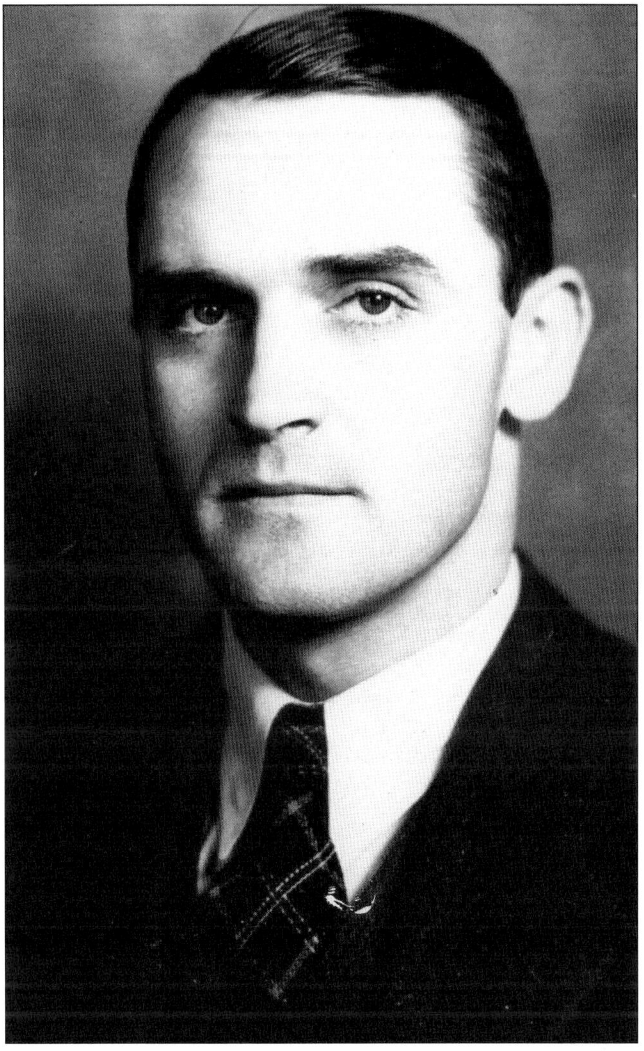

Edwin Rudisill (1909–1988). Lawrence Edwin Rudisill was the son of John Henry and Sarah Frances Rudisill. His first job was washing windows and sweeping floors at the Carlton Yarn Mills for his uncle, Carl Rudisill, founder of the Carlton Yarn Mills. In 1934, Carl Rudisill went to England to visit the fine yarn mills. There he studied brass bobbins yarn, a unique system necessary to produce fine-blended yarns for lace manufacturing. Very fine lace required the best-grade cotton and a high-count yarn, especially prepared for winding on brass bobbins. Upon his return, Edwin Rudisill helped his uncle develop brass bobbin yarn in Cherryville. In 1942, Edwin Rudisill became superintendent of both the Carlton Yarn Mills and NuWay Mills. The Rhyne-Houser Manufacturing Company (shown below on the right) was the seventh textile mill founded in Cherryville. It was incorporated in 1919 by D. E. Rhyne, Dr. W. H. Houser, and C. A. Rudisill.

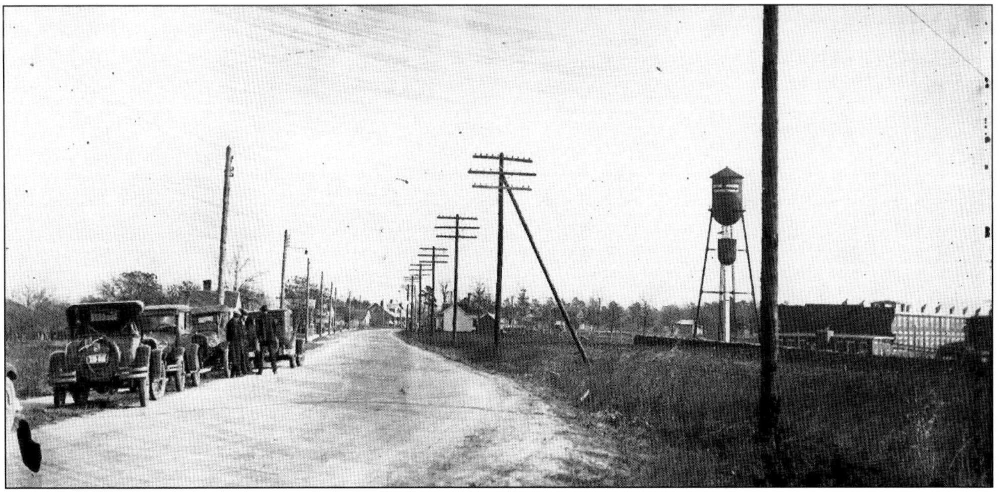

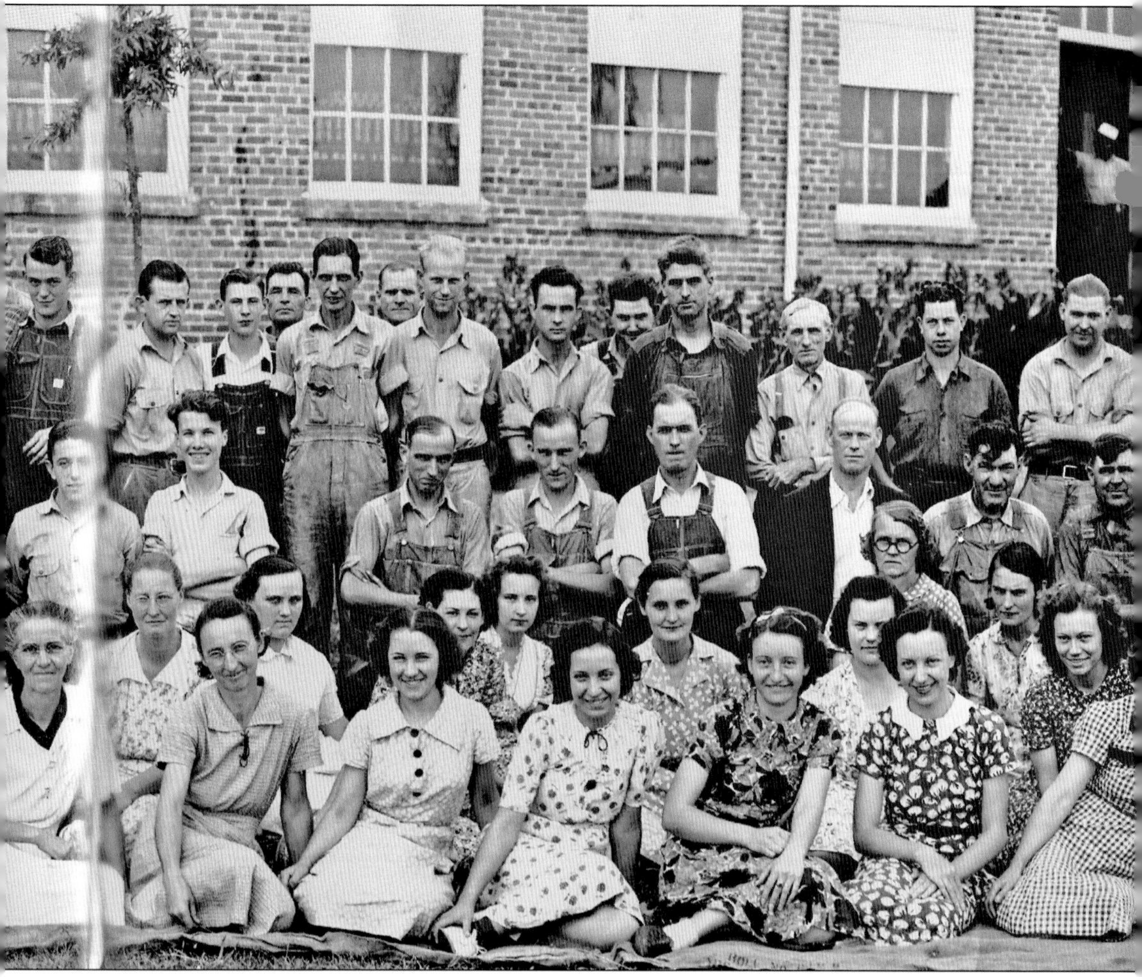

Before the Last Whistle Blows. The fifth cotton mill in Cherryville was Howell Manufacturing Company, incorporated in 1907 by A. W. Howell, Moses Stroup, B. F. Costner, J. C. Ballard, A. H. Huss, J. S. P. Carpenter, G. D. Huss, J. F. Bynum, and E. C. Sullivan. The mill was built a short distance west of town on Wert Street along the Seaboard Railroad tracks and directly north of the Melville Mill. In 1915, it was sold to D. E. Rhyne, and Carl Rudisill became head

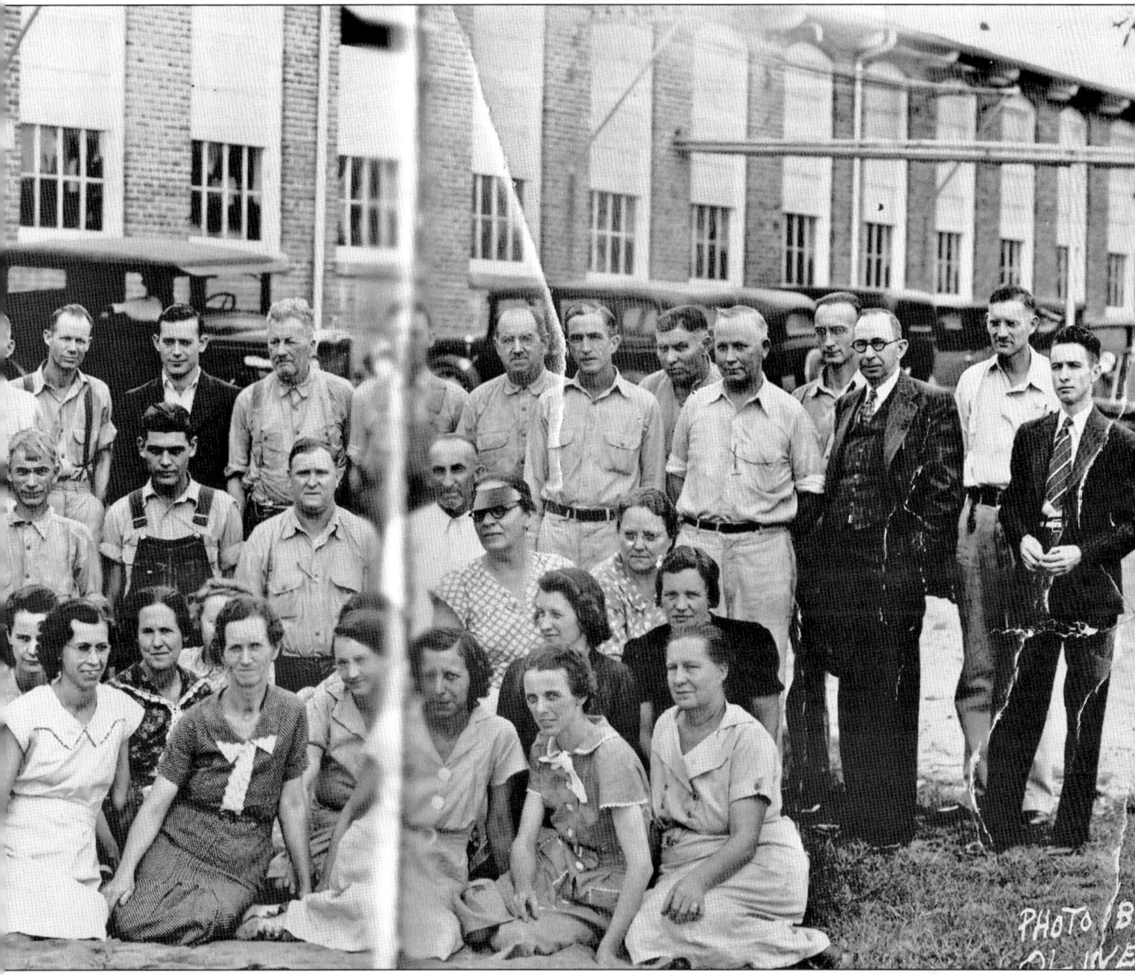

of operations. In 1918, Paul Conrad Rhyne was president, J. W. Howell was secretary-treasurer, and J. C. Ballard was superintendent. By 1925, the plant's size had doubled. Management was under D. E. Rhyne's direction until his death in 1933. Employees of the Howell Manufacturing Company are shown here in 1938.

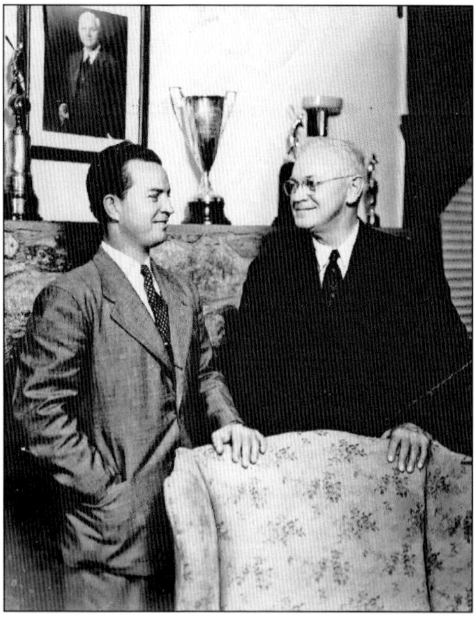

Father and Son. Carl A. Rudisill, one of the foremost textile manufacturers in the South, established the Carlton Yarn Mills in Cherryville and pioneered many new fields in the industry. He served in the North Carolina Legislature from 1937 until 1941. He later gave the reins to his son, Ben Richard Rudisill, who continued his work in the textile industry.

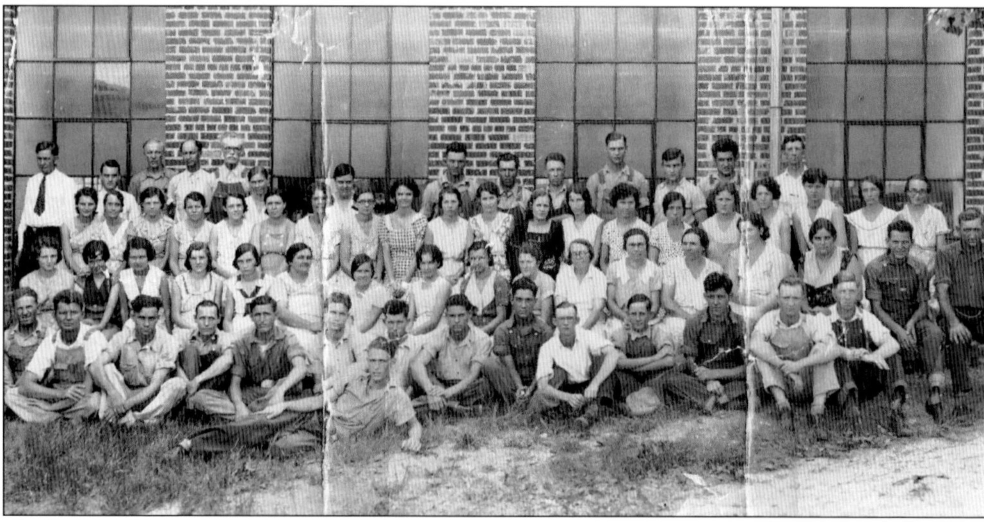

Carlton Yarn Mills Employees, 1931. From left to right are (first row) Clyde Arrowood; (second row) Phil Homesley, Steele Allran, Houston Quinn, Darius Randall, Guy Timmons, Pete Quinn, Lewis McCurry, Gene Devenny, Willis Hendrick, Floyd Beal, Andy Devine, Lonnie Peeler, John Hovis, Bud Devine, and Odus Lankford; (third row) Avalene H. Farris, Novella Q. Metcalf, Bence J. Jones, Pauline Barker, Locie Shuford, Mrs. L. C. (Junie) Ford, Bessie Forrester, Lillian R. Franklin, Mrs. Garland Stroup, Mert Boyles, Mrs. Jim Harris, Frank Henkle, Blanch Beam, Bryte Humphries, Mary Quinn, Carl Hicks, and Larry Beal; (fourth row) Mrs. Forrest Ford, Mrs. Lindo Randall, Bessie Wyant, Mrs. Jim Black, Mrs. Henry Lee Baxter, Edna George, Mrs. Lloyd (Geneva) Wyant, Buice McCurry, Knox Wyant, Verna Boyles, Mrs. Roy Carpenter, Ella Forrester, Minnie Beam, Della Forrester, Mable London, Susan Randall, Deed Sneed, Mrs. Jim Friday, and Lilliam Randall; (fifth row) W. B. Putnam, Edwin Rudisill, P. B. Forrester, Frank Henkle, Ed McCurry, Mrs. C. M. Willis, Alda Leonhardt, Roy Quinn, Dewey Humphries, Lloyd Wyant, Henry Sisk, Forrest Ford, Lee Devenny, and Nathe Barker. The original photograph included Ed Peeler, but he is not shown here.

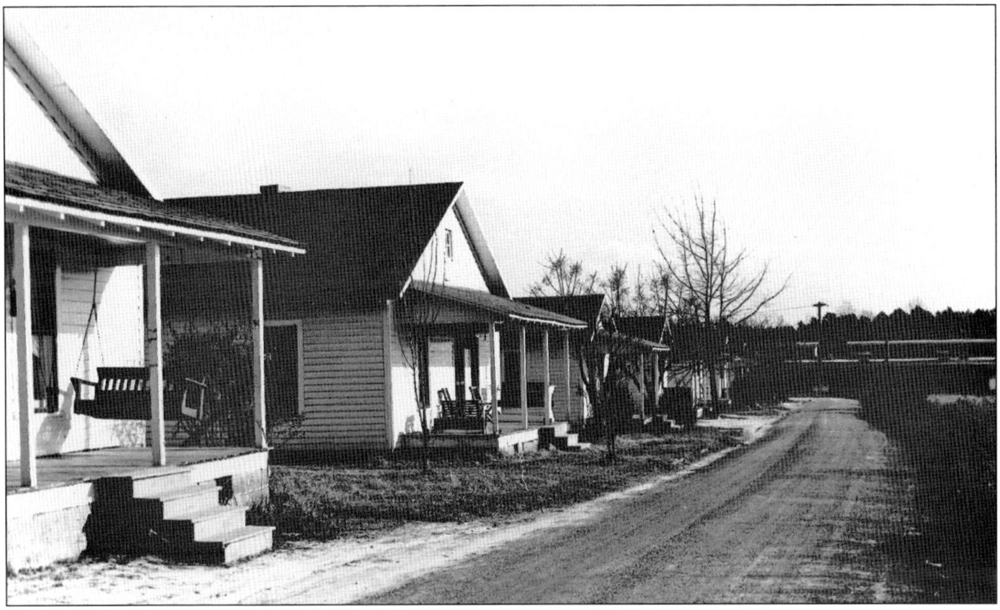

Black Avenue, Carlton Mill Village Houses. D. A. Thompkin's mill cottage designs were published in his *Cotton Mill Commercial Features.* They were used in cotton mill villages across the South. A two-room mill house cost $250 to build. This style was known as a "shotgun house" because it was possible to shoot from the front door in a straight line through the house and out the back.

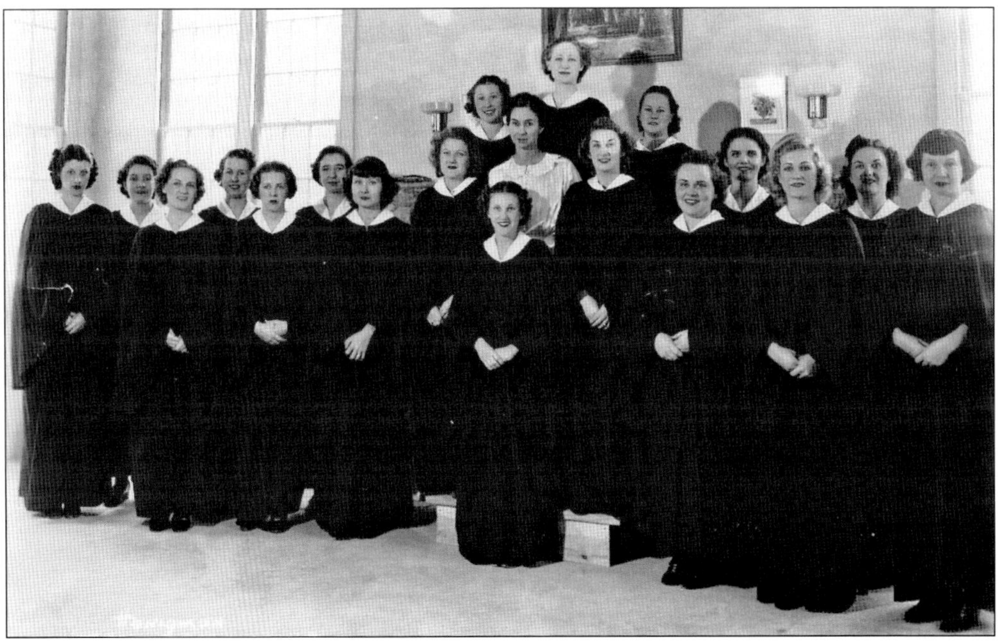

Carlton Yarn Mills Women's Choir. Choir members who gathered to practice around 1938 are, from left to right, (first row) Fannie H. Black, Evelyn W. Carpenter, Knox Wyont, Bence Quinn, Virginia Carpenter, Angelita Beam, Ruth Randall, and Novella Quinn; (second row) Nettie Dellinger, Gathel E. Waters, Katherine Dellinger, Myrtle Boyles, Carmen Frye, Bunis McCurry, and Eva Ford; (third row) Emma Foster, Gladys W. Brown, and Bessie Foster.

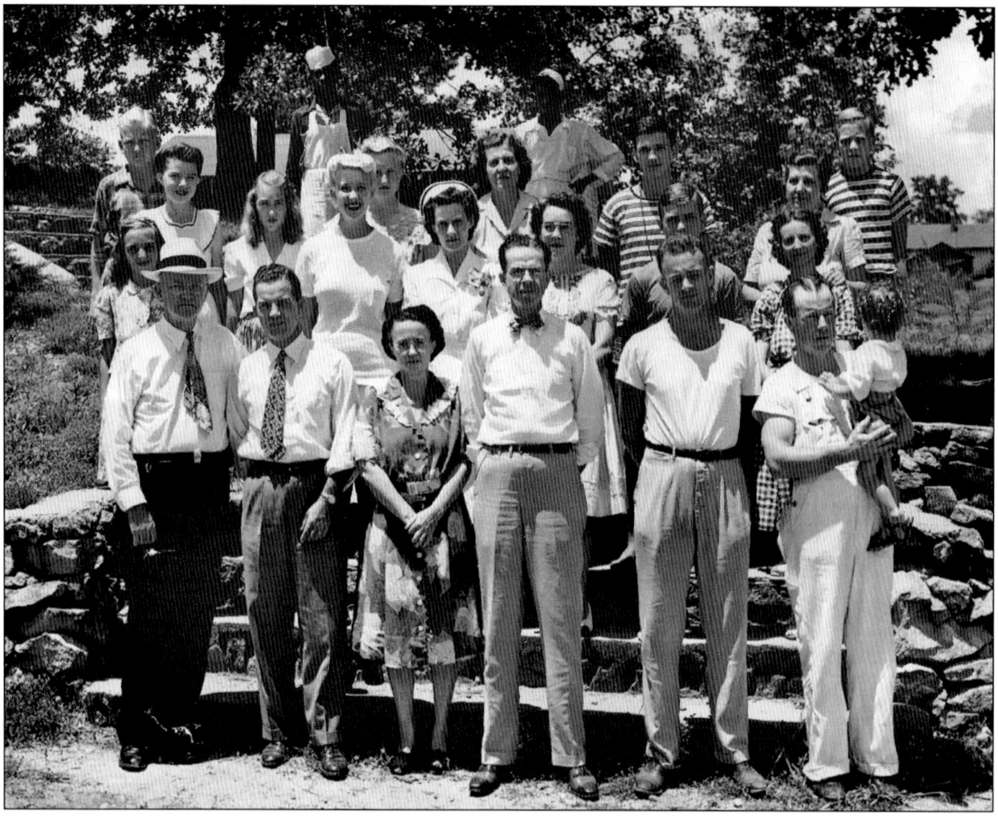

CAMP RUDISILL STAFF, 1947. Located about two miles from Cherryville on the Carl Rudisill Farm, Camp Rudisill was a modern and well-equipped summer camp for the children of Carlton and Rhyne-Houser mill employees. Swimming, nature study, folk-dancing, and various outdoor sports were enjoyed. The staff included a nurse, a director of social recreation, and lifeguards.

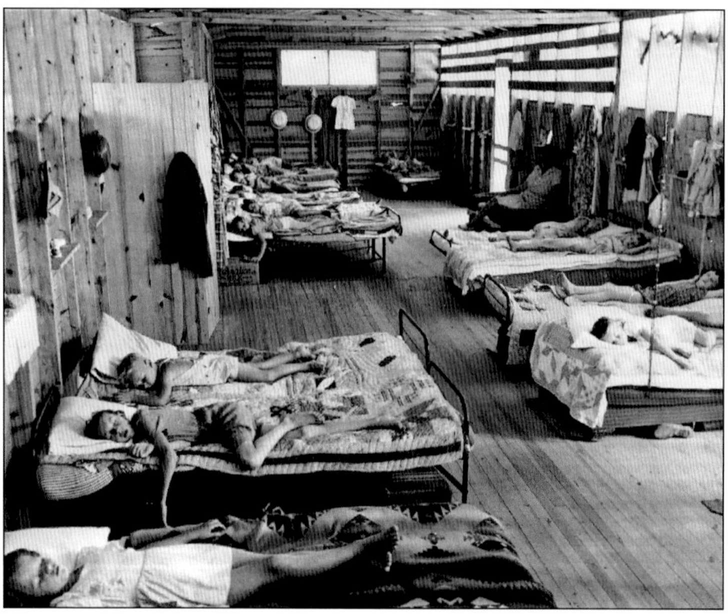

NAP TIME AT CAMP RUDISILL. When the children arrived at camp on the mill-operated bus, they were assigned to a cabin and to a counselor who would be in charge of them during their stay at Camp Rudisill. At the close of camp, parents were given charts as a means of showing them that every effort was made to ensure the best possible care for their children.

Six

Portraits of Faith

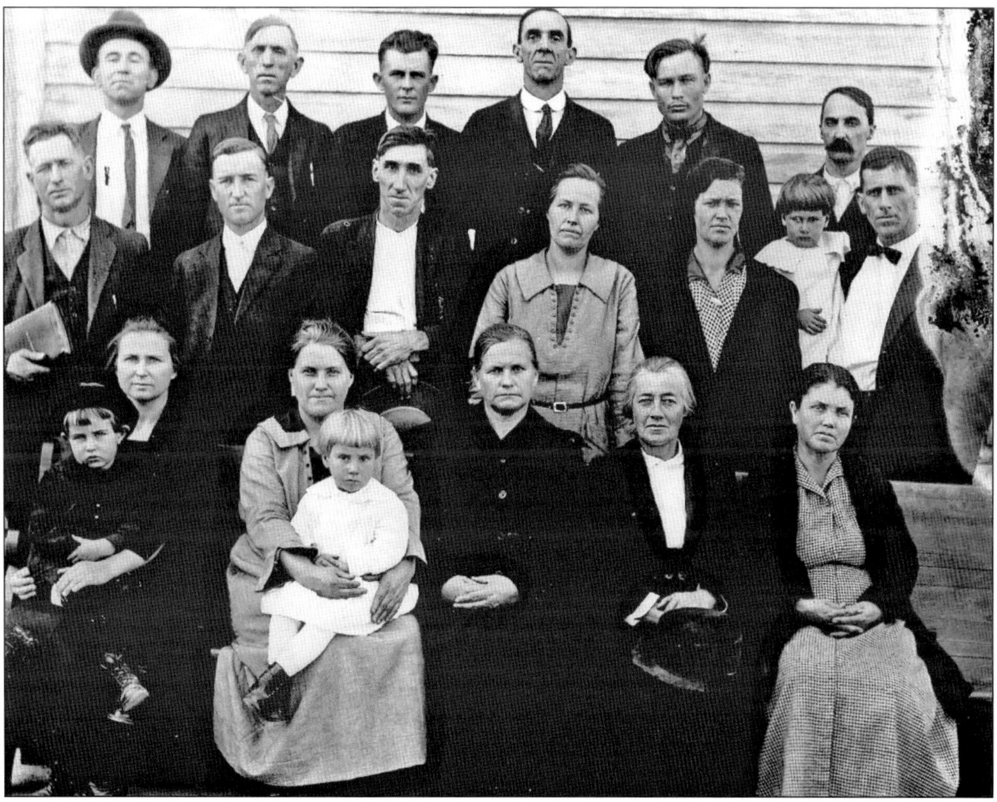

First Wesleyan Methodist Church. Organized around 1907, charter members were Mr. and Mrs. Clayton Sisk, Mr. and Mrs. C. A. Spencer, Mr. and Mrs. Sidney Beam, Mr. and Mrs. Oliver Sisk, Mandy Armstrong, Laura Self, Cora Carpenter, Mr. and Mrs. G. F. Beam, Mr. and Mrs. Lee Beam, Jessie Carpenter, Emma Beam Harvey, Mr. and Mrs. John Short, Mr. and Mrs. Jim Short, Mr. and Mrs. Grover Carpenter, Mr. and Mrs. Joe Sisk, Mr. and Mrs. Frank Robinson, and Bertha Black. Some are seen here.

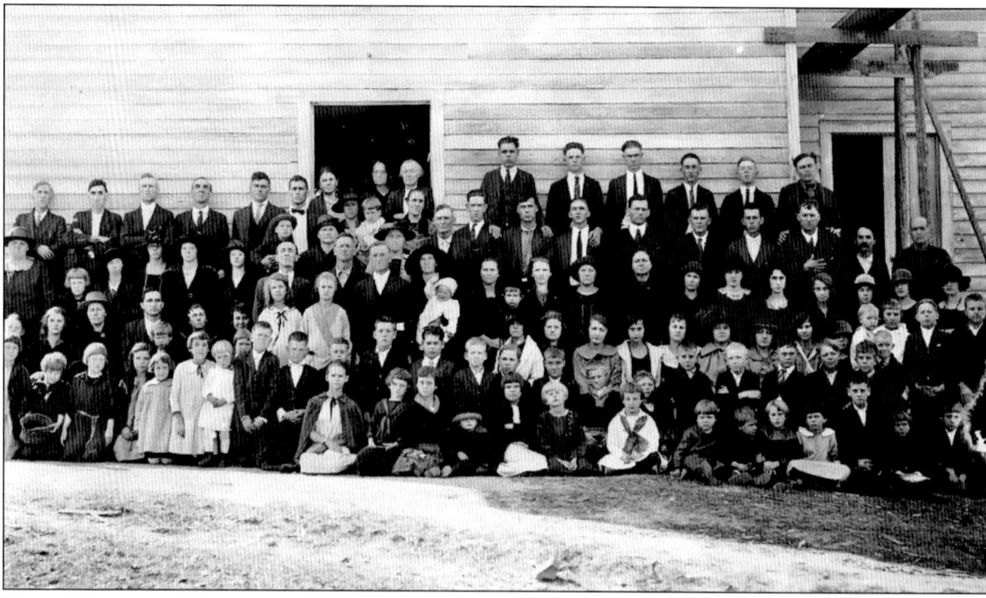

First Wesleyan Methodist Church. The congregation grew out of a revival meeting held by Rev. Zeb Grigg in an old frame store building. The church had a membership of 85 members. Reverend Grigg and his wife also served the Free Saints Tabernacle around the beginning of the 20th century. Ford Grigg sang at the Tabernacle, and Rev. A. P. Robinson and Rev. Ross B. Palmer also served there.

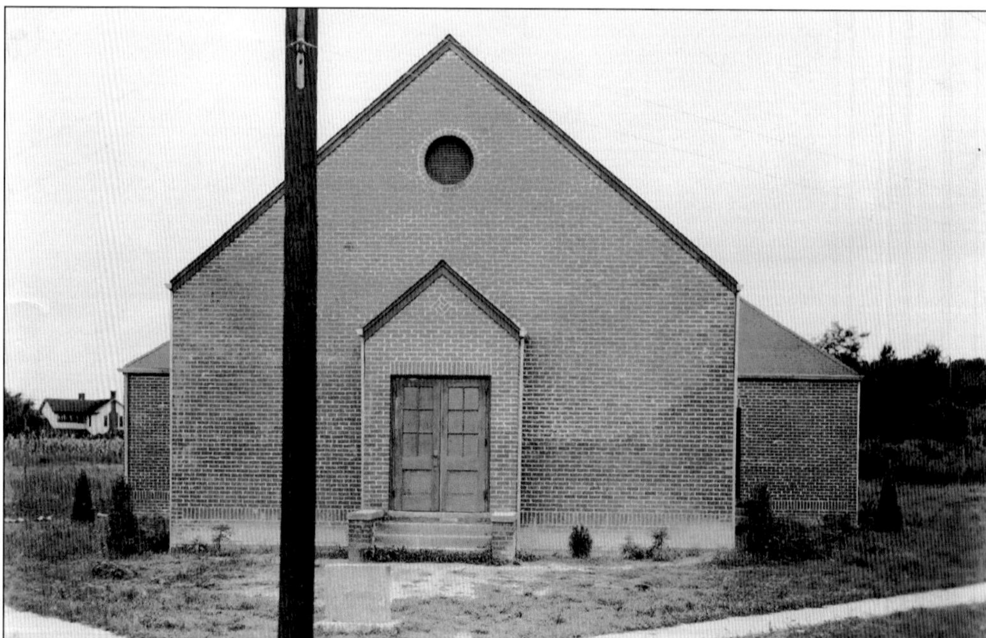

Cherryville Wesleyan Methodist Church. Seen here on North Elm and West Second Streets in 1938, the church had just been completed. It was built under the leadership of Rev. R. A. Christenbury, pastor at that time, who died before the first sermon was preached in the new church. The church's organization resulted from a revival conducted by Rev. Zeb Grigg and Rev. W. G. Cobb. In the 1970s, a new church was built on North Pink Street.

REV. W. G. COBB. Reverend Cobb came to Cherryville in 1927 as pastor of St. John's Lutheran Church and stayed for 24 years. He was an outstanding minister and was loved by all in town. His daughter, Mildred, married Dr. Marshall Agner and made her home in Cherryville. St. John's Lutheran Church was organized in 1881 and is the oldest church in Cherryville. It sprung from St. Mark's Lutheran Church (Old Beaver Dam Church).

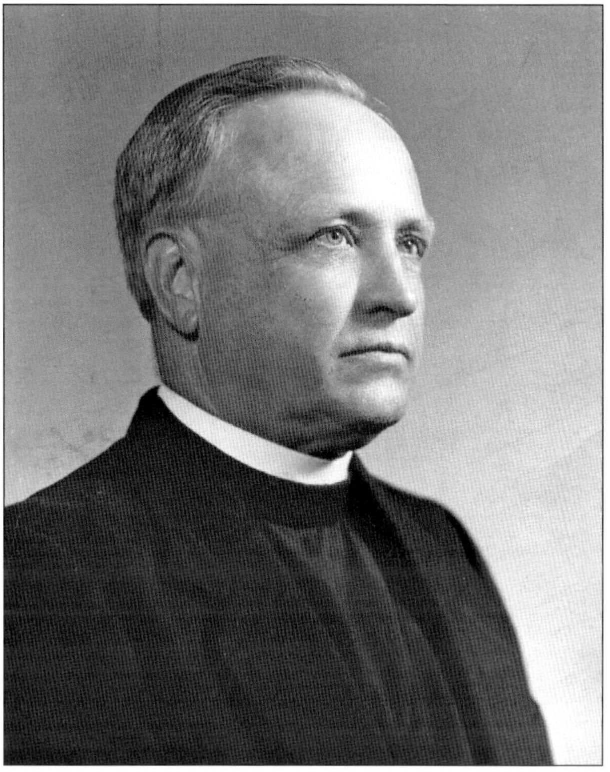

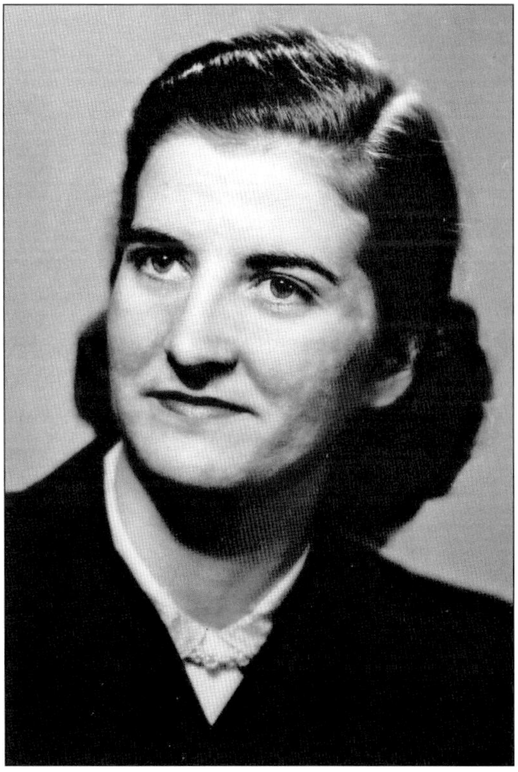

BARBARA YOUNT RUDISILL. Barbara Yount of Hickory came to Cherryville in 1949 after graduating from Lenoir-Rhyne College to become the first full-time parish worker at St. John's Lutheran Church. She married Edwin Rudisill and was active in the civic and religious life of Cherryville. She has done much to support the Cherryville Historical Museum, where she is on the board of directors.

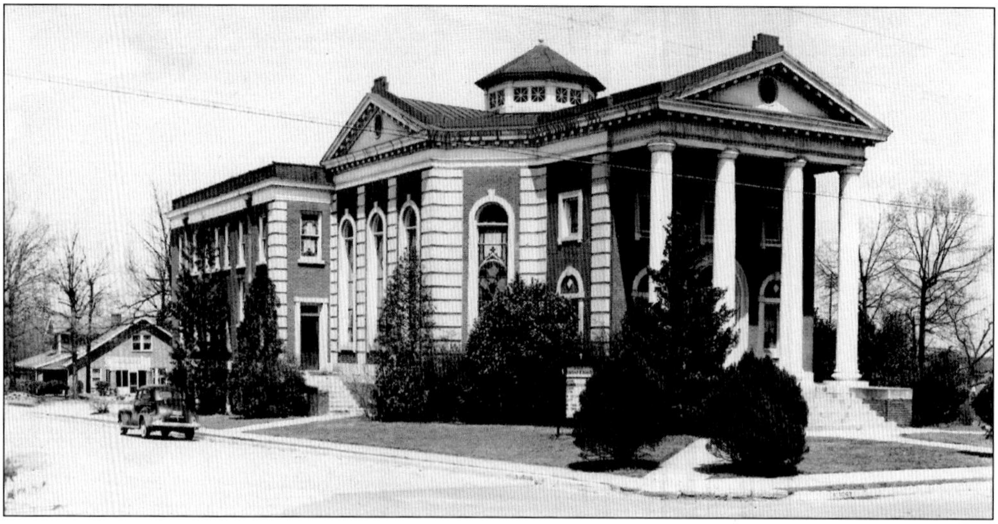

First Baptist Church of Cherryville. The church was organized in 1893 with 24 charter members. Originally located on Mountain Street near Church Street, this location was later disposed of for a more suitable location on First Street. The first church was a 40-by-60-foot wooden building. The beautiful brick church shown here was completed in 1921, but on the morning of January 30, 1961, the sanctuary building was destroyed by fire.

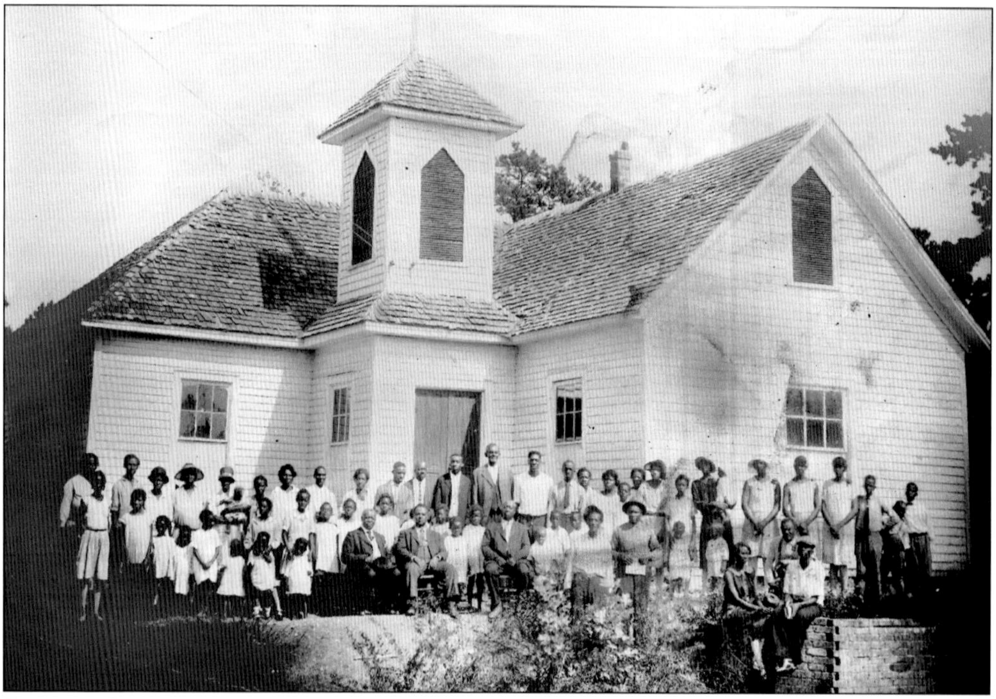

Rudisill Chapel AME Zion Church. The congregation of Rudisill Chapel AME (African Methodist Episcopal) Zion Church on South Mountain Street stands in front of the church around 1925. The first church was built around 1896 and was named for church member Calvin Rudisill. The first AME churches were started in Philadelphia and New York in the early 1800s, but Bishop James Walker Hood was the first missionary preacher of the AME Zion Church in the South. He was also the first black assistant superintendent of education in North Carolina.

Rev. George L. Riddle. The First Presbyterian Church was organized in 1893 with 29 charter members but had no resident pastor until 1922. Lee Dellinger and Rufus Carroll donated a plot of land on West Academy Street in the 1890s, and a small church was erected. A new stone church was built in 1945–1946. Rev. George L. Riddle was called and began his work at the church on August 8, 1937.

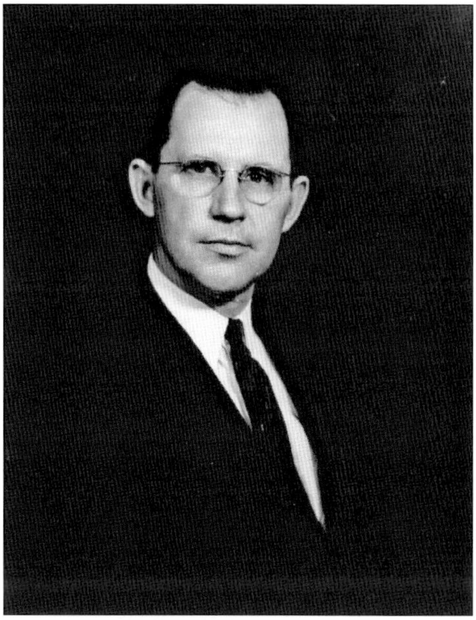

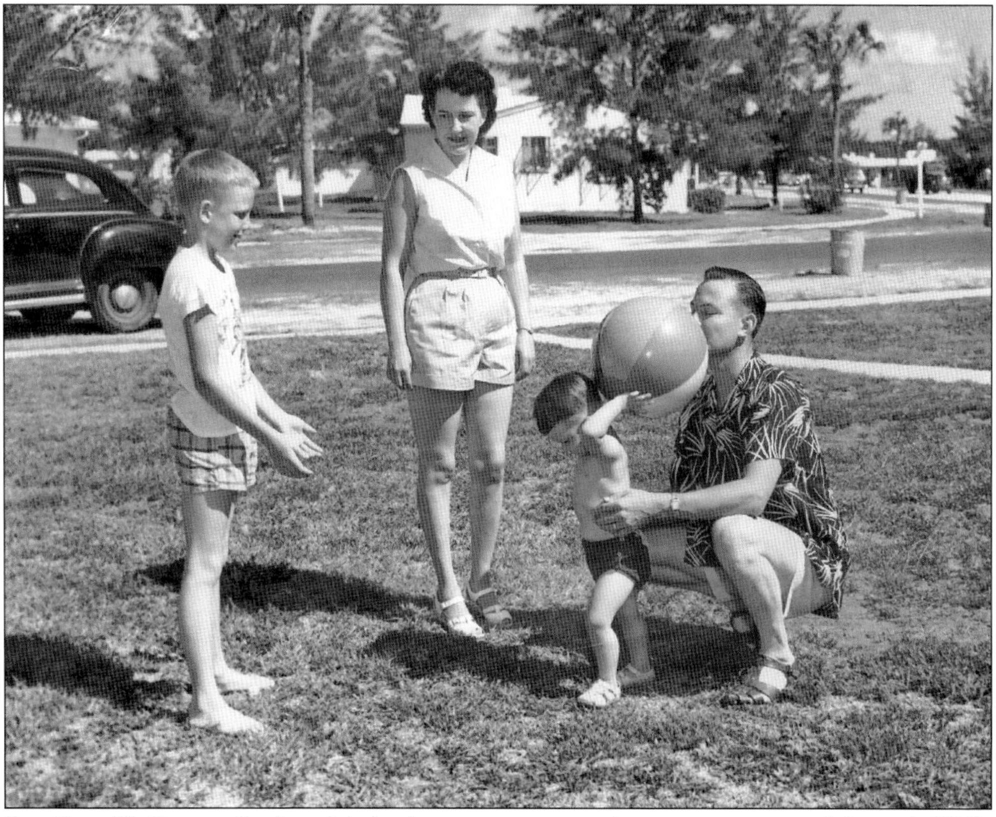

Rev. Jack H. Cooke. Cooke, a Methodist minister, is seen here vacationing with his wife, Willa Cauble Cooke, and children, Jack Jr. (left) and William, in Daytona Beach, Florida, during the 1950s. Reverend Cooke was chaplain at Carolina Freight Carriers Corporation for many years and was named pastor emeritus of the First United Methodist Church.

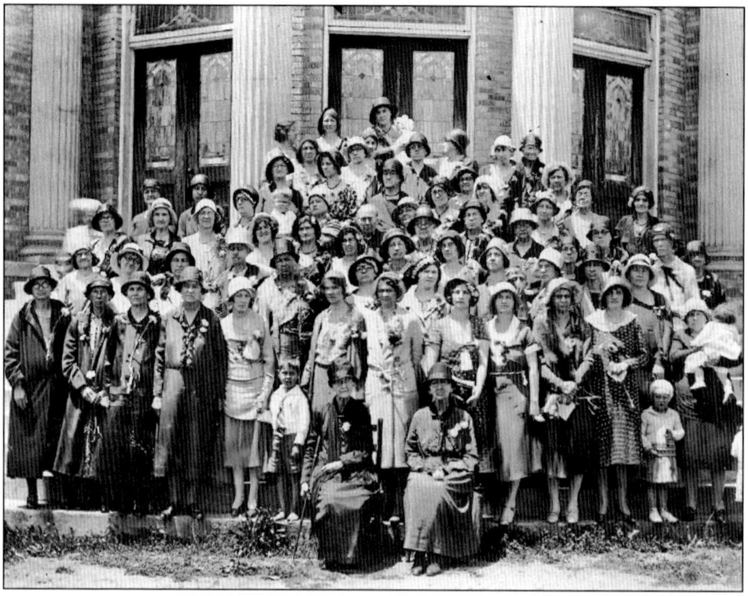

First Methodist Church. The women of the First Methodist Church gather on the front steps of the church for a photograph on Mother's Day 1932. Note the carnations in hand and the beautiful architecture of the church, completed in 1922. This church, originally organized in 1883, was located on the corner of West Second and North Mountain Streets.

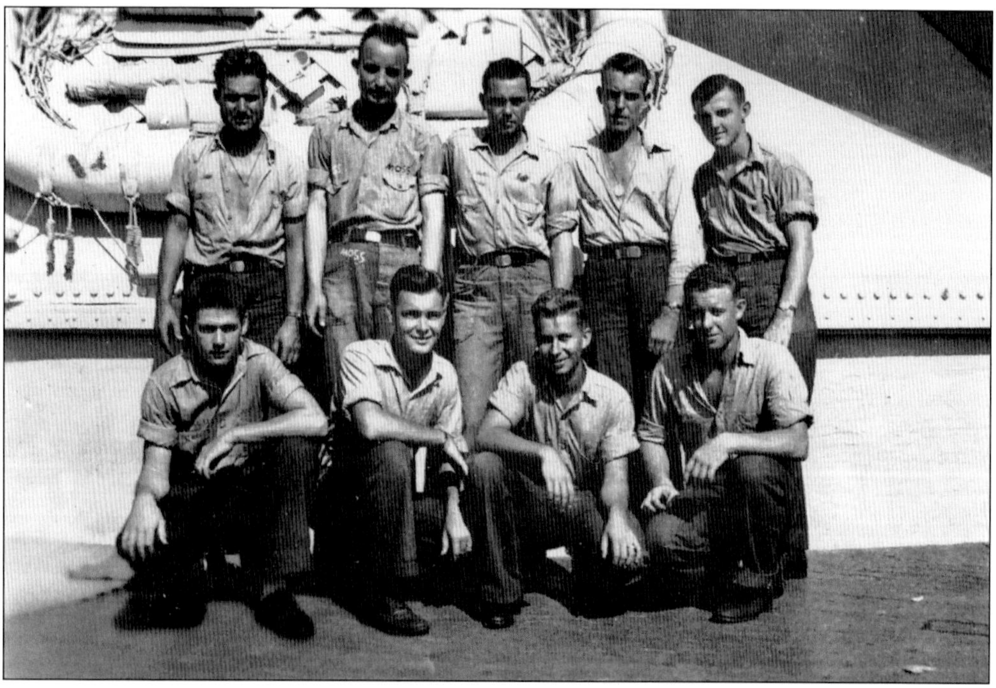

World War II Heroes. These nine brave sailors from Cherryville all served together on the USS *New Mexico* in the Pacific during War World II. Max Carpenter and Robert Franklin were killed in action in Okinawa on May 12, 1945. Pictured from left to right are (first row) Robert "Bobby" Franklin, Ruben Ramsey, Jack Jenkins, and J. L. Carroll; (second row) Lloyd Hastings, Robert Moss, Max David Carpenter, Fred Neill, and Jimmy Boyles.

Seven

Some Coming, Some Going

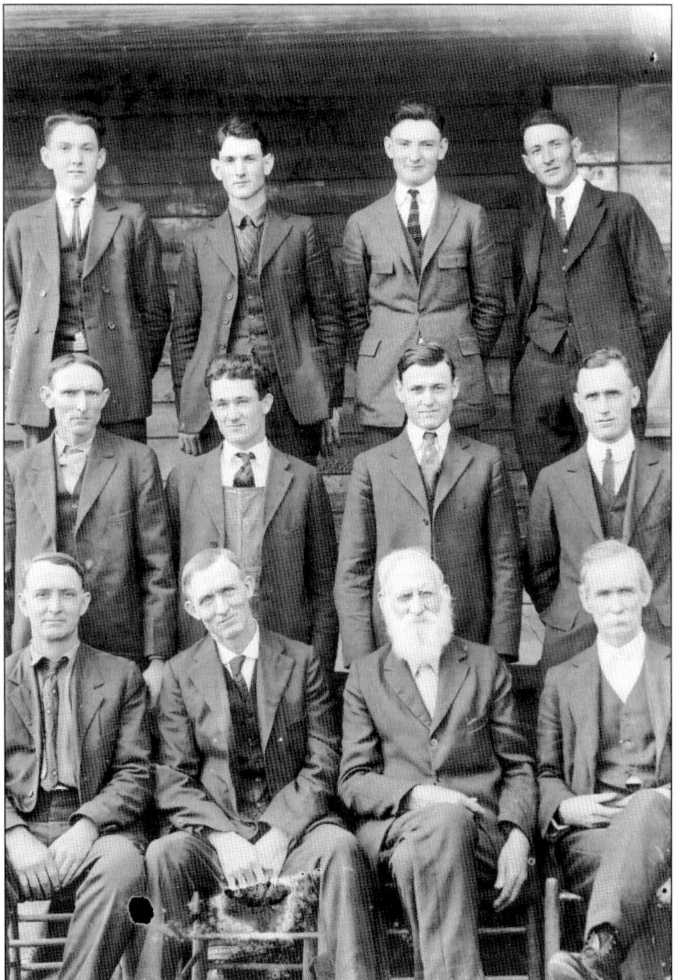

The Gift of History. Everyone has a history, an account of where they come from and how they got to be who they are. This gift of history was often shared from one generation to the next on the front porches of America as families gathered there. Some people were born in Cherryville and never left; others were here for a short while, left their mark, and moved on.

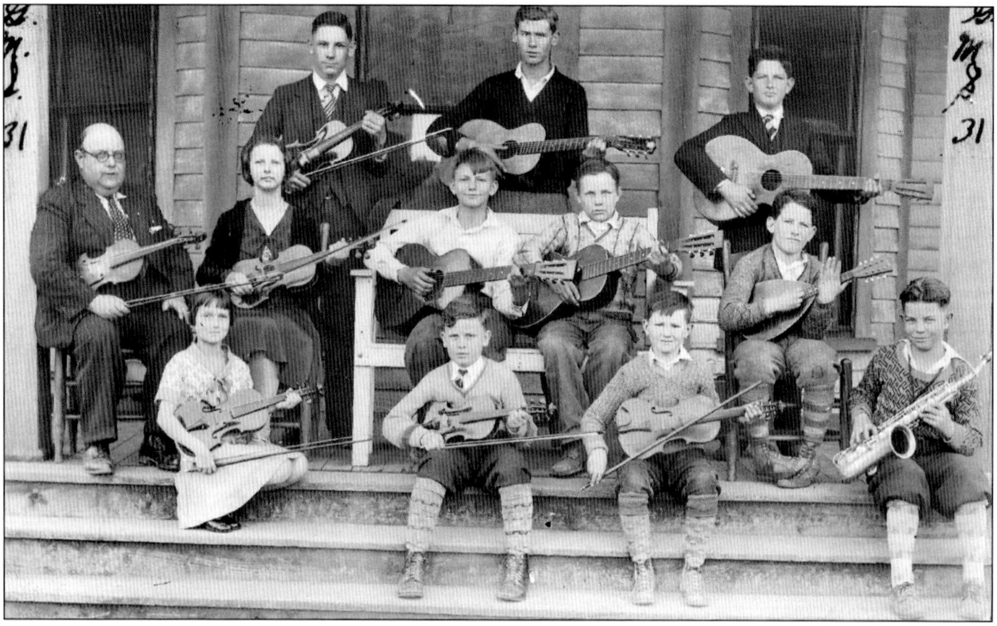

GOLDMAN MUSIC SCHOOL, 1931. Sitting on the steps of the Hoover House, across the street from the Cherryville Foundry Works on Mulberry Street, in 1931 are Bill Goldman's music students. Pictured in no certain order are Bill Goldman, Bobby McLurd, James Allran Jr., John Henry Howell, Ben Rudisill, Louie Baber, Howell Stroup, Lawrence Stroup, Kenneth Nixon, Edith McGinnis, Jack Stroup, and Joe R. Nixon Jr.

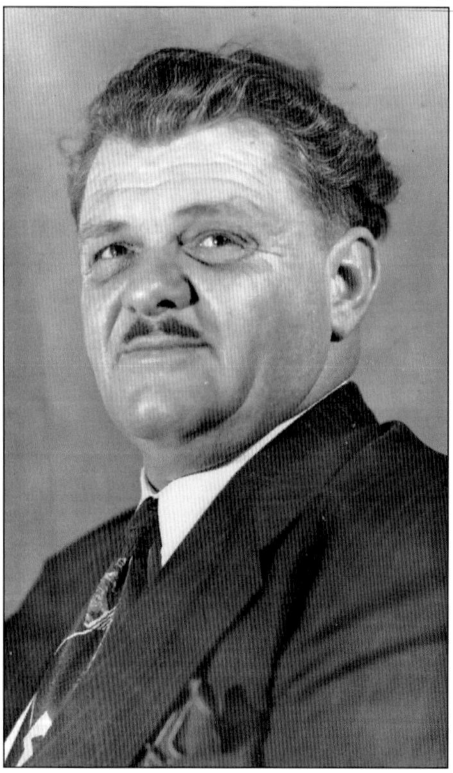

HOBSON P. "HOB" HENDRICKS. A cotton mill employee and a Bible scholar, Hob had polio as a child. His love was music, and it is said that he had great musical talent and once directed a brass band at First Baptist Church. He was the leader of the Hendricks Brothers Band and organized the Nu-Way Choir. After his death in 1959, soft South Sea Island music was played at his wake, as he had requested.

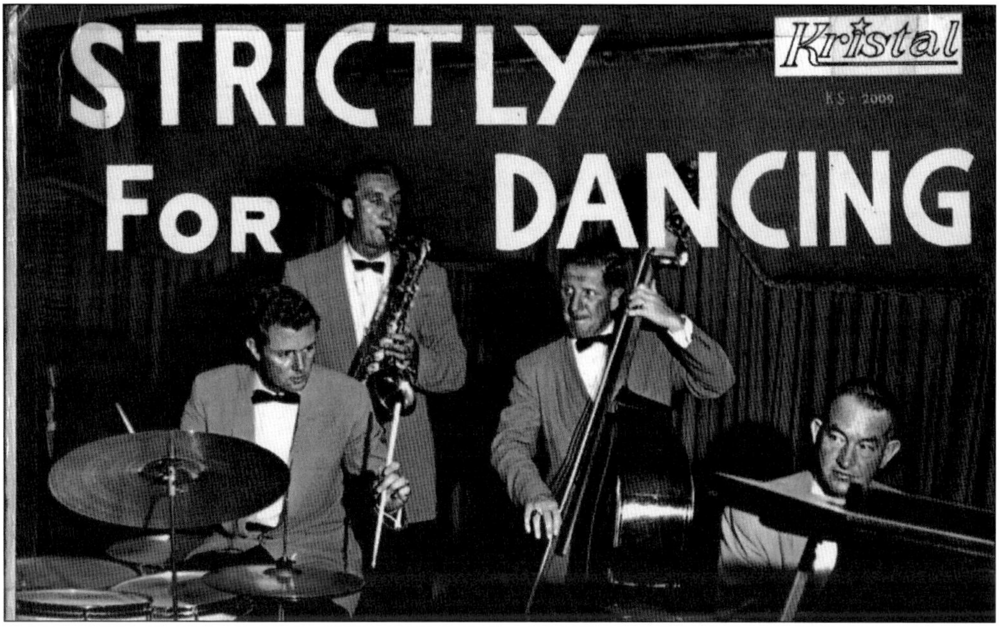

Gene Bookout. Growing up in Cherryville, Bookout started playing drums at age 12 and organized his first swing band in high school. Afterward he joined the air force and played USO shows, later joining the Frank Lane Orchestra. In 1949, he went to Miami and performed in nightclubs. This album, recorded in Cuba, included two original songs, "Like How So?" and "Blue Gene," a blues number. The photograph below appeared in the *Charlotte Observer* on January 31, 1958. Members of the Cherryville jazz band the Southerners are, from left to right, Gary Summers (pianist); Harlan Howell (guitar), who later performed with the Howell Brothers; Butch Blackwelder (drummer); Jerry Summitt (tenor saxophone); Tommy Howell (trumpet); and John H. Black Jr. (baritone saxophone). John later played with the U.S. Army Band and the Original Shakers, and had a long career at Cherryville National Bank.

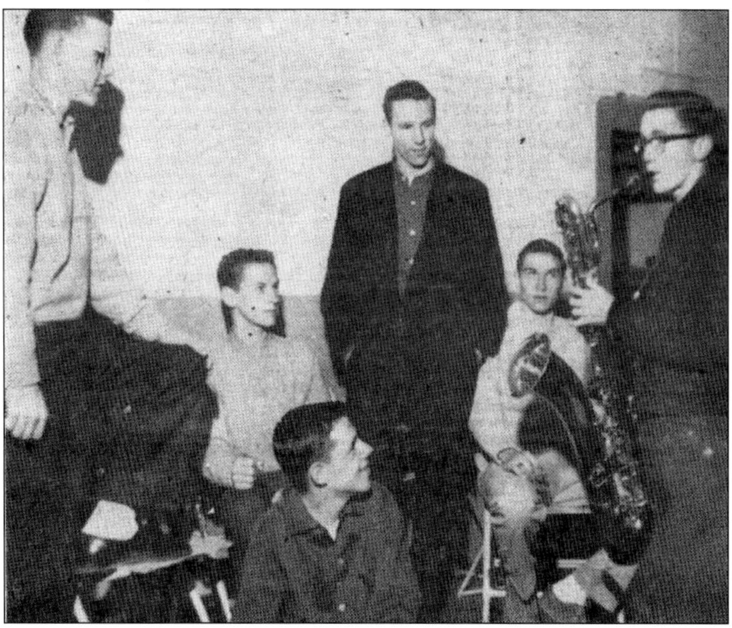

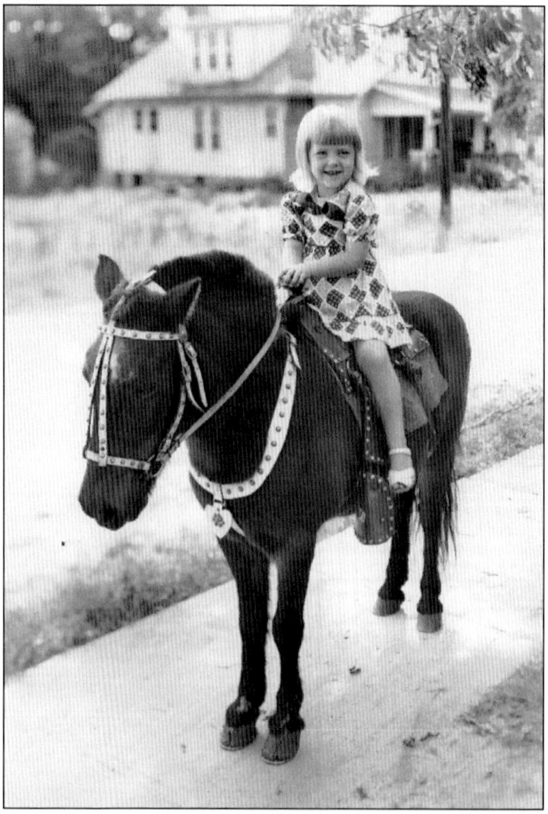

BEVERLY BARTS, 1950s. M. M. Barts (1888–1977), a World War I veteran, moved quite often around the United States with his wife, the former Marie Brown, and their large family. The early 1950s found him living in Cherryville, where his youngest child, Beverly, had her picture made on a photographer's pony on Pine Avenue. (Courtesy of Beverly Barts Gantt.)

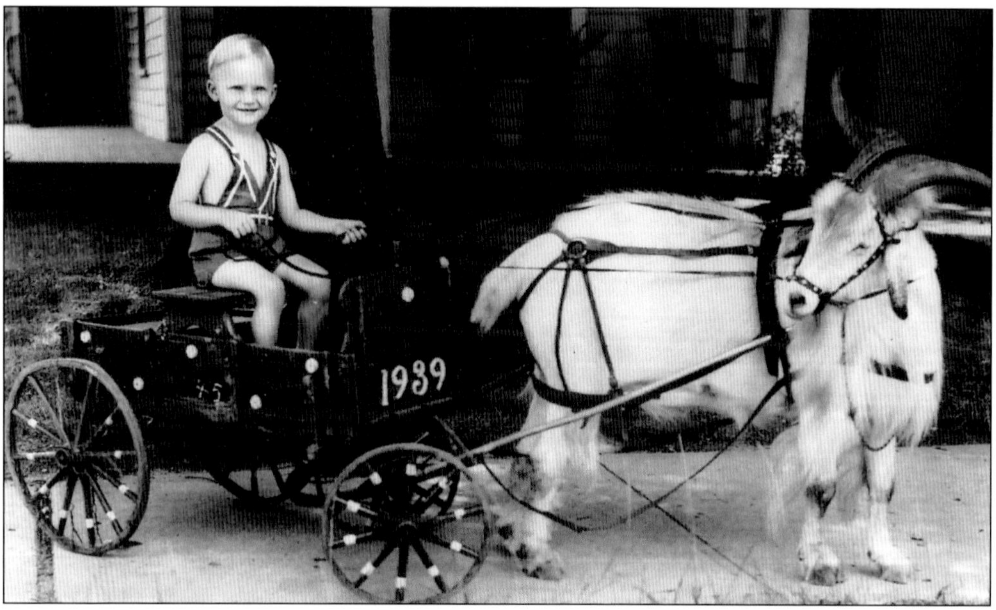

CHARLES DELLINGER SHERRILL, 1939. Charles Sherrill, son of Garland Sherrill and Ruth Dellinger Sherrill, is seen here in 1939 on a goat cart. Photographers would go from neighborhood to neighborhood in small towns with their cart and draft goat taking pictures, for a price, to the delight of the children and parents. (Courtesy of Charles and Pat Sherrill.)

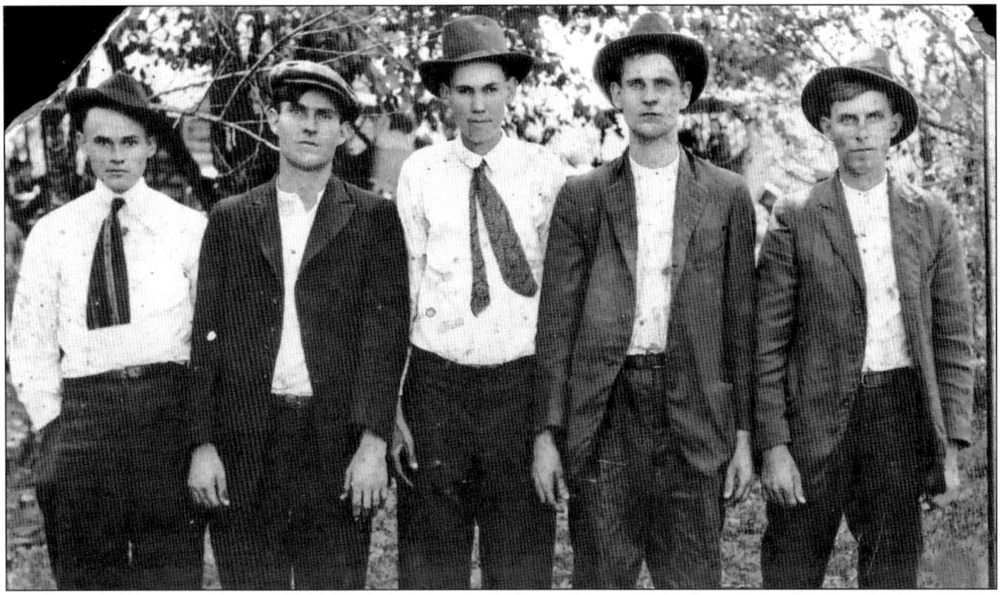

THE NEAL BROTHERS. Descended from Irish immigrant Adam O'Neal, the Neal brothers grew up on Indian Creek near Crouse. Their father was John Andrew Neal (1860–1900). Pictured here around 1913 are, from left to right, Ira Odell Neal, Noah Jacob Neal, Caleb Milton Neal, Daniel Charles Neal, and Green Berry Neal.

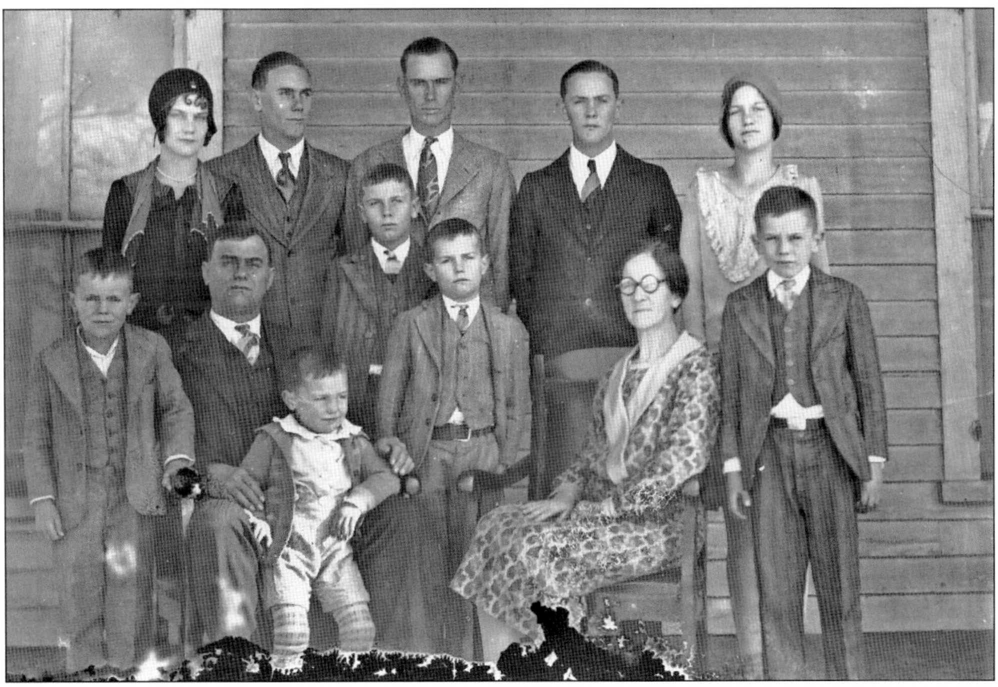

THE CARPENTER FAMILY. The Clayton Carpenter family sent six sons—Lloyd, Troy, Hubert, Colon, Fred, and Max—to war during World War II. The youngest, Max Carpenter, joined the U.S. Navy and was killed in action on Mother's Day, May 12, 1945, at Okinawa. Pictured around 1929 are, from left to right, (first row) Harold, Clayton, Max, Troy, Colon, Sarah, and Fred; (second row) Connie, Everett, Hubert, Lloyd, and Ruby.

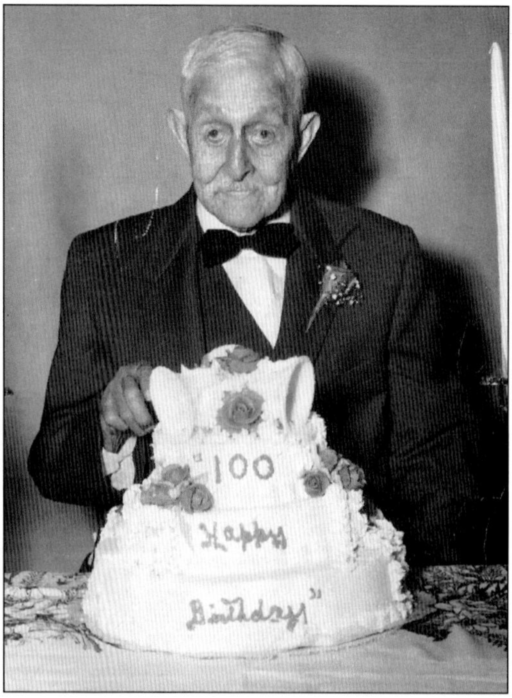

DAVID ANDREW CRAFT (1857–1958). A prominent citizen of the Panhandle area north of Cherryville, Craft was the son of John Philip Craft (1802–1894) and Margaret "Peggy" Neal. He died in 1958 at the age of 100, leaving many descendants in the Cherryville area. The first documented Craft in Old Lincoln County was Michael Craft, born in 1756.

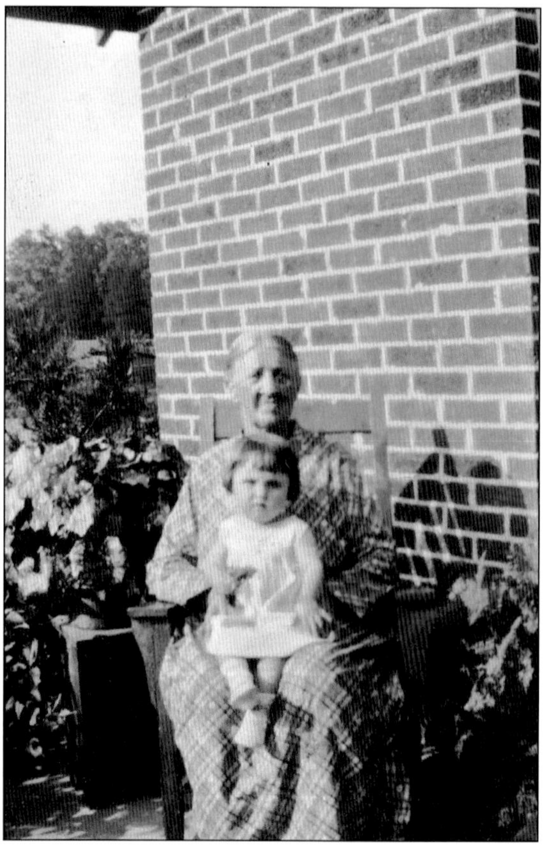

SUSAN CRAFT DELLINGER (1855–1938). Married to Stephen Dellinger, Susan was the daughter of David Craft (1814–1862) and Roxannah Leonhardt (1817–1902). Her daughter Mima Dellinger married Austin Beam, and they were the parents of Cherryville businessmen Kenneth Beam and Woodrow Beam. Her other daughter, Sarah ("Sallie") Dellinger (1879–1914), married P. Sherrill Wehunt. Susan is seen here with great-great-granddaughter Dorothy Wood Wehunt in 1934.

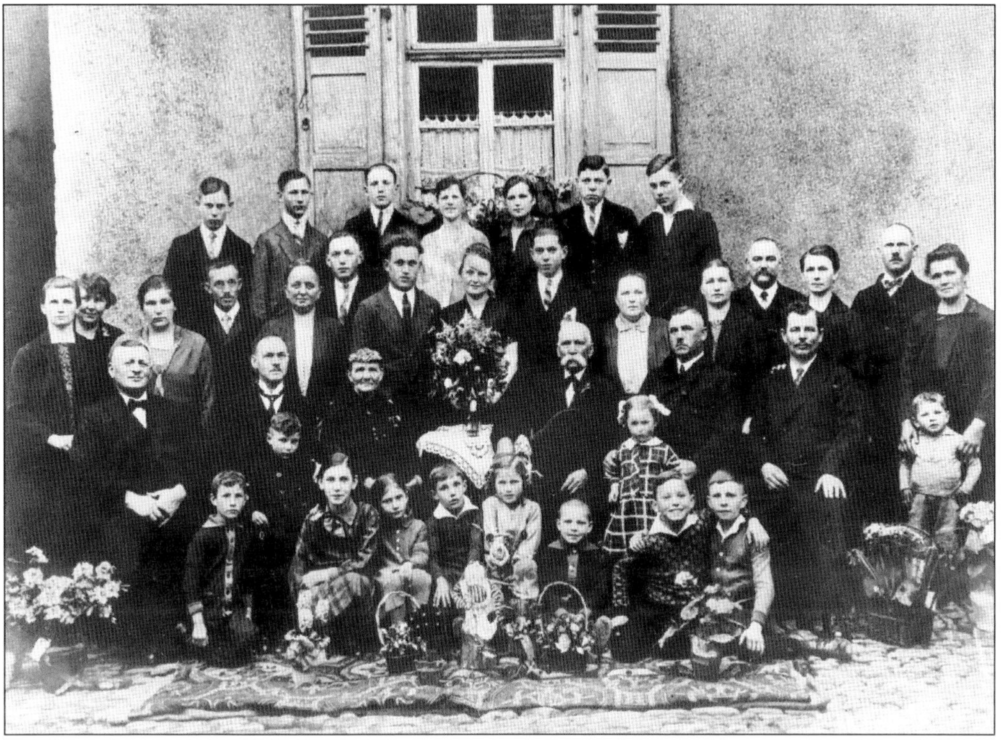

Wiegandt Family. Johann Friederich Wiegandt, who served in the Revolutionary War and was stationed at Camp Security in York County, Pennsylvania, came to North Carolina in 1787. He died in 1800 in Rowan County, and his wife moved her family to Little Long Creek near Paysour's Mountain. Many Wiegandts did not migrate to the New World from Germany. Shown above is the Wiegandt family in Freinsheim, Germany, in 1939. The name was anglicized to Wehunt around 1820.

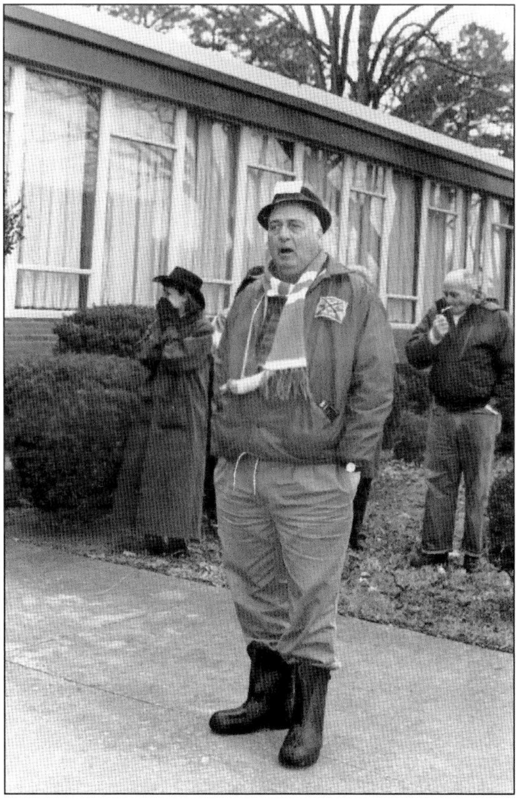

Carl Dellinger. A descendant of German settlers, Carl "Boozie" Dellinger delivers the New Year Shooters Chant: "Good Morning to you, sir. We wish you a happy New Year, good health, long life, which God may bestow so long as you stay here below. May He bestow the house you are in, where you go out and you go in. Time by moments steals away, . . . and for good luck, we'll fire our guns."

Bibliography

Allran, Von Eva, et al. *Cherryville, Past and Present*. Cherryville, NC: Ken Rollins Printing and Publishing, 1996.

Andrews, Mildred Gwin. *The Men and the Mills*. Macon, GA: Mercer University Press, 1987.

Atkins, Garland. *Carolina Freight Corporation: A History 1932–1985*. Herald Publishing, 1985.

Brengle, Kim Withers. *The Architectural Heritage of Gaston County, North Carolina*. Gastonia, NC: Commercial Printers, 1982.

Cope, Robert F., and Manly Wade Wellman. *The County of Gaston: Two Centuries of a North Carolina Region*. Gastonia, NC: Gaston County Historical Society, 1961.

Gaston County Heritage Book Committee. *Gaston County Heritage*. Winston-Salem, NC: Jostens, 2002.

Hanchett, Tom, Ryan Sumner, and the Levine Museum of the New South. *Charlotte and the Carolina Piedmont*. Charleston, SC: Arcadia Publishing, 2003.

Harpe, Jason. *Lincoln County Revisited*. Charleston, SC: Arcadia Publishing, 2003.

Mauney, Mary Frances, and Rev. John D. Mauney Jr. *Beaver Dam Lutheran Church Cemetery: A Challenge for Our Time*. Cherryville, NC: 1992.

Osborne, Adrienne Beam. *A Surprise, a Joy, and a Blessing*. Cherryville, NC: Gradual Joy Books, 2007.

Ragan, Robert Allison. *The Textile Heritage of Gaston County, North Carolina 1848–2000*. Charlotte, NC: Loftin and Company Printers, 2001.

Wehunt-Black, Rita. *Gaston County, NC: A Brief History*. Charleston, SC: History Press, 2008.

———. *They Didn't Blow in on the Wind*. Hickory, NC: Hickory Printing Company, 1976.

Williams, Robert L. *Gaston County: A Pictorial History*. Norfolk, VA: Donning Company, 1981.

INDEX

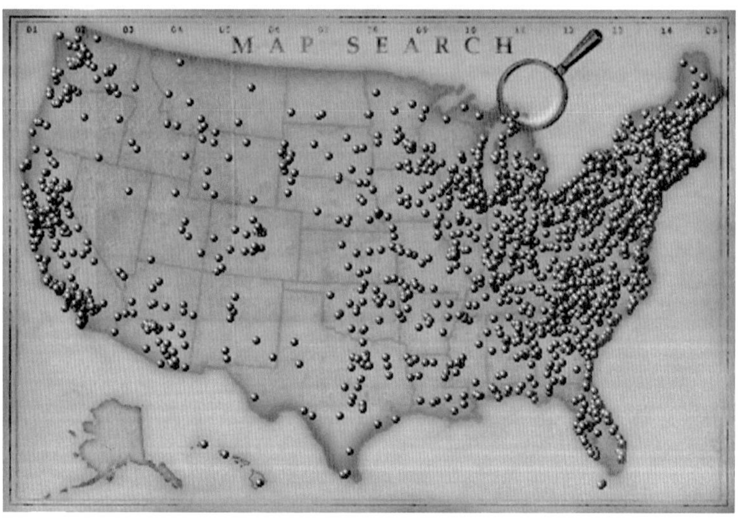
MAP SEARCH